HOW MASTER MOU

REMOVES OUR DOUBTS

SUNY SERIES IN BUDDHIST STUDIES
MATTHEW KAPSTEIN, EDITOR

HOW MASTER MOU

REMOVES OUR DOUBTS

*A Reader-Response Study and Translation
of the* Mou-tzu Li-huo lun

John P. Keenan

*A study conducted with support from
The Pacific Cultural Foundation
The Republic of China*

STATE UNIVERSITY OF NEW YORK PRESS

Published by
State University of New York Press, Albany

For information, address State University of New York
Press, State University Plaza, Albany, N.Y., 12246

Production by E. Moore
Marketing by Dana E. Yanulavich

Library of Congress Cataloging-in-Publication Data

Keenan, John P.
    How master Mou removes our doubts : a reader-response study and
translation of the Mou-tzu Li-huo lun / John P. Keenan.
        p.   cm.—(SUNY series in Buddhist studies)
    Includes bibliographical references and index.
    ISBN 0-7914-2203-8 (alk. paper).—ISBN 0-7914-2204-6 (pbk. : alk.
paper)
    1. Mou-tzu. Li huo lun. 2. Buddhism—Relations—Confucianism.
3. Buddhism—Relations—Taoism. 4. Buddhism—China. I. Mou-tzu
Li huo lun. English. 1944. II. Title. III. Series.
BQ4610.C6K44   1994
294.3'42—dc20   93-47099
                                                                         CIP

10 9 8 7 6 5 4 3 2 1

Dedicated to the memory of
my ancestors
and my parents
John P. Keenan, Sr.
and
Mary Connelly Keenan

Contents

2. Source Codes (Background textual images
   and ideas)
3. Reader-Response Criticism (What the
   argument accomplishes in each of its
   progressive steps)

Preface

I first grew interested in the *Mou-tzu Li-huo lun* (牟子理惑論) long ago in the golden days of graduate school at the University of Wisconsin. There, under the able direction of Professor Francis Westbrook, I attempted a first study and translation of the text and its meaning. Subsequently I used sections of the *Li-huo lun* in a seminar on the translation of Chinese Buddhist texts at the University of Wisconsin when I taught there as a leave replacement for Professor Minoru Kiyota during 1980–81. I thank participants in that seminar for the comments and criticisms they offered more than a decade ago. Since then the *Li-huo lun* has sat in my file cabinet, for I was unsure just what to do with it.

The idea for this book dawned only after I had spent some time studying scriptural exegesis in connection with another project and learned something of the new hermeneutical approaches being employed by Western Christian scholars such as Elizabeth Struthers Malbon, Robert M. Fowler, and John Dominic Crossan. I find that the methods of literary criticism they have employed so profitably in the interpretation of Christian texts are equally applicable to Buddhist writings.

My ability to complete this project benefited greatly from a grant from the Pacific Cultural Foundation, under the directorship of its president, Yu-sheng Chang. I am also grateful for the congenial atmosphere among my colleagues at Middlebury College, whom I thank.

In an attempt to make the book readable I have kept the use
of Chinese characters to a minimum, citing them only when they
are needed to clarify a point. The Sinologist, I presume, has access
to the tools of the trade and can easily find references to cited materials in university library catalogs.

On textual issues, this study of the *Mou-tzu Li-huo lun* relies
on the work of other scholars. I have taken Makita Tairyō's study
Gumyōshū kenkyū (Research on the *Hung-ming chi*) as my guide
in translating the text of the *Li-huo lun* in the Ssu-pu pei-yao edition of the *Hung-ming chi* collection and in the *Taishō shinshū
daizōkyō*. Furthermore, I enter only briefly and cursorily into the
tangled issues of the text's authenticity as a late Han document
and the historicity of its main character, Mou-tzu. My focus lies
elsewhere: on the impact of the rhetoric of the text upon its implied readers. In a word, I seek to learn what this tractate
achieves for its original readers.

Reading the *Mou-tzu Li-huo lun*: Socioliterary Strategies

The *Mou-tzu Li-huo lun* is a narrative text that presents the story of the Chinese Buddhist scholar Mou-tzu, and reports in thirty-seven articles a dialogue between him and an unnamed critic or critics. The overall aim of the work seems crystal clear, for the text begins with a statement of Mou-tzu's intent and ends in the conversion of Mou-tzu's hitherto critical interlocutors and their adoption of lay vows (*pañcaśīla*). The work has often been described as a Buddhist apologetic, and yet that description seems unwarranted, for one finds in it no developed argument for the truth of Buddhist doctrines.

THE INTENT OF THE *LI-HUO LUN*

The Preface of this text depicts Mou-tzu as a Confucian gentleman who is well versed not only in the classics but also in the works of such philosophers as Mencius, Hsün-tzu, and Lao-tzu. He has fled the chaos at the end of the Han dynasty to Chiao-chou, on the Gulf of Tonkin (modern Hanoi), in the southernmost region under Chinese political control, where circumstances lead him to seek retirement and to ponder the Buddhist Path through an examination of the *Book of Lao Tzu*. The Buddha Path for Mou-tzu is an amalgam of "dark learning," fusing Buddhist ideas with Taoist notions. Mou-tzu is criticized by his lit-

erati colleagues for turning his back on the classics he has so assiduously studied and for adopting the strange and heterodox path
of Buddhism. In a word, he is regarded as a cultural heretic. Despite his desire to remain in seclusion, he is forced to respond to
his critics. So he uses his leisure to collect citations from the Chinese sages and worthies to convince his critics of the validity of
being a traditional Chinese scholar and at the same time a devout
Buddhist. Mou-tzu's strategy is to address the literate elite, alluding to and citing the Chinese classics, which they know and
whose authority they recognize.

The winding path of dialogue leads from question to question
until at the end his critics are finally converted:

> When the doubters heard this, they became nervously defer-
> ential, paled, clasped their hands together, and backed away
> from their mats. Shrinking back in humility and prostrating
> themselves, they said, "We are really backward and blind
> persons, born into a benighted backwater. We have pre-
> sumed to utter foolish words and have not distinguished
> happiness from sorrow. But now, upon hearing your pro-
> nouncements, as suddenly as hot water melts the snow, we
> beg to change our feelings, cleanse our minds, and reform
> ourselves. May we please receive the five precepts and be-
> come lay followers?

On the surface, then, the intent of the *Mou-tzu Li-huo lun* does
seem quite clearly to be apologetic: to recommend acceptance of
the Buddha Path to the cultured Chinese aristocracy. Yet there is
an underlying dissonance, for the rhetoric of the text does not
occupy itself with issues of the truth of specifically Buddhist
doctrines. Thus, the unqualified assertion that the *Li-huo lun* is
a doctrinal apologetic for Buddhism needs reexamination, for it
has functioned as an interpretive assumption underlying most
of the modern scholarship on this text, focusing attention too
exclusively on doctrinal issues. The text itself does not attempt
to present the normative teachings of Buddhism. Rather, the *Mou-
tzu Li-huo lun* assumes the truth of the Buddha's Path and is
designed to enculturate that Path as a valid option for cultured
Chinese readers.

MODERN SCHOLARSHIP

Scholars assume that the *Mou-tzu Li-huo lun* is a doctrinal apologetic because it argues for the Path of the Buddha, and yet they find it rather deficient in its grasp of Buddhist doctrinal notions. Yet not every argument for Buddhism need be focused on doctrine. The questions about the text that have occupied the scholarly community to date have focused less on the rhetoric of the text itself than on extratextual issues of doctrine and provenance.

In particular, scholars have asked, Who was Mou-tzu? When did he write his treatise? Such a person is not reported in any of the historical records of the time. His literary product purports to represent the efforts of a figure from the waning years of the Later Han dynasty, that is, right after the death of Emperor Ling in 189. However, the earliest catalog of Buddhist literature, the *Tsung-li chung-ching mu-lu* of Tao An (d. 374) makes no mention of the *Li-huo lun*. The first reference to the work appears much later—almost three hundred years after its purported date of composition. It is included in the *Fa-lun*, a collection of Buddhist titles compiled by Lu Ch'eng (425–94) at the direction of the devout Emperor Ming (465–73) of the Liu Sung Dynasty. The *Fa-lun* itself is now lost, but its table of contents was included in chapter 12 of Seng Yu's (435–518) *Ch'u-san-tsung chi chi*, published in 515.[1] It is also cited in the commentary to the *Shih-shuo Hsin-yü* by Liu Chün (426–521) and its version of the coming of Buddhist scriptures to China is discussed.[2] Seng Yu also edited the *Hung-ming chi*, the collection of Buddhist apologetic works that is our source for the full text of the *Mou-tzu Li-huo lun*. After Seng Yu, the text apparently gained in popularity; there are later editions from the Sung, Yüan, and Ming dynasties. The *Taishō shinshū daizōkyō* includes a critical edition of the *Mou-tzu Li-huo lun* in its edition of the *Hung-ming chi* (T. 2102), and a modern critical edition is presented by Makita Tairyō.[3]

This absence of early, independent attestation regarding the date and authorship of the *Mou-tzu Li-huo lun* has led scholars to question its historical authenticity. In such a vacuum of corroborating witnesses, it is perhaps natural that the first issue becomes that of authenticating the text. "All the Chinese texts before the fifth century are silent about Mou-tzu and his work. Thus a first question must be posed: that of the authenticity and date of the work."[4] Henri Maspero argued that the *Li-huo lun* is to be dated not from the Later Han, but from around the year 250.[5] His principal argument is that portions of Article 1 of the *Li-huo lun* appear to have been borrowed from the *T'ai-tzu jui-ying pen-ch'i ching* (T. 185), a Chinese translation of an Indian text made between the years 222 and 229. The two texts are so close that clearly some borrowing has taken place, and since the *Pen-ch'i ching* is a translation from Sanskrit, it would appear that the *Li-huo lun* must be dependent on it. Maspero further argues that a mention of the state of the samgha in Khotan in Article 34 of the *Li-huo lun* must be an anachronism, since the situation of Buddhism in Khotan was not well known in China, particularly in the far south, before the monk Chu Shih-hsing brought back Mahāyāna scriptures and information from there in 260.[6] Maspero, however, does hold that the Preface of the *Li-huo lun* is historically authentic, demonstrating how it harmonizes with events described in the *Hou-han shu* and the *San-kuo chih*. As the Preface reports:

> Just then the Governor of [Chiao-]chou [learned that] he (i.e., Mou-tzu) was a highly cultured scholar living in retirement and summoned him. Again he feigned illness and excused himself. When that governor's younger brother became grand administrator of Yü-chang and was murdered by the Chief Commandant Tse Yung, the governor sent Cavalry Captain Liu Yen to take troops and go to [Yü-chang]. But he was afraid that, since the outlying areas were suspicious of one another, the troops would be unable to get through. The governor then made a request of Mou-tzu: "My younger brother has been murdered by a rebel and the pain in my bones and flesh has engendered anger in my heart. I wanted to send Captain Liu there, but he was afraid that, being suspicious, the outlying regions would make it difficult for our men and they would not get through. Only you, sir, well skilled in both letters and tactics, have the talent to take the initiative. Now, I wish you would be my chancellor and consent to go to Ling-ling and Kuei-yang to obtain passage along the open road. What do you say?"

Mou-tzu consents to go, but then is unable to do so when his mother dies, for he must observe the proper period of mourning.

Maspero argues that the two brothers, whose names are not given in the *Mou-tzu Li-huo lun*, are identified respectively in the *Hou Han shu* and the *San-kuo chih* as Chu Fu and Chu Hao, which provides independent confirmation that the report of them as brothers in the Preface to the *Li-huo lun* is historically accurate.

Paul Pelliot takes issue with Maspero's dating of the *Li-huo lun* at around the year 250. He argues that if Mou-tzu indeed wrote his work in the middle of the third century, he would have been quite an old man, unlikely to have been interested in, or able to record with such accuracy, the events of his youth. Furthermore, Pelliot argues that since Khotan was on the trade routes between India and China, knowledge of the state of Buddhism there was quite possible early in the second century. Thus, even if one accepts Maspero's argument that the *Li-huo lun* could not have been written until after the *T'ai-tzu jui-ying pen-ch'i ching* was translated from Sanskrit in 225, Mou-tzu, whose birth Pelliot assigns to 165–70, could himself have written the *Li-huo lun* after 225, when he would be approaching his sixties. However, Pelliot does not accept the dependence of the *Li-huo lun* on the *Pen-ch'i ching*, arguing instead that a now-lost tradition about the life of the Buddha existed in southern China and was the source for the parallel sections in Article 1 of the *Li-huo lun*. Thus, Pelliot gives full weight to the historical accuracy of the Preface and dates the text to the waning years of the second century, for the events recorded in the Preface occurred no later than 190–94.[7]

The Japanese Buddhologist Tokiwa Daijō takes a bolder tack, arguing that the *Li-huo lun* was concocted by the Buddhist monk Hui T'ung (ca. 426–ca. 478). Tokiwa bases his argument on parallel passages in the *I-hsia lun*, a Taoist work by Ku Huan (ca. 470), which in the course of exalting Taoism over Buddhism mentions a Buddhist monk called Hui T'ung. Tokiwa speculates that this monk wrote the *Li-huo lun* to refute Ku Huan's *I-hsia lun* and in the process copied some sentences from it, reproducing them in Articles 1 through 7.[8] As in all cases of parallels, the direction of dependence can go either way, and Pelliot argues that, on the contrary, it is the *I-hsia lun* that borrows from the *Li-huo lun*.

These scholars, despite their different conclusions as to the historical accuracy and textual authenticity of the *Mou-tzu Li-huo lun*, are in unison in assuming that the Preface was at least intended to be read as a historical document, whether actually reporting events or concocted to give that impression. Erik Zürcher bolsters Tokiwa's argument, contending that "Mou-tzu" is an imaginary figure created by a later author who provided this person with a historical background by linking him with some events and personalities known from other sources. Zürcher supports this view by pointing out that the Preface could not be autobiographical, because of its eulogistic nature. Who could believe that a Chinese scholar would compare himself with Mencius, "refuting the (perverse doctrines) of Yang Chu and Mo Ti," that he would claim that he was entrusted with a mission to Chingchou "on account of his wide learning and great knowledge," that he "has a complete understanding of civil as well as military affairs, and the talent to react independently (to any situation)"? Zürcher concludes that the Preface is "an idealized description of the scholar-official who leads a retired life far from the bustle of the world, repeatedly declines the official posts which are offered to him, finally feels constrained on moral grounds to accept an honorific mission, giving it up again when his mother dies, to spend the rest of his life in study and meditation."[9] Thus, in Zürcher's view, the Preface could not have been written by Mou-tzu himself and affords no entry into the provenance of the ensuing Dialogue.[10]

The discussions outlined above adopt a historical-critical approach to textual study, attempting to excavate and examine the historical realities underlying the text in question. The focus of academic interest in the *Mou-tzu Li-huo lun* has turned to these complex issues about its historicity, and it has been generally assumed that it was meant to be a doctrinal apologetic, despite its lack of doctrinal specificity. Yet that is perhaps a flawed approach. As formulated, the issue of the historical authenticity of our text is "an almost insoluble problem,"[11] for it is certainly possible either that, even without independent attestation, a real historical person named Mou-tzu who lived during the final days of the Later Han could have written a Buddhist tract or that an unnamed Han author could have constructed the Dialogue under the name of an idealized image of a Buddhist Master Mou. Even if Zürcher is correct, and there was no historical person called Mou-tzu to write the Preface, his argument is aimed only at the Preface. One could without fault imagine that a historical Mou-tzu did indeed write the Dialogue, but that the Preface came from the hand of a knowledgeable disciple or a later Buddhist author, as an example of the hagiographic introduction appended to many Buddhist texts. Yet, on strictly historical grounds, it is equally possible, in light of the dearth of corroborating evidence, that the work was a later creation of an unknown author. Historical argumentation alone seems unable to settle the issue—for lack of conclusively persuasive evidence.

THE APPROACH OF LITERARY CRITICISM

The goal of the present study of the *Mou-tzu Li-huo lun* is to clarify the rhetorical moves whereby this text itself, not its supposed author, accomplishes its literary task. I adopt an approach in literary criticism, more specifically in Reader-Response Criticism, that will focus on just how this text is constructed to render the Buddhist teachings congruent with Chinese cultural assumptions, and how it attempts to elicit the desired response from its intended readers. The meaning of the text and its contextual milieu is not seen as something to be unearthed by ever more exact and discerning extratextual study, but as the product of a careful reading of the text itself. That meaning is not an inherent property of the text, but rather an event that occurs during an interpretation of the text within its rhetorical context. And its context is more a function of that meaning than of dubious conclusions reached on inadequate evidence almost two thousand years after the event. I propose to replace the question "What does this text mean?" with the question "What does this text do?"[12] To uncover the *Li-huo lun's* literary structure and its impact on early Chinese Buddhism, we will examine both how the text itself is constructed and how that structure works to draw the reader to read his or her own experience into the text and to repeat the proffered experience of conversion. The text is not a stable, self-contained entity awaiting the scrutiny of the modern scholar, but is itself the record of an event, of a process meant to involve its readers.[13] To appreciate the significance of the *Mou-tzu Li-huo lun*, one needs to enter into the role of its intended readers, reconstructing as far as possible their response.

The literary approach employed here throws a new light on the *Mou-tzu Li-huo lun* and calls into question the assumptions of previous scholarship. In the first place, this reading of the *Li-huo lun* casts doubt upon the widely shared notion that early Chinese Buddhists simply misunderstood Buddhism because of the cultural filters they possessed. Modern scholarship has tended to regard early Chinese descriptions of Buddha and Buddhism as demonstrating Chinese misunderstanding of Indian Buddhism. For example, Fung Yu-lan thinks that the Taoist assumptions of early Chinese Buddhists prevented them from seeing any difference in the new teachings:

> The early stages of the Period of Disunity (221–589) ... witnessed a major revival of Taoism. It is characteristic of the thought of this time that many Neo-Taoists failed to realize that there was any fundamental difference between Lao Tzu and Chuang Tzu on the one hand and Buddhism on the other.[14]

Scholars have long appreciated the importance of the practice of "matching concepts" (*ko-yi*) in domesticating Buddhism, the equation of Indian Buddhist notions with familiar Taoist ideas. However, that appreciation has been accompanied by the conviction that such a practice resulted merely from syncretic misunderstandings, from a failure to recognize fundamental differences between Indian Buddhism and Chinese Neo-Taoism.

By contrast, I argue that the rhetorical strategy employed by the *Li-huo lun* in filtering Buddhist notions through Chinese cultural patterns of thought is a consciously adopted and creative strategy, intended to weave Buddhism into Chinese culture. Indeed, the successful passage of Buddhism into the "high" culture of China is a curious phenomenon, a unique event in the history of religious traditions, for most successful missionary endeavors have been bolstered by the "higher" status of the missionary culture over the indigenous culture.

A second assumption I wish to qualify is that the *Mou-tzu Li-huo lun* is simply a Buddhist apologetic, as it has been characterized by virtually all scholars who have treated the text to date. Kenneth Ch'en states that "the *Mou-tzu* was written as a sort of defense of Buddhism, supposedly by an author bearing the same name, to explain why he was converted."[15] Zürcher concurs, writing that the *Li-huo lun* is "one of the most detailed and interesting specimens of early Chinese Buddhist apologetic."[16] Pelliot agrees: "During his stay in Tonkin, so it seems, our young scholar was taken with Buddhism. When the troubles of the times made him renounce all desire for public life, Mou-tzu, despite the criticism he received, persisted in his faith. It was to defend that faith that, at an undetermined date, he published the small apologetic tract which has come to use under his name."[17] Arthur Wright repeats the refrain: "The earliest [Buddhist] apologetic which has come down to us was written at the end of the second century by a Chinese scholar-official who had fled to Chiao-chou (in modern Tongking) to escape the social and political upheavals in his native province. His volume is a kind of cyclopedia of the points at which Buddhism had to be reconciled with or adapted to Chinese tradition. In question-answer form he considers the claims of an alien tradition versus the claims of a native tradition."[18]

Yet the *Mou-tzu Li-huo lun* contains very little that might be labeled a direct defense of Buddhist doctrine, and thus simply and without qualification to characterize it as an apologetic is to cloud the issue. Indeed, the Buddhist ideas presented in this text are almost without exception assumed to be valid, taken on faith, as it were. The Buddha and his Tao are praised and eulogized, but reference to specific Buddhist doctrines does not form any major part of the dialogue. Neither the Four Noble Truths nor the Eightfold Path is mentioned. The foundational doctrine of dependent co-arising is never brought up. The Buddha's awakening is described, but the nature of that awakening never becomes the topic of any discussion. The focus of this text is not upon the defense of Buddhist doctrine against its critics, but upon the interpretation of the classical Chinese traditions in terms that are compatible with the Buddhist teachings. The argument is not over Buddhism itself, but over the validity of a Buddhist interpretation of the Chinese classics. The *Li-huo lun* is not, then, a Buddhist apologetic arguing for the doctrinal truth of Buddhism over against the Chinese traditions, but rather a culturally Chinese hermeneutic about how to interpret China's classical tradition, about the validity of a Buddhist hermeneutic of its classics. It is hermeneutics, not apologetics. It contends for a Buddhist hermeneutic of the classics as against the Han Confucian classicism that obtained among the literati. It is not an apologetic for Buddhism, but

rather an argument for a Buddhist interpretation of the classical
Chinese tradition.

The overall problematic is cultural, not conceptual. Mou-tzu
cannot argue for the validity of Buddhist doctrine on a level playing field as if Buddhist notions, even if familiar to his readers,
were culturally acceptable alternatives to be considered in light
of their logical persuasiveness. Rather, from the beginning of the
text, Buddhism is seen and depicted by the critics as a culturally
marginal option, strange to the *Li-huo lun's* Chinese readers. The
task of the text is, then, to gain a hearing for Buddhism within a
Chinese cultural ambiance. The rhetorical tension is between the
foreignness of the Buddhist understandings of the Chinese classics
and the familiarity of the Chinese traditions about those very classics. The Preface describes Mou-tzu as a classical scholar committed to the Buddha Tao. The validity of his stance is the point
at issue throughout, and the Dialogue is designed to persuade
its readers to accept a Buddhist interpretation of the classical
Chinese tradition.[19]

The *Li-huo lun* reveals its conceptual strategy for mediating
Buddhism within Chinese culture in Article 1, where it presents a
sinified version of the myth of the Buddha, describing the Buddha
in classical Taoist terms as having amassed the power of the Path
(*tao-te*) for countless aeons and showing the way to attain nonaction (*wu-wei*). Yet I would contend that this identification of
Buddha and his doctrine with Taoist notions does not, as is often
argued, represent a misunderstanding of Buddhism. Rather, it is a
conscious and creative rhetorical strategy of cultural adaptation
(presaging the later "matching concepts" methodology), whereby
the foreign Buddha and his doctrine are progressively mediated in
terms of Chinese culture. If, as some have argued, Chinese culture
is centered on an ineffable but all-encompassing Tao,[20] the task is
to draw Buddhist understandings into the sphere of Chinese cultural options by understanding them as embodiments and manifestations of a Tao long recognized as the ineffable source of all
that is. The effort to enculturate Buddhism into China, I would
suggest, moved within an all-encompassing framework centered
on the Tao: depicting Buddha and Buddhist doctrine as expressing the immanence of a reinterpreted Tao. Thus, the *Li-huo lun*
serves as a prime example, not of early Chinese Buddhist doctrinal apologetic, but of a patterned approach to the enculturation
of Buddhism in terms of a reinterpreted Chinese classical tradi-

tion, setting the stage and determining the context for later developments in Chinese Buddhism.

READER-RESPONSE CRITICISM

Philological-historical studies of the *Mou-tzu Li-huo lun*, such as Paul Pelliot's well-annotated "Meou-tseu ou les doutes levés," Fukui Kōjun's "Mou-tzu no kenkyū,"[21] and Makita Tairyō's *Gumyōshū kenkyū* offer detailed examinations of the text of the *Li-huo lun*. The many allusions and citations in the text have been traced with thoroughness, and the thorny issue of historical setting has been, if not resolved, at least discussed with a thoroughness that all but exhausts the available evidence.

I do not intend to argue over details with, or duplicate the efforts of, these scholars. My intent is rather to build upon this work and to focus on the experience of reading the text, adopting a language of reading and readers that may coax new insights from the text and broaden our understanding of just how such ancient texts wove their spell over their intended readers. Such a shift in approach entails a number of related shifts.

Reader-Response Criticism, as I attempt to practice it herein, is a species of structuralist hermeneutics that introduces a new set of interpretive terms into the analysis of narrative texts. Following Seymour Chatman's *Story and Discourse*, and trimming his method where appropriate, I distinguish a narrative text into the *what* of the text and the *how* of the text. The *what* is the *story* level, the content or the chain of events that happen to the characters. The *story* is bound by the beginning and end of the text itself. The *how* of the text, or its *discourse* level, is the rhetorical or symbolic expression by means of which that story is communicated, and it moves beyond the confines of the text itself to exercise its impact within an expanded horizon. In a word, the *discourse* is the telling of the *story* in its broad cultural context. The import of any text, in our case of the *Li-huo lun*, the message that it is valid to be both Buddhist and culturally Chinese, extends beyond the particular artistic or literary form of the text itself to the culture at large. The form chosen by the author of the *Li-huo lun*, an initial Preface followed by a Dialogue, is but one rhetorical form among many. Biography is another literary form that might convey the same discourse, for the biographies of Chinese Buddhist monks and sages offer paradigms of religious figures who are both Buddhist and Chinese. Chinese Buddhist pictures and statues offer yet another manifestation of this process in the visual depiction of Buddhist sages.[22] Thus the basic discourse about how to be both Buddhist and Chinese can take many different forms of expression: cultural hermeneutics, hagiography, statuary, even popular chanting and storytelling. The same discourse can have many stories. If the form had been available, second-century Chinese Buddhists might well have written a novel about the adventures of a cultured Chinese gentleman's quest for truth, an early version of *The Journey to the West* perhaps. Perhaps the *Mou-tzu Li-huo lun* is an early example of just such an endeavor. The discourse underlies the story and is not simply to be identified with the story, for the same discourse can be expressed in various stories and sundry manners.

Whatever form is chosen, it must have closure. Pictures must be finished, stories must be self-regulating, never leading beyond the system chosen, lest the final outcome of the narrative be lost in clouds of confusion.[23] Particularly if the point is to convince, the story must come to a conclusion. The *Li-huo lun* announces that its basic intention is to validate the option of being a cultured Chinese Buddhist, and this objective is woven into the design of the narrative from beginning to end. It concludes, appropriately, with the conversion of Mou-tzu's critics and the resolution of all their doubts and delusions.

And yet one may perhaps discern an even deeper design underlying the telling of the *Mou-tzu Li-huo lun*. Beneath its dialogue literary form, underneath its attempted demonstration of how scholars like Mou-tzu can adopt the Path of Buddha and still be culturally Chinese, lie deeper issues of personal and social identity. Geographically, Mou-tzu is located on the very margins of Chinese political and social control in Chiao-chih, at the very point where Chinese territory gives way to the lands of the "barbarians." The times are described as totally chaotic, for the Preface says that "after the death of Emperor Ling, the world was in disorder. Since only Chiao-chou remained relatively secure, strangers from the north came and settled there." I would suggest that this is something of an overstatement, for although the waning years of the Han did witness vast social unrest and warfare, the majority of the Chinese upper classes retreated not to the far south, but to the area just below the Yangtze. Yet Mou-tzu is located at the very farthest reaches of the realm—not because that area alone afforded safety from the troubles, but because it represented the extreme limits of the cultural and social sphere, marking the border between civilized Chinese order and barbarian chaos. Underlying the antinomy between the foreign Buddhist Path and the ancient Path of the Chinese sages is this more universally present chasm between chaos and order.

If I may take a clue from the work of Elizabeth Struthers Malbon on the New Testament, the starkness and irreconcilability of such a basic antinomy tends to be lessened and mediated when expressed in more manageable cultural divides. One might not know how to cope with chaos, but one can deal with barbarians, even to the point of adopting a foreign religion. From the latter days of the Han, and on through the subsequent dynastic shifts and social dissolution that characterized China for the next four hundred years, the specter of chaos loomed just over the next horizon. Thus, the deeper issue for the author of the *Li-huo lun* was not just about being a Buddhist Chinese. Rather, the threat, and at times the experience, of chaos and social "nothingness" haunted the entire age. Such an existentially frightening antinomy between chaos and order is transformed and transposed in the narrative of our text, first being expressed as the antinomy between Indian Buddhist notions and accepted Chinese cultural norms, then being collapsed into the image of a devout Chinese Buddhist. It is conceptually easier to mediate Buddhism and Chinese culture than to mediate chaos and order.[24]

The discourse that embodies itself in the story of Mou-tzu suggests a new way to mediate the threatening antinomies between chaos and order in an age of increasing strife and warfare. Expand your horizon, Mou-tzu invites; become truly a classical scholar by adopting the Path of Buddha. The *Li-huo lun* is attempting to broaden the cultural horizon in which Chinese social and personal identity can be constructed. By focusing not on the story level, but on the discourse, one is led to examine not the historicity of the story, as in the traditional scholarly attempts of Pelliot, Maspero, Fukui, and Tokiwa, but rather the rhetorical strategies whereby the underlying discourse communicates its meaning and tries to attain its desired result.

Yet, each and every time, it is the reader or the audience that has to provide that result. "They must respond with an interpretation: they cannot avoid participating in the transaction. They must fill in the gaps in essential or likely events, traits or objects which have gone unmentioned."[25] The *Li-huo lun* has more than its share of such gaps. Its stylized form of argumentation omits any reference to where the dialogue takes place or who the critic is, for in reality the conversation is to take place wherever a reading of the text occurs. We are not offered a description of Mou-tzu's appearance or told whether he was sitting at a table or pacing about the room. The information provided is extremely sketchy, yet sufficient for the purposes intended. The reader may fill in the gaps however she wishes without changing the calculated impact of the story. More-significant gaps do occur throughout the Dialogue, as when arguments set forth by Mou-tzu fail to elicit any response from the critic, who proceeds simply to ask his next question. The critic evinces no reaction to what he hears, no "uptake." Here again the reader is meant to fill in the gap, this time drawing away from the critic's position and internalizing the point of Mou-tzu's reasoning.[26] In the end, the *Li-huo lun* leaves no doubt of its intent: that the reader/hearer take up its underlying meaning and be converted himself, thus creating in microcosm a harmonious Buddhist-Chinese culture, able more effectively to mediate the stark dichotomy between order and chaos that all China was experiencing when the *Mou-tzu Li-huo lun* was written.

The real impact of Chatman's distinction between the discourse level and the story level of a text is seen in his analysis of narratives as communications. "Narratives are communications, thus easily envisaged as the movement of arrows from left to right, from author to audience. But we must distinguish between real and implied authors and audience: only the implied authors and audiences are immanent to the work, constructs of the narrative-transaction-as-text. The real author and audience of course communicate, but only through their implied counterparts. What is communicated is *story*, the formal content element of narrative; and it is communicated by *discourse*, the formal expression element. The discourse is said to 'state' the story."[27] One works through the story to the meaning of the discourse, trying to decode the underlying dilemmas mediated by the choice and development of the particular expression that is the text.

The narrative-communication situation entails the distinguishing of real author, implied author, narrator, narratee, implied reader, and real reader. Chatman illustrates the function of these critical entities by means of a diagram:

Real Author →	Implied Author → (Narrator) → (Narratee) → Implied Reader	→ Real Reader

"The box indicates that only the implied author and the implied reader are immanent to a narrative, that narrator and the narratee are optional (parentheses). The real author and real reader are outside the narrative transaction as such, though, of course, indispensable to it in an ultimate practical sense."[28]

One should perhaps start with the distinction between the narrator and the narratee. The narrator is the person who is supposed within the text to be telling the story. For instance, in *Huckleberry Finn* the implied author is distanced from the narrator, who is Huck himself, telling his own story. By contrast, in *War and Peace* the narrator is identical with the voice of the implied author, knowing the actions, feelings, and inner thoughts of all the characters as they move through the account. He is an unidentified but always-present storyteller. In the *Li-huo lun* the role of narrator shifts between the Preface and the Dialogue. In the Preface the narrator stands out clearly as the overt teller of the story of Mou-tzu, informing the reader where Mou-tzu comes from and what he is like. He informs the reader of things a character such as Mou-tzu would be too modest ever to claim about himself, for the mere act of doing so would disqualify him as a Confucian gentleman. This overt narrator in the Preface hovers over his presentation, omniscient not only as to the course of events, but also as to the inner thoughts of Mou-tzu. The narrator even reveals what Mou-tzu thinks when he steels himself to accept the governor's mission, as well as which text from the *Lao Tzu* he cites when he is compelled to retire from his assigned task: "Sighing, he said to himself, Lao-tzu wrote, 'Exterminate the sage, discard the wise.' If one cultivates himself and protects his essence, then the ten thousand things will not oppose his resolve...."

The narrator in the Preface is a constructed detached observer who tells us the story (history) of Mou-tzu. He tends to fade and become an effaced narrator, however, for he provides only the bare hagiographic bones of a description. He does not identify himself, nor does he provide much detail beyond what is needed to establish Mou-tzu as a bona fide classical gentleman.[29] By contrast, in the body of the text, when the narrative switches its rhetorical form to a dialogue, the narrator all but disappears from view. He becomes a covert presence, an almost objective lens focused on the give-and-take of the Dialogue, until the very end, where he emerges once again in the brief Postscript to report that the critics have been persuaded and the mediation successfully completed.

The narrator of the *Mou-tzu Li-huo lun* thus presents a third-person narrative in the Preface and in the conclusion of the Dialogue, and a first-person dialogue in the body of the work, where both Mou-tzu and his critics speak for themselves. The rhetorical construction of the Dialogue requires no intrusion by the narrator, and thus he fades to the role of merely presenting what is "said" by the interlocutors.[30] Indeed, the distinctions between covert, effaced, and overt narrators form a spectrum along which the narrator of the *Li-huo lun* moves back and forth. At the beginning he emerges to describe the troubling events at the end of the Han, Mou-tzu's flight to the south of China, and his relationships with the local officials there. Then our narrator fades into the background to become almost the stenographer for the Dialogue, finally reemerging at the end to report on the happy final outcome.

Narratee is a term coined by the literary critic Gerald Prince to refer to the story-level character to whom the story, not the discourse, is directed.[31] No narratee is identified on the story level in the Preface of the *Li-huo lun*. On that same story level, the Dialogue is carried on between Mou-tzu and an anonymous interlocutor (or interlocutors), who raises objections and receives answers to his questions. Yet this interlocutor is not really the narratee as defined by Reader-Response Criticism, for he (or they) is but a character in the story. He has been given specificity, for he raises questions that indeed characterize the initial reaction to Buddhism in China. We can judge from his argument that he is a Chinese gentleman familiar with the classical codes of Confucian and Taoist texts, aware of the presence of Buddhist monks in Khotan, and able to remember a visit to the Lo-yang library. Nevertheless, this critic (or critics, it is not clear how many there are) is so underdeveloped a character as to be a nameless cipher, merely raising issues for Mou-tzu to answer. The critic acts in his own right only in the last article, when he capitulates and begs to receive the lay vows of Buddhism. Otherwise, this figure functions merely as a mouthpiece for the furtherance of Mou-tzu's argumentation. He is so empty of defining traits that he serves merely as an intra-story model for the implied reader, and the story narrative has, in effect, no identified narratee.

Moving out from the center of Chatman's diagram, we next consider the implied author and the implied reader of the text. The implied author of a narrative text is not explicitly present, but has to be inferred, reconstituted by the reader from the act of reading. As Wayne Booth explains,

> As he writes, [the real author] creates not simply an ideal, impersonal "man in general" but an implied version of "himself" that is different from the implied author we meet in other men's works ... [or perhaps in other works of the same real author!]. Whether we call this implied author an "official scribe," or adopt the term revived by Kathleen Tillotson—the author's "second self"—it is clear that the picture the reader gets of this presence is one of the author's most important effects. However impersonal he may try to be, his reader will inevitably construct a picture of the official scribe.[32]

The implied author is different from the narrator, for he is the unstated presence who creates that narrator, together with all the rhetorical development of the text, "that stacked the cards in their particular way, had these things happen to these characters in these words and images. Unlike the narrator, the implied author can *tell* us nothing."[33] The only voice the implied author has is the narrative expression of the text, the how of its plot and arrangement. He informs only through the construction of a narrative disclosure. In the *Li-huo lun*, the identity of the implied author can be surmised only by attending to his narrative, to the notions and events portrayed in that narrative. Clearly he is a Chinese gentleman, familiar with the classics and himself a convert to the Buddha Path. He is cognizant of the "dark learning" that was popular from late Han times and through the subsequent dynastic changes, culminating in the florescence of Sui and T'ang

Buddhism. It is difficult to identify this implied author in any more detail, for we are limited to what can be gleaned from the construction of this one, rather brief text. Indeed, the *Li-huo lun* has been so successful in masking its implied author that modern attention has all but ignored his presence, focusing almost single-mindedly upon the actual historicity of Mou-tzu, who is simply a character on the story level.

The implied reader is the reader encoded in the rhetorical expression of the narrative, the persona we must be willing to adopt, at least for the duration of reading the text, so that we may experience the rhetorical impact of the narrative. The discourse of the *Li-huo lun* takes as its implied readers Chinese literati, who can be presumed to be familiar with the numerous classical allusions and citations scattered throughout the text. To enable a modern reader to share somewhat in this role of the *Li-huo lun's* implied readers, this study will attempt to decode the relevant classical allusions and citations, pointing out their relevance to the ongoing dialogue. In its own time and place, our text functioned so as to wean its original implied readers away from the cultural biases of the narratee/character of the critic, until the final moment when both he and they accept Buddhism and receive the lay precepts.

Chatman's terminology, awkward as such abstractions tend to be, does provide a way of talking about the difference between the narratee/character of the critical interlocutor and the implied readers, for whereas the story-level dialogue is directed to this narratee/character, the rhetorical discourse and its impact are directed to the implied readers. It is they who are to elicit the "uptake" to Mou-tzu's arguments and they who are to be convinced by his rhetoric. The meaning of the *Li-huo lun* thus lies not in the text itself, but in the minds of its implied readers, even to modern readers to the extent that they are able to reconstruct and fill that rhetorical role.[34] If indeed, as I maintain, the *Mou-tzu Li-huo lun* is constructed not simply to argue apologetically for its own world of Buddhist meaning, but to validate its Buddhist reading of the classical Chinese canon, thereby mediating the personal and social chaos of the times, then it is more in harmony with the text to attend to its rhetorical discourse and its impact on those readers than to glean whatever remnants of historical information it might have strewn in its wake.

Finally, the real author and the real readers are the flesh-

and-blood people who write and read the text. The real, flesh-and-blood author stands outside the text, because the text, once written, has an existence independent of that author. The real reader also stands outside the text, because she comes to the text from some other context, and is, initially at least, not an immanent part of the textual transaction. When we, as real readers, actually read a text, we do not encounter the real author. In a text like the *Mou-tzu Li-huo lun*, we cannot then conclude that its main character is a flesh-and-blood person at all! What we do encounter— or, said better, what we do construct—is the implied author, the persona implied in the text itself, a kind of second self created by the real author for the purpose of telling the story—in this case, of presenting a dialogue on how to read the classical Chinese tradition.

The *Li-huo lun* is a narrative about how to read narratives, about how to understand the stories that constitute the classical traditions. Often its implied author jumps out of the text to speak over the head of his character, the critic, to the implied reader, attempting to convince him that Buddhism is indeed congruent with Chinese culture. Often the character Mou-tzu offers arguments that would be immediately countered by any intelligent critic in a real-life dialogue. Mou-tzu makes comments that are ignored by his interlocutor, that have no uptake in the story development. These are not, I think, simply lapses in cogent argumentation, but rhetorical devices through which the implied author is speaking not to the intra-story, constructed interlocutor, but to the intended, implied reader. After all, the *Li-huo lun* aims not to give an objective account of an afternoon of dialogue, but rather to convince its implied readers to redefine their cultural norms and give Buddhism a second look. The real reader, of course, is anyone who takes up the text to read. One supposes that at the time when the *Li-huo lun* was written, its real readers were by and large identical with the implied readers envisaged by the text—that is, cultured Chinese gentlemen who were at once conversant with the classics and thus able to recognize the *Li-huo lun's* many classical allusions and citations, and also doubtful of the worth of the strange foreign Dharma teaching recommended by the character Mou-tzu. Today, however, the real readers of this text are for the most part scholars. They take critical stances vis-à-vis the text and attempt to interpret it through a variety of methods.

Modern scholars have all focused upon the *story* level of the *Mou-tzu Li-huo lun*: the account of Mou-tzu's life given in the Preface and the question of its historical validity; the Dialogue between the main character Mou-tzu and his interlocutor; and within the Dialogue the historical sources for individual articles, such as the story of the Buddha in Article 1 or the introduction of Buddhism to China in Article 21. By contrast, I would like to focus on the *discourse* level, or the *rhetoric* of this text: the way in which the language of the text weaves its spell over the reader. By and large, critical scholarship has attended to the story of Mou-tzu arguing for the truth of the Dharma with his cultured interlocutor. In so doing, scholars have, I think, overlooked the rhetorical structure of the narrative and "misread" it as a source of historical information. One can of course validly read a narrative text with an agenda different from that intended by its author. Yet I think more care must be taken to perform such a "strong reading" with an awareness that we are trying to coax historical information from a text that is rhetorically designed to lead elsewhere.[35] The text does indeed provide historical clues, but they are entwined in its rhetoric and must be carefully and sensitively lifted out of their literary context. Questions about who Mou-tzu in fact was, about the sources from which "he" drew, about the conceptual meaning of the text in itself—in a word, all the issues addressed by critical scholarship—must be grounded upon a prior appreciation of the text's self-contained rhetorical structure. If one attends not only to the story of the *Li-huo lun*, but also to its discourse, its meaning is seen to be not an internal property of the story awaiting scholarly cross-referencing to the Chinese classics and histories, but rather a dynamic event in the process of enculturating Buddhism in China. Its language is not merely referential or informative, but rhetorical, affective, and—in its time—powerful.

However, the rhetoric of the *Li-huo lun* has lost its punch for the modern reader. In terms of any modern interest in Buddhist thought, it no longer persuades, for the context of the modern reader is so far removed from that of the *Li-huo lun* as to blunt its impact. The main reason for this is that so much time has passed and the efforts of the early Chinese Buddhists have been so successful that there is no longer any cultural dissonance in viewing Buddhism as Chinese. Readers of the *Li-huo lun* today live with traditions and within interpretive communities far removed from those of Mou-tzu's time. The issues of personal and social chaos that face us are vastly different from those of the *Li-huo lun's* time, with nuclear holocaust, ecological disaster, and the social dissolution of overpopulated cities in the forefront of our consciousness. Thus, any attempt to recover the rhetorical power of the *Li-huo lun* must be an exercise in literary reconstruction, an attempt, first and foremost, to read the *Li-huo lun* as its implied readers would have done. That is indeed a daunting task, and on one's own it would be impossible to reconstruct putative responses for third- or fourth-century Chinese readers.[36] Happily, there is no need to do this, for the text itself encodes its implied reader for us in the description of the interlocutor. He is a Chinese gentleman schooled in the classical tradition and biased against the foreignness of Buddhism.

A Reader-Response approach is not simply an antiquarian literary endeavor. A creative "misreading" of a text such as the *Li-huo lun* can illuminate the cultural patterns of early Chinese Buddhism. A Reader-Response approach, while not disregarding the ideological syncretism of the concepts matched through the *ko-yi* procedure, is more focused on identifying the rhetorical function of the endeavor. It might also be able to shed some light on the social context within which the text's rhetorical strategy could have been effective. The recognition that the *Li-huo lun* consciously adopts Taoist categories to interpret the Buddha Path does not prevent one from gathering the gleanings the author has strewn throughout his narrative and coaxing out some social and historical conclusions about where this text came from, who wrote it, and what role it played in the history of Chinese Buddhism.

For example, one cannot fail to notice that the centrist Buddhism advanced by the *Li-huo lun* did fail to introduce principal Mahāyāna themes. To cite but the main example, the central doctrine of dependent co-arising finds scant representation in the *Li-huo lun*. And the understanding of emptiness was interpreted not through the Indian rejection of Abhidharma essentialism, but in terms of Taoist "empty nothingness" (*hsü wu*). The overall pattern of Chinese Buddhism was centrist, seeing the Dharma as Tao, the ineffable yet identified source for all things. Such a pattern could not long remain unchallenged by Buddhists engaged in the reading of the Mahāyāna scriptures, and this led directly to the stress on emptiness in the later Prajñāpāramitā school of Tao An.

One result of employing a Reader-Response approach to reading a text like the *Li-huo lun* can be the clarification of the dynamic movement behind early Chinese attempts to enculturate Buddhism, and thus clearer insight into the patterns against which subsequent Chinese forms of Buddhism developed.

The first task, however, is to examine the discourse of the text, the how of its rhetorical strategies. Which brings us to the question of plot: What is it that happens here? To whom does it happen? Is it significant? Employing the tools of Reader-Response Criticism sketched above, we now turn our attention to the dynamic rhetoric of the *Mou-tzu Li-huo lun*.

THE PLOT OF THE *MOU-TZU LI-HUO LUN*

As a narrative text, the *Li-huo lun* tells a story, presents an unfolding of events involving its characters, and moves from a beginning point to a conclusion. As the story moves, it invites the reader to move into and along with it. The story is constructed by the discourse and entails events and characters. Things happen and people are changed. In schematic form, the narrative is composed of two levels, the discourse level constructing the story level with its events and characters.

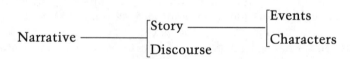

The author creates a discourse in the form of a story composed of events and characters, developing a plot and leading the implied reader into the story and, in the end, into engaged participation in the issue that constitutes the meaning of that story. The story begins with the life of Mou-tzu, who then serves as the central, and only developed, character of the main story. He is a paradigm of traits, in Chatman's phrase, a "relatively stable and abiding" personality.[37] He is described in the Preface as a Confucian scholar intent on the practice of the path of Han Confucianism, who (after an interlude of *hsien* Taoist practices mentioned in Article 31) subsequently devotes himself to the Buddha Path. And later he becomes a proponent of that Path to his fellow literati.

This character stands out not only against the background of orthodox Chinese learning, but, more profoundly, in contrast to the social and personal chaos of his times. He proceeds to mediate the antinomies inherent in his situation. First he transforms the contradictions into issues of spatial civilization, located as he is in this narrative on the very margins of Chinese civilization, and treats them in terms that challenge the tradition of the civilized/barbarian dichotomy. He responds directly to Chinese ethnocentric claims by negating them, urging his critic to broaden his cultural assumptions of ethnic superiority and to identify the center of the world not with China, but with India. In doing so, he invites the implied reader to reevaluate the old notion that only the Chinese are civilized, for in his time and for some centuries thereafter—whether precisely at the end of the Han or throughout the Three Kingdoms, the Eastern or Western Tsin, or during the North and South Dynasties—the heartland of Chinese civilization was in distress, often under the direct political control of non-Chinese Emperors. Strict claims for Chinese ethnocentrism were scarcely believable in a situation where the Chinese literati were themselves emigrés in a hitherto strange and humid hinterland. One could only hold on nostalgically to a long-past age of Chinese cultural hegemony or reinterpret and adjust the cultural codes to open up the world to the so-called barbarians—at least this was Mou-tzu's contention. Having made the latter move himself, Mou-tzu can then recommend the religion of the "barbarian" Buddha as a cultural option entirely in harmony with the classical tradition, reinterpreted. From a literary perspective, the setting of the story performs a crucial rhetorical function and is not any more, or any less, grounded in actual Chinese history than is *War and Peace*, for example, grounded in Russian history.[38]

The events of such a story are called a "plot," defined by Aristotle as the "arrangement of incidents."[39] The working out of such a plot is a process of delimiting or narrowing the options for the reader. "The choices become more and more limited until the final choice seems not a choice at all, but an inevitability."[40] If the reader has entered into the plot of the *Li-huo lun*, the final conversion of the critic seems but the natural outcome of what is learned through the Preface about Mou-tzu's sterling character and throughout the Dialogue about the issues that challenge the old cultural codes.

But plots must be believable. Not just any concatenation of

incidents will do the deed. They must be arranged skillfully and elicit on the part of the reader an assent that, "yes, indeed, this does represent the way things actually are!" Such believability is ordinarily achieved by arranging the events and incidents according to accepted cultural codes so as to lend verisimilitude to the plot's unfolding. "The convention of filling in by verisimilitude is ... basic to narrative coherence.... Audiences come to recognize and interpret conventions by 'naturalizing' them,"[41] by seeing them against or within a believable framework. The reader of *War and Peace,* knowing something of the history of Russia and Napoleon's failed invasion, recognizes that Tolstoy's narrative reflects what actually happened, even if the characters are all literary creations. One naturalizes something by seeing it as probable, by at least temporarily buying into its verisimilitude. Mou-tzu's location on what is, according to the old codes, the margins of the civilized world, and his status as a Confucian gentleman add to the verisimilitude of the *Li-huo lun's* plot, and are indeed absolutely necessary for its successful outcome. The Preface, then, is not merely an appendage to the text, but part and parcel of the overall rhetorical strategy of the narrative. This Preface is not incidental or extraneous information for later literati, but an essential part of the rhetorical effectiveness of the whole. Only if the reader has accepted the verisimilitude of the story's plot will she "fill in the gaps in the story, adjusting events into a coherent whole, even when ordinary life expectations are called into question."[42] If the reader is to perform "uptake" on the story, to move beyond the surface content to the meaning of the underlying discourse—mediating order and chaos first through the broadening of cultural geography and then through the Buddha Path—she must acknowledge the verisimilitude of the plot.

Gérard Genette has shown that the artistic construction of such verisimilitude is grounded in public opinion, in the commonly accepted cultural codes that establish human order, "what would be today called an ideology, that is, a body of maxims and presuppositions which constitute at once a vision of the world and a system of values."[43] Perhaps rather than an ideology, it would more aptly be called a version of commonsense expectations. A new system of such maxims and values is precisely what the *Li-huo lun* attempts to establish, drawing the reader to accept Mou-tzu's reinterpreted version of the Chinese classics in light of the Buddha Path. And yet it must accomplish this in terms of the accepted Chinese notions of meaning and value. It is for this reason that our text is a hermeneutical essay and not an apologetic tract.

One cannot then begin with the question of the historical authenticity of the *Li-huo lun*. The situation is rather like that presented in the riddle of the explorer who comes suddenly upon a strange island in the middle of the ocean. On this island live two tribes, one of whose members always tell the truth and one of whose members always lie. The explorer comes ashore to find the members of the two tribes intermingled as they await his arrival. He says to the first person he meets, "What tribe do you belong to?" The fellow mumbles something unintelligible. A second island person says, "He said that he belongs to the True tribe." Yet a third comments that the second is lying. The hearer of the riddle is then directed to determine which tribe the third person in fact belongs to. Eventually one realizes that what must first be ascertained is the veracity of the second, and then the first, islander, for this in turn determines whether the third is speaking truth or falsehood. In the end, it dawns on one that the first person had to have said: "I am a member of the True tribe." One does not know if in fact that is true, only that this is what he must have said, for, if he belongs to the False tribe, he lied and claimed to be a member of the True tribe, or, if he is of the True tribe, he told the truth and does in fact belong to that tribe. One may then quickly deduce that the statement of the second person is true, and that of the third a lie. In the case of the *Li-huo lun* it is similarly difficult to ascertain whether or not the events reported are truly historical, for if it is a work of fiction, it strives to present things as authentically as possible, and if it is a work of factual history, it also strives to present things as authentically as possible. I imagine finding Balzac's *Lost Illusions* in a corner at some dusty garage sale. If one had no access to the commentarial studies on its author or his works, one might have a similarly difficult time adjudicating whether or not its characters were actually flesh-and-blood persons.

INTERPRETATION AS A FUNCTION OF
AN INSTITUTIONAL COMMUNITY

The *Li-huo lun* argues for a new interpretation of the classical Chinese tradition. As such, it stands in contrast to the more or less established and normative traditions of Han Confucianism.

Those traditions were the result of long and at times painful argumentation and themselves incorporated many Taoist and Neo-Taoist notions.[44] The Han dynasty had witnessed intense political and cultural debate over the issue of how to interpret the classics. In the year 135 B.C.E. the Emperor Wu had established a system of Erudites, one scholar specializing in each of the recognized five classics, and in 124 B.C.E., at the suggestion of the philosopher Tung Chung-shu, he set up the Imperial Academy to institutionalize their scholarship and lend them official support. Indeed, *The History of the Han Dynasty* reports that Tung Chung-shu even proposed a ban on all non-Confucian schools of thought:

> The teachers of today have diverse ways, men have diverse doctrines, and each of the philosophic schools has its own particular position, and differs in the ideas it teaches. Hence it is that the rulers possess nothing whereby they may effect general unification, the government statutes having often been changed, while the ruled know not what to cling to. I, your ignorant servitor, hold that all not within the field of the Six Disciplines [*Chun Qiu, I Jing,* books of *Poetry, History, Rites,* and *Music*] or the arts of Confucius should be cut short and not allowed to progress further. Evil and licentious talk should be put to a stop. Only after this can there be general unification, and can laws be made distinct, so that people may know what to follow.[45]

As Peerenboom remarks, "When Emperor Wu, following Dong Zhongshu's advice, established the Imperial University and examination system with the Confucian classics as core curriculum, the eventual victory of Confucianism was assured."[46] Yet all dispute was not thereby ended. Under Emperor Hsüan there arose a conflict over which commentary to use in interpreting *The Spring and Autumn Annals,* and a group of scholars were convened at the Shih-ch'ü Pavilion to discuss and determine the issue. As Homer Dubs reports:

> The proceeding took the form of summoning the outstanding scholars from all over the empire and fixing authoritatively and by imperial authority, the correct interpretation of the various classics. . . . In the development of Confucianism, the

discussions in the Shih-ch'ü Pavilion fill a place corresponding to that occupied in the occident by the first General Council of the Christian Church at Nicea (325 A.D.). In the time of Emperor Hsüan the *Tso-chuan* had not yet become canonical; the *Chou-li* was later also added to the canon; these official additions and other changes (made by Wang Mang) necessitated another revision of the Confucian tradition. This discussion was summoned by Emperor Chang on December 23, 79 A.D., and met in the White Tiger Lodge (Po-hu Kuan). Its procedure was modeled on that in the Shih-ch'ü Pavilion; Emperor Chang similarly attended it and himself decided disputed points.[47]

The White Tiger Lodge Council resulted in victory for the New Text School of Tung Chung-shu (179?–104? B.C.E.), which had combined the Confucianism of Confucius with a cosmology based on yin-yang and Five Elements theory and thereby developed not only a universalizing theoretical framework, but also a normative hermeneutical method for reading the classics. This was codified under Tung Chung-shu's "ten guiding principles" for interpreting the inner meaning of *The Spring and Autumn Annals*.[48] The orthodoxy established by Tung Chung-shu, and seconded by the efforts of such scholars as Yang Hsiung, shaped the mind of medieval China for more than a thousand years.[49] Ancient Chinese literature became the literature of Confucianism and was interpreted to teach Confucian lessons. Scholars "naturally gravitated to the Confucians, for they possessed the scholarly traditions of the country, and anyone who acquired a scholarly education was inevitably given a Confucian indoctrination."[50] Thus Confucianism became the normative orthodoxy, with "the advantage of unifying the country intellectually by making one system of thought current among all educated men."[51] The ancient literature thus became the province of the Confucian elite. Tjan Tjoe Som explains:

The Classics were not just ancient books containing descriptions of the past. They were *ching* 'canons', literally the 'warp', which provided the standards for man to arrange his life, for the ruler to govern his people. The study of these canons was not for the sake of historical knowledge alone; this knowledge should teach the student how to behave, how to order his actions so as to be in harmony with the sacred rules of antiquity.... The books which in the Han were assigned official teachers were no longer ordinary documents, but sacred writings containing messages from the past, to be respectfully preserved and guarded against adulteration, and to be understood in a spirit of pious reverence.[52]

The Confucian reading of the classics was erected into a normative orthodoxy by such Han scholars as Tung Chung-shu and Yang Hsiung, and all other teachings were seen as worthless by comparison. Yang Hsiung writes:

The Way of Confucius is like the four main rivers: they flow through the middle land and eventually enter the great sea. But the courses of other men are streams of the northwest, treading their way back and forth among the lands of the Yi and Mo barbarians. Some enter into the T'o river, some drain into the Han.[53]

Yang Hsiung here elevates the classics to a new level of normative value. "Throughout the Han men had venerated the classics, but in asserting that they were the only works of value, Hsiung was calling for a Confucian fundamentalism of new proportions."[54] He writes:

Never has there been anyone who set aside ships and barges and crossed a watercourse. And there will never be anyone who sets aside the Five Classics and crosses the Way. Should someone who would abandon the constantly precious and crave after rare delicacies be regarded as a man who understands taste? And could someone who would discard the great sages and fall in love with the philosophers be regarded as a man who understands the Way?[55]

Supported by imperial institutions and enjoying control of the interpretation of the classics, Han Confucianism became the dominant interpretive community of the time. The normative value of the classics was determined not by the texts themselves, but rather by the collective decision of the Han Confucianists as to what they mean and what in them is of special importance. Those decisions constituted the standard story and laid a bedrock of belief, the denial of which threatened cultural chaos.[56] The values enshrined by this interpretive community derived not from the ancient texts themselves, but from their institutional adoption, and "while no institution is so universally in force and so perdurable that the meanings it enables will be normal for ever, some institutions or forms of life are so widely lived in that for a great many people the meanings they enable will seem 'naturally' available and it takes a special effort to see that they are the products of circumstances."[57] What counts as valuable in the ancient literature is not what the old texts themselves say, as if they could speak apart from the interpretive reading of later thinkers. Their language is not constative, striving to be accountable to an objective world, but performative, aimed in particular circumstances to achieve a desired effect. The values and truths of the classics, thus understood, were constrained by the interpretive community of Han Confucianism.[58] Thus, the reading of the classics in Han times was not a matter of open possibilities. "The dominance of tradition as the source of practical and affective norms leads to a restriction of the novel contributions of persons as individuals who would break with continuities of the past and establish new directions in thought or institutional practice. History thrives on the actions of rebels, idiosyncratic creators and innovators. Traditional societies prize continuities as embodiments and elaborations of the thinking and action of the past."[59] The shape of such a tradition was determined by a normative institution that authorized only a finite number of acceptable strategies.[60] The principles enshrined in the normative version of the classics led to a reading of the old texts that was to take precedence over other interpretations, which were, according to Tung Chung-shu, to be discouraged and suppressed.[61]

The notion of "interpretive communities" is one of the central themes of Stanley Fish's literary criticism and can, I think, help us to understand the immense force of the official community of Han interpreters in setting the meaning of the classical texts. Having abandoned the stability of the text as an illusion, and being forced to look beyond the text for the source of interpretive agreements,[62] Fish saw such communities as constituted by those who, belonging to the same group, share the interpretive strategies that constitute the properties of texts.[63] Such "interpretive strategies are not put into execution after reading (the pure act of perception in which I do not believe); they are the shape of reading, and because they are the shape of reading, they give texts their shape, making them rather than, as it is usually assumed, arising from them."[64]

What is normative for one community, seen as a matter of common insight and immediate assent, may appear strange and outlandish to another community. Indeed, Mou-tzu's reading of the classics appeared strange to his Chinese contemporaries. However, if in fact there is no single, objective way of reading a text, of interpreting the classics, then all interpretations are functions of such communities. When disagreements arise among competing communities, Fish tells us,

> the assumption in each community will be that the other is not correctly perceiving the 'true text,' but the truth will be that each perceives the text (or texts) its interpretive strategies demand and call into being. This explains ... why there are disagreements and why they can be debated in a principled way: not because of a stability in texts, but because of a stability in the makeup of interpretive communities and therefore in the opposing positions they make possible. Of course this stability is always temporary (unlike the longed for and timeless stability of the text). Interpretive communities grow larger and decline, and individuals move from one to another; thus, while the alignments are not permanent, they are always there, providing just enough stability for the interpretive battles to go on, and just enough shift and slippage to assure that they will never be settled.[65]

THE ARGUMENT OF THE *LI-HUO LUN*

The *Li-huo lun* is engaged in challenging the interpretive patterns of Han Confucianism, arguing for the validity of a Buddhist strategy. To achieve its goal, however, it must move within the patterns of the interpretive community of Chinese literati, recognizing the givenness of "the consensual background."[66] Confucius had looked back with longing to the time of the Duke of Chou, the golden age of benevolence and harmony. The Confucianism of Tung Chung-shu and Yang Hsiung had championed the past as the norm and source for present insight. Indeed, when the Chinese literati "wanted to demonstrate or explain, when they intended to narrate or describe, the more original authors employed historical stereotypes and conventional expressions, drawn from a common fund."[67] The style of reasoning was not the presentation of a sequential chain of points leading to a final all-embracing logical conclusion. "The movement is entirely concrete, leading from one example to another."[68] It is a kind of reasoning that moves from case to case, assuming an analogy of present concerns with paradigmatic examples from the past.[69]

The Dialogue of the *Li-huo lun* is constructed in this same fashion. The first three articles establish the basic stance of the text, setting forth the normative story of the Buddha's life, Mou-tzu's equation of Buddha with the Tao, and a brief, very Chinese, description of Tao. These articles set the stage for the disagreements that follow by outlining what is normative tradition for the two different communities, Chinese and Buddhist, to which Mou-tzu belongs.

Articles 4 through 8 move to a presentation of the overall cultural conflict. Article 4 answers the objection that Mou-tzu's Buddhism is in basic contradiction with Confucius and the classics. Articles 5 and 6 treat the culturally dissonant style and abundance of Buddhist scriptures. Article 7 answers the claim that there is no historical precedent for the adoption of Buddhism. And Article 8 deals with the strangeness of the physical description of the Buddha that Mou-tzu presented in Article 1.

Articles 9 through 13 attempt to show that Mou-tzu's Buddhist practice contradicts only specific interpretations of accepted behavior, but not the classics themselves. Articles 9 and 10 contrast filial piety with the Buddhist practices of tonsure and celibacy, arguing that Buddhist practices do not violate authentic filial piety. Article 11 defends Buddhists from the charge that they violate the rules of propriety. Articles 12 and 13 contrast Buddhists' belief in reincarnation (life after death), and their preoccupation with spirits, with the Confucian advice to keep the spirits at a distance, adducing counterexamples from the accepted tradition. Article 12 comes close to arguing for the Buddhist doctrine of life after death (i.e., for the continuance of the spirit). And yet, even here, the focus is not on the relative merit of notions about an afterlife, but on whether such an idea violates the classical norms.

Articles 14 and 15 tackle the fundamental cultural criticism faced by Chinese Buddhists. In Article 14 Mou-tzu answers the critic's claim to Chinese cultural hegemony over barbarian teachings, while in Article 15 he responds to an argument against Buddhist practice and for the primacy of the Confucian family.

In Articles 16 through 24 Mou-tzu's interlocutor turns a critical eye on particular Buddhist practices. Article 16 answers the accusation that Buddhists practice a phony brand of nonaction. Article 17 similarly refutes the critique that the Buddhist practice of giving (*dānapāramitā*) is done only for show. Article 18 argues for the validity of the Buddhist usage of analogy, demonstrating the impossibility of sticking to the literal sense of things. Article 19 counters criticisms about Buddhist renunciation. Article 20 answers the interlocutor's challenge to Mou-tzu to either put up or shut up—to preach Buddhist teachings at the court or withdraw into his private quarters and stop bothering people. Article 21 breaks the pattern, for it asks a simple question about the circumstances of the introduction of Buddhism into China, eliciting from Mou-tzu an account of Emperor Ming's famous dream, demonstrating that Buddhism is itself a revered, imperially sanctioned Chinese tradition. The thread of the argument is taken up again in Article 22, where Mou-tzu's challenger charges that Buddhists like to talk more than practice. Article 23 reiterates the point, refuting the idea that Buddhists prefer rhetoric over virtue. Article 24 answers the critique that Buddhists have an uncontrolled literary style and doctrine.

Articles 25 through 29 introduce the basic hermeneutical issue underlying the entire Dialogue. In Article 25 the critic objects specifically to the use of the Chinese classics for the explanation of the Buddha's teachings. His point is perhaps more that he objects to a Buddhist reading of those classics because he wants to keep the two traditions separate and distinct. But in his response, Mou-tzu continues on his previous tack, making numerous allusions to Lao-tzu and to Mencius. In Article 26, the critic asks why Mou-tzu prefers to use the Chinese texts rather than the Buddhist scriptures, thus confusing things that were meant to be kept apart. Article 27 responds to the assertion that the representatives of official orthodoxy in the capital do not even mention the Buddha, while in Article 28 Mou-tzu answers criticism that the flowery words of Buddhist praise ill accord with the reality of Buddha.

Mou-tzu is constantly engaged in defending Buddhist practice, and yet his arguments make no attempt to show the truth of Buddhist teachings. He is solely concerned with demonstrating that they do not violate the Chinese classics. His task is much more a question of hermeneutics than of apologetics.[70] The remaining articles, 29 through 37, all treat Neo-Taoist notions of *hsien* practices. Article 29 affords Mou-tzu an opportunity to reject the immortals (*hsien*). Articles 30 and 31 treat Taoist dietary practices, also rejected. In Article 32 Mou-tzu criticizes the Taoist attempt to dispense with medicine. Article 33, which forms the central discussion in this last section, allows Mou-tzu to differentiate Buddhist nonaction from the nonaction of *hsien* practitioners. Article 34 similarly allows him the chance both to reject *hsien* immortality and to maintain his orthodox Chinese stance. Article 35 treats the shallowness of the monks of Khotan, who I will later argue are to be seen as symbols for naturalized Buddhist practitioners of magic and *hsien* ways. In Article 36 Mou-tzu rejects *hsien* practices of tranquillity. Article 37 asserts the inevitability of death against the Taoist belief that the immortals never die.

The Postscript reports that the previous thirty-seven articles are modeled on the thirty-seven chapters of the first book of the *Lao Tzu* and the thirty-seven factors of awakening. It then reports the conversion of the critics and their request to become lay Buddhist practitioners.

The Dialogue is not structured as a tight logical process that moves by building its argument point by point. Rather, its sequence of arguments charts a broad area, often circling back to or recalling earlier arguments. Within the charted area, at any time, the implied reader might get the point, might see the validity of reading the classics as Mou-tzu does. The overall aim is to persuade the reader that Buddhist readings of the Chinese classics are indeed valid and represent no abandonment of things Chinese. The story-level critics all acknowledge the point at the end. On the discourse level, the implied reader is likewise expected to see the point.[71]

The character Mou-tzu is presented as belonging simultaneously to two communities: he is both a cultured Chinese gentleman and a Buddhist. And he wants to be the former in light of the latter. Throughout the narrative, in both the Preface and the Dialogue, maxims, citations, and allusions from the Chinese classics abound. Indeed, the *Li-huo lun* suffers from an excess of such intertextuality. Interestingly, only a few references are made to Buddhist scriptures or commentaries, and even these do not directly cite those texts. The argument is not, then, about the relative merits of doctrine, but about how to read the Chinese classics. No Chinese literati could function within Chinese society if seen as abandoning the traditions wholesale.[72] If indeed, as argued above, the intent of the *Li-huo lun* is to present a narrative with all the marks of verisimilitude, such an option was neither reasonable nor possible. The task of the *Li-huo lun* was to "naturalize" its presentation of the implications of being both Buddhist and Chinese. Chatman explains this phenomenon:

> The norm for verisimilitude is established by previous texts—not only actual discourses, but the "texts" of appropriate behavior in society at large. Verisimilitude is an "effect of corpus" or of "intertextuality." . . . It is a form of explication, pointing from effect to cause, and even reducible to a maxim. Further, because maxims are public, that is, "tend to go without saying," they may be implicit or backgrounded.[73]

The *Li-huo lun* establishes its verisimilitude by alluding to and citing the ancient texts of classical orthodoxy, presenting the "texts" of proper Han Confucian behavior, such as those on filial piety and the proper observance of propriety. It wants the reader to read its recommendations in light of these texts, for, as Article 26 states, one could not speak to cultured non-Buddhists by citing texts and examples of which they have no knowledge and to which they feel no affinity. That would condemn the enterprise to certain failure, since it would seem to them that Mou-tzu was not talking in terms of any civilized (i.e., accepted) system of cultural codes of truth and value.

The *Mou-tzu Li-huo lun's* impact on its reader is heightened by the design of the Dialogue. In the Preface, the narrative does establish a sense of present movement, for the reader hears the narrator, more or less overtly, tell the story of Mou-tzu's life. In the Dialogue, where the narrator all but disappears, the immediate sense of overhearing a conversation is intensified, as if one were actually listening to the give-and-take of the argument.[74] The restriction of the narrative to the direct statements of Mou-tzu and his critics (at least until the Postscript) is a "kind of over-hearing by the audience," a mimesis or direct showing to the reader of what takes place before her literary eyes.[75]

For all this to be effective, the reader must adopt the role of the implied reader, allowing herself to be read into the text, so that she can read out its meaning. Any reader, however disengaged, can follow the story line and note how it moves "objectively." But this is not to take on the role of the implied reader. Real readers of the *Li-huo lun* may indeed refuse to take on the role of the implied reader, and as a result they are likely to dismiss the text as inane or uninteresting. But in that case the text will withhold its secrets, offering only the detritus of historical hints against which to measure one's previous views about the history of early Chinese Buddhism. The implied author of this text employs the narratee/character of Mou-tzu's critic(s) as a device to show his reader how to perform as the implied reader, which point of view to adopt. And yet the real reader may refuse, or simply be unable, to fulfill that role. Indeed, the difficulty with ancient texts is that the cultural codes have shifted so immensely over time and space that reading an ancient text requires the reconstruction of these codes, insofar as it is possible. Even in the *Li-huo lun's* own time and place, not all readers appear to have played the game, as least if we may judge from the continuing criticism of Confucian Chinese against the Buddha Path. Not all readers received the lay vows.

The *Li-huo lun* does make clear its point of view. Indeed, "a philosophical treatise on abstract issues ... may express quite eloquently the author's personal interests in the matter along with his ideology."[76] The narratee, in the *Li-huo lun*, collapsed into the character of the critic, performs as an audience for the implied author, however effaced "he" lurks behind the scene. It is that critic/narratee upon "whom the various artifices of narrative rhetoric may be practiced. Recalling that rhetoric in fiction has to do with verisimilitude rather than arguable "truth," the acquiescing narratee can show that the narrator's efforts "to win acceptance of his version are in fact successful."[77] Yet the real reader has the option of marching to a different drummer and refusing to play the role of a converted former critic, whose only function in the final analysis is meant to be to strengthen the force of Mou-tzu's rhetoric. Nevertheless, "such direct communication of values and opinions between narrator and narratee is the most economical and clearest way of communicating to the implied reader the activities required by the text."[78]

Not all ancient readers who picked up our text fulfilled the requisites for reading out the inner message of the text. Similarly, modern scholars, in their commitment to objective norms of research, have often disallowed themselves the possibility of becoming caught up in its rhetoric, for they insist upon the decidedly modern stance of remaining outside the rhetorical transaction and observing its historical contours. In so doing, they have all but made themselves—in obedience to the cultural codes of unbiased scholarship—immune to the text's attempts to draw them into the story. And so they talk about the historical accuracy of the text, or the failure of its doctrinal argument to measure up to what they consider to be the true Buddhism of more sophisticated works. I do not mean to say that these issues are invalid, only that they too represent a "strong reading" of the text, a refusal to enter into its literary structure.[79]

One should not be too harsh in faulting modern scholars, however, for the discourse meaning of the text is no longer directly applicable. No Japanese scholar worries about the cultural validity of being both Buddhist and Japanese. Yet worry they do about the validity of being both modern scholar and Buddhist. Indeed, scholars of religion the world over frequently dispute the relative merits of taking an objective stance versus entering into the texts they study. Some claim that, without entering, one cannot truly understand, and can only, like Śāriputra in the Prajñāpāramitā literature, get the words right. Others claim that entering into a text engenders a sectarian bias that prevents one from reading it within the larger perspective of overall doctrinal development, the history of ideas, or solid textual research.

By highlighting the rhetorical strategy of a text, a Reader-Response approach can identify more clearly the role that the implied reader is to play—a role that any interpreter must adopt, at least provisionally, in approaching a text. This approach would also caution that a subsequent "misreading" of a religious text for historical information—while valid and indeed a fecund source for sketching the movement of thought—functions best when it recognizes that it is indeed a "misreading" of the text.

In the analysis that accompanies the translated text of the *Li-huo lun* below, pride of place will go to the Reader-Response approach, and comments on the text will focus on the issues described above. But questions of history will also be treated from time to time as they arise, reading the text on those occasions not as it was intended to be read by its implied author, but in an attempt to suggest patterns of thought that help identify the concrete *Sitz-im-Leben* for the *Li-huo lun*. I do not believe that the information supplied by this text can lead to any definitive conclusion about its dating. Yet the structure of the argument does suggest to me that, whether it is the record of an actual hermeneutical dialogue or a creative and fictional work of hermeneutics in response to actual issues, it is quite early—either, as it claims, from late Han or not too long after the fall of the Han dynasty. In short, I will try both to reconstruct and play the role of the *Li-huo lun's* implied reader and, from time to time, shifting roles, to briefly revert to the critical scholar's concern with questions of textual and historical relationships. It should be mentioned beforehand, however, that, having identified Mou-tzu as a character in the text, I doubt that he is its author, or that he is a historical person. If the very rhetorical structure of the *Li-huo lun* requires a high degree of verisimilitude, any excavation of the historicity of the Preface can do nothing more than note the successful achievement of such verisimilitude. Yet that does not lead to the conclusion that the text has been "concocted," as Tokiwa claims,[80] for this would suggest that its author embraced the same norms of objective scholarship under which modern scholars work, and then tried to foist his work upon an unsuspecting readership. An unwarranted supposition, if ever there was one!

One can sketch the figure of the real author of the *Li-huo lun* only indirectly and obliquely, by posing questions that the text never intended to treat. But by asking such questions about the text's assumptions and the discourse crafted by the implied author, and how these square with what we in fact know from other sources, one can reach prudent and probable judgments as to its time and author.

The Reader-Response approach will be employed below to reconstruct the probable response of the *Mou-tzu Li-huo lun's* intended audience. Each article of the text of the *Mou-tzu Li-huo lun* will be examined in three steps. The first step is my English translation of the text, based on Seng Yu's version in the *Hung-ming chi*.[81] Paul Pelliot's masterful French translation in his "Meou-tseu ou les doutes levés" is richly and diversely annotated, and thus I will refrain from duplicating his efforts, limiting the "Source Codes" sections to treating the cultural assumptions of the classical tradition. My aim is to decode the *Li-huo lun's* argument by identifying some of the relevant background information from the classical Chinese tradition that its intended readers were assumed to possess. In the third step I will employ Reader-Response Criticism in an attempt to determine the intended effect of the various articles upon the reader.

NOTES TO INTRODUCTION

1. For a brief discussion, see Zürcher, *The Buddhist Conquest of China*, 13.

2. *Shih-shuo Hsin-yü*, Ssu-pu pei-yao ed., shang chih hsia, ch'eng-shih chapter, 12b. Mather, *Shih-shuo Hsin-yü: A New Account of Tales of the World*, 104–5.

3. Makita Tairyō, *Gumyōshū kenkyū*.

4. Aurousseau, Review of "Meou-tseu ou les doutes levés," by Paul Pelliot, 278. Aurousseau argues that some passages are suspect, probably later additions.

5. See Maspero, "Le songe et l'ambassade de l'empereur Ming: Étude critique des sources."

6. For Chu Shih-hsing's pilgrimage to Khotan, see Tsukamoto Zenryū, *A History of Early Chinese Buddhism*, 138–41. But see the discussion under Article 34, below, where the "monks of Khotan" are taken to represent naturalized Chinese practitioners of the Taoist *hsien* arts.

7. See Pelliot, "Meou-tseu ou les doutes levés: Traduit et annoté."

8. Tokiwa Daijō, *Shina ni okeru bukkyō to jukyō dōkyō*, 89–100; and "Kan-min guhosetsu no kenkyū," 16–25.

9. Zürcher, *The Buddhist Conquest of China*, 15.

10. If indeed the text is the creation of a later author, it would seem that the "prime suspect" would be Seng Yu himself, who included the *Mou-tzu Li-huo lun* in his collection of apologetic tractates, for that *Hung-ming chi* collection is its literary Sitz-im-Leben. If the Seng Yu reference in the *Ch'u-san-tsung chi chi* in 515 is the first reference (and Liu Chün citation in the commentary to the *Shih-shuo Hsin-yü* was made shortly thereafter before he died in 521), it is possible that Seng Yu himself wrote the text. Schmidt-Glintzer, in his *Das Hung-ming Chi und die Aufnahme des Buddhismus in China*, 212, notes that the *Hung-ming chi* includes almost the entire range of arguments found in the later texts. On this hypothesis, one would begin, as does Schmidt-Glintzer, with a study not of the *Li-huo lun* itself, but of Seng Yu's collection and the role it played in the development of the changing attitudes of the southern Chinese gentry in regard to the Buddhist saṃgha, and the harmonization of Buddhism with Confucian cultural norms.

11. Zürcher, *The Buddhist Conquest of China*, 13.

12. Fish, "Introduction, or How I Stopped Worrying and Learned to Love Interpretation," in *Is There a Text in This Class?*, 2–3. For an insightful essay on the impact of Fish on scriptural hermeneutics, see Stephen Moore, "Negative Hermeneutics, Insubstantial Texts: Stanley Fish and the Biblical Interpreter."

13. Fish, *Is There a Text in This Class?*, 312.

14. Fung Yu-lan, *History of Chinese Philosophy*, 2:240. On the mingling of doctrinal notions, Hakamaya Noriaki in his *Hongaku shisō hihan*, *Hihan bukkyō*, and *Dōgen to bukkyō*, argues for a doctrinally normative Buddhism, in light of which he criticizes such ideas as "original enlightenment." Within the context of modern Japanese Buddhism, I find his critique engaging and incisive. Yet I do differ from Hakamaya in holding that no universal Buddhism exists. Rather, "Buddhisms" exist, each embedded in its particular cultural context.

15. K. Ch'en, *Buddhism in China*, 38.

16. Zürcher, *The Buddhist Conquest of China*, 14.

17. Pelliot, "Meou-tseu," 257.

18. Wright, *Buddhism in Chinese History*, 38.

19. Fish, "Demonstration vs. Persuasion," in *Is There a Text in This Class?*, 365: "In short, we try to persuade others to our beliefs because if they believe what we believe, they will, as a consequence of those beliefs, see what we see; and the facts to which we point in order

to support our interpretations will be as obvious to them as they are to us. Indeed, this is the whole of critical activity, an attempt on the part of one party to alter the beliefs of another so that the evidence cited by the first will be seen *as* evidence by the second."

20. See Derk Bodde, "Harmony and Conflict in Chinese Philosophy," 21; and John P. Keenan, "The Doctrine of Buddha Nature in Chinese Buddhism," 132–34. Also Bodde, "Dominant Ideas in the Formation of Chinese Culture," in *Essays on Chinese Civilization*, 138, who emphasizes "the fundamental oneness and harmony of the Chinese Weltanschauung." In "The Chinese Cosmic Magic Known as Watching for the Ethers," *Essays on Chinese Civilization*, 351, Bodde reminds us of the prevailing Chinese worldview, formulated during the Han dynasty, according to which the universe "is a harmoniously functioning organism consisting of multitudinous objects, qualities and forces which, despite their seeming heterogeneity, are integrated into coherent patterns by being subsumed under one or another of many numerical categories." Again in his *Chinese Thought, Society, and Science*, 194, Bodde discusses Joseph Needham's notion of Chinese organism, and, on 324, of the essence of Chinese mysticism as a wholly receptive approach to nature, in which humans are related organically to the entirety of the cosmos.

21. Appendix to his *Dōkyo no kisoteki kenkyū*.

22. See Tsukamoto, *Early Chinese Buddhism*, 14–21, "The transmission of Buddhism after the Appearance of Icons."

23. Chatman, *Story and Discourse: Narrative Structure in Fiction and Film*, 20–22.

24. See Malbon, "Structuralism, Hermeneutics, and Contextual Meaning."

25. Chatman, *Story and Discourse*, 28.

26. See J. L. Austin, *How to Do Things with Words*, 17–18: "I cannot be said to have worked an audience unless it hears what I say and takes what I say in a certain sense. An effect must be achieved on an audience if the illocutionary act is to be carried out [i.e., if the words are to perform their function]. How should we best put it here? How can we limit it? Generally the effect amounts to bringing about the understanding of the meaning and of the force of the locution. So the performance of an illocutionary act involves the securing of *uptake*."

27. Chatman, *Story and Discourse*, 31.

28. Ibid., 151.

29. Ibid., 196: "A quantitative effect applies: the more identifying features, the stronger our sense of a narrator's presence.... Covert or effaced narration occupies the middle ground between 'nonnarration' and conspicuously audible narration. In covert narration we hear a voice speaking of events, characters, and setting, but its owner remains hidden in the discursive shadows. Unlike the 'nonnarrator' story, the covertly narrated one can express a character's speech or thoughts in indirect form. Such expression implies an interpretative stenographer of non-narrated narratives."

30. In a similar vein, ibid., 169: "Of all forms of literary narrative those that pretend to be constituted by found letters and diaries least pre-suppose a narrator. If we insist on an agent beyond the implied author, he can only be a mere collector or collator.... His presence can only be made known by means of footnotes or a preface." In the *Li-huo lun*, the narrator likewise all but vanishes in the Dialogue, only making himself known in the Preface and Postscript.

31. Gerald Prince, "Notes Toward a Categorization of Fictional 'Narratives,'" *Genre* 4 (1971): 100–105.

32. Booth, *The Rhetoric of Fiction*, 70–71.

33. Chatman, *Story and Discourse*, 148.

34. Ibid., 149: "The counterpart of the implied author is the implied reader—not the flesh and bones you or I sitting in our living rooms reading the book, but the audience presupposed by the narrative itself. Like the implied author, the implied reader is always there."

35. Fowler, *Let the Reader Understand: Reader-Response Criticism and the Gospel of Mark*, 235–37.

36. Chatman, *Story and Discourse*, 95, treats the issue of the macrostructure of the plot of a narrative, the question of whether we can explicate the structures of the plot into an overall typology that can do justice to all the cultural codes at work. He writes: "In short, the characterization of plot into macrostructures and topologies depends on an understanding of cultural codes and their interplay with the literary and artistic codes of ordinary life. It relies heavily on verisimilitude. Until we can begin to formulate *all* the cultural codes, our deliberations must remain impressionistic."

37. Ibid., 126: "I argue—unoriginally but firmly—for a conception of character as a paradigm of traits; 'trait' in the sense of 'relatively stable or abiding personal quality,' recognizing that it may either unfold, that is, emerge earlier or later in the course of the story, or that it may disappear and be replaced by another."

38. Ibid., 138: "Characters exist and move in a space which exists abstractly at the deep narrative level, that is, prior to any kind of materialization.... Abstract narrative space contains, in clear polarity, a figure and a ground. Just as we can distinguish, in a painted portrait, the person from the background against which he or she is posed, so we can distinguish the character from the setting in the story. The story 'sets the character off' in the usual figurative sense of the expression; it is the place and collection of objects 'against which' his actions and passions appropriately emerge."

39. Ibid., 43.

40. Ibid., 46.

41. See Culler, "Convention and Naturalization," in *Structuralist Poetics: Structuralism, Linguistics, and the Study of Literature*, 131–60.

42. Chatman, *Story and Discourse*, 49.

43. Genette, "Vraisemblance et motivation." *Communication* 11 (1968): 6.

44. Dubs, "The Victory of Han Confucianism."

45. *Han shu*, 56:20, F(1), 1:16. Translation from Peerenboom, *Law and Morality*, 250.

46. Peerenboom, *Law and Morality*, 250.

47. Dubs, "The Discussion of the Classics in the Shih-ch'ü Pavilion," 272–74.

48. The New Text School relied on a version of the classics written in Han script, while the Old Text School proffered a version supposedly discovered in the first century B.C.E. and written in the old script of the Chou dynasty. These textual issues were accompanied with larger ideological differences, the New Text people arguing for a more cosmological worldview and a numinous vision of Confucius as a "divine" sage. See Fung, *History of Chinese Philosophy*, 2:7–167; on the ten guiding principles, see p. 76; on the unification of writing, see Bodde, *China's First Unifier*, 147–61.

49. Pokora, "Notes on New Studies on Tung Chung-shu," 264.

50. Dubs, "The Victory of Han Confucianism," 351–52.

51. Ibid., 352.

52. *Po Hu T'ung: The Comprehensive Discussions in the White Tiger Hall*, 95.

53. *Fa-yen* 12.12a. See Doeringer, "Yang Hsiung and His Formulation of a Classicism," 144, from whose translation I diverge slightly.

54. Doeringer, "Yang Hsiung," 162.

55. *Fa-yen* 3.1a. Doeringer, "Yang Hsiung," 162.

56. Fish, "How to Do Things with Austin and Searle," in *Is There a Text in This Class?*, 199: "While the world given by the standard story is no less a constructed one than the world of a novel or a play, for those who speak within it (and indeed as an extension of it) the facts of that world will be as obvious as one could wish. In short, the standard story and the world it delivers rest on a bedrock of belief, and even if that bedrock were challenged, it would be so from the vantage point of a belief (and a world) that had already taken its place."

57. Fish, *Is There a Text in This Class?*, 309.

58. Fish, "How to Do Things," 198. Again in "Demonstration vs. Persuasion," 357: "The mistake is to think of interpretation as an activity in need of constraints, when in fact interpretation is a *structure* of constraints. The field interpretation covers comes complete with its own internal set of rules and regulations, its lists of prescribed activities which is also, at the same time, a list of activities that are proscribed."

59. Hall and Ames, *Thinking Through Confucius*, 23.

60. Fish, "What Makes an Interpretation Acceptable?" in *Is There a Text in This Class?*, 342. See also p. 241: "In large part, my argument follows from Wittgenstein's notion of a 'language game' in which words are responsible not to what is real but to what has been laid down as real (as pickoutable) by a set of constitutive rules: the players in the game are able to agree that they mean the same things by their words not because they see the same things, in some absolute phenomenal sense, but because they are predisposed by the fact of being in the game (of being parties to the standard story) to 'see them', to pick them out."

61. Wright, *Buddhism in Chinese History*, 14–16.

62. Fish, "Interpreting the Variorum," in *Is There a Text in This Class?*, 171: "Why should two or more readers ever agree, and why should regular, that is, habitual differences in the career of a single reader ever occur? What is the explanation on the one hand of the stability of interpretation (at least among certain groups at certain times) and on the other of the orderly variety of interpretation if it is not the stability and variety of texts? The answer to all of these questions is to be found in a notion that has been implicit in my argument, the notion of *interpretive communities*. Interpretive communities are made up of those who

share interpretive strategies not for reading (in the conventional sense) but for writing texts, for constituting their properties and assigning their intentions. In other words, these strategies exist prior to the act of reading and therefore determine the shape of what is read rather than, as is usually assumed, the other way around."

63. Fish, "Introduction," in *Is There a Text in This Class?*, 14.

64. Fish, "Interpreting the Variorum," 168.

65. Ibid., 171–72.

66. The phrase from Antonio Cua, "Uses of Dialogues and Moral Understanding," 134.

67. Granet, *La Pensée chinoise*, 54.

68. Richards, *Mencius on the Mind*, 55. See also p. 57: "The finality of the ritual social system may perhaps also explain the fourth mark of these arguments—the exclusive use of concrete examples. A Western thinker will appeal to abstract logical principles because these are to him the most certain and ultimate considerations. Thus St. Thomas will appeal to the principle that an effect must resemble its cause. Kao Tzu and Mencius appeal instead to concrete instances of universally recognized correct behaviour."

69. Cua, *Ethical Argumentation*, 96–97. Also see Cua, "The Concept of Paradigmatic Individuals in the Ethics of Confucius," 41: "The ethics of Confucius contained in the *Analects*, a major authoritative source of Chinese moral education, does not present a systematic scheme for conduct. There is a lack of an explicit and coherent ordering of moral ideas. This unsystematic character in part reflects its concern with and emphasis on the concrete and particular."

70. Thus I differ from those who see Mou-tzu as simply misunderstanding Buddhist doctrinal notions. Jiahe Liu writes in "Early Buddhism and Taoism in China," 37: "Mouzi defended the spread of Buddhism in China, but, unavoidably, he misunderstood certain Buddhist doctrines. The problem of Chinese Buddhist monks misunderstanding the original meanings of Buddhist doctrine existed throughout the period A.D. 65–420." No doubt, misunderstandings were common. Yet it seems to me that doctrinal orthodoxy should not serve as a central interpretative concern in reading the *Li-huo lun*. More to the point perhaps would be the perspective of Gadamer, who insists that all interpretation takes place in light of preunderstandings, prejudices. Mou-tzu's task was then to confront cultural prejudices and expectations that invalidated the Buddha's path as alien and thus irrelevant.

71. Obviously not all were moved by the argument, for many of the issues Mou-tzu treats are raised again and again in later critiques of Buddhism. See Han Yü's "Memorial Bone of the Buddha," in *Sources of Chinese Tradition*, ed. de Bary, 1:372–73. Also see Wright, "Fu I and the Rejection of Buddhism."

72. Searle, *Speech Acts*, 186n: "Standing on the deck of some institutions one can tinker with constitutive rules and even throw some other institutions overboard. But could one throw all institutions overboard? ... One could not and still engage in those forms of behavior we consider characteristically human."

73. Chatman, *Story and Discourse*, 50.

74. See Genette, "Time and Narrative in *A la recherche du temps perdu*," 93–118.

75. Chatman, *Story and Discourse*, 146. See Genette, "Frontières du récit."

76. Chatman, *Story and Discourse*, 152.

77. Ibid., 258.

78. Ibid., 261.

79. Harold Bloom, *The Anxiety of Influence: A Theory of Poetry*, 5, discusses the wrestling match that a strong poet engages in with his predecessors, supplanting them (i.e., his poetic predecessors) through creative and powerful misreadings of their texts. He explains: "*Clinamen* ... is poetic misreading or misprision proper; I take the word from Lucretius, where it means a 'swerve' of the atoms so as to make change possible in the universe. A poet sways from his predecessors, by so reading his predecessor's poem as to execute a *clinamen* in relation to it. This appears as a corrective movement in his own poem, which implies that the precursor's poem went accurately up to a certain point, but then should have swerved, precisely in the direction that the new poem moves." *Mutatis mutandis*, the modern reading of ancient texts like the *Li-huo lun* parallels such a clinamatic procedure, reading them for the light they shed, not on their own rhetorical interests, but on modern questions of scholarly concern. Thus, both Pelliot and Maspero, who set the stage for the discussion among Western Buddhologists, focus not on the rhetoric of the text, but on what gems of truth they can cull from its borders, wishing all the while for a firmer and more accurate confirmation from the text itself. Their readings, I suggest, although indeed valuable in terms of these questions that are so important in modern scholarship, do in fact represent strong readings, creative misreadings, of the text.

80. Tokiwa Daijō, *Shina ni okeru bukkyō to jukyō dōkyō*, 89–100.

81. Taking into account the critical edition of Makita's *Gumyōshū kenkyū* and noting the emendations of Pelliot.

The Preface to the *Li-huo lun*

BACKGROUND AND CONTEXT

The classics and commentaries Mou-tzu is reported to have studied are the classical texts of Confucian orthodoxy. The writings of the philosophers are those works not regarded as classics but prized in literate circles, notably the texts of the *Lao Tzu* and the *Chuang Tzu*. The development of Han Confucianism included both, for, under the influence of Huang-Lao thinking, the classical canon had been expanded to include much more than the Confucian orthodox lineage of texts.[1] The Preface of the *Li-huo lun* makes a distinction between such philosophers and the more popular books about practices aimed at becoming immortal (*hsien* 仙), although such notions are contained at least in an inchoate form in the *Lao Tzu* and the *Chuang Tzu*. The military manuals refer to such works as the *Sun Tzu*, concerned with the conduct of warfare.

The events recorded in this Preface have a high degree of verisimilitude. They present historical conditions and happenings that are either verifiable or highly probable. They are quite accurate. Our text reports that after the death of Emperor Ling (189) the world was in chaos. In point of fact, it was—for this was the time of the T'ai P'ing Tao Rebellion of the Yellow Turbans. In the year 184, during the reign of Emperor Ling, the realm, already under stress from internal economic and political pressures,[2] was

47

shaken to its roots by the uprising of rebels under the leadership of Chang Chüeh, whom they regarded as a *hsien*.[3] He preached from village to village, recruiting thousands of followers and promising them not only healing through the drinking of magical potions, but also the beginning of a new age, to be signaled by the ascendancy of the color yellow over that of the Han blue. Han Confucianism, as seen in the writings of Tung Chung-shu, had incorporated a belief in the cyclical progression of the five elements, each associated with a specific color.[4] Thus the cry of the rebels was, "The blue heaven [of the Han] is already dead. All-under-Heaven shall now be yellow. The year is chia tzu [the first in the sexagenary cycle], and All-under-Heaven shall be much blessed!"[5] Even though the Han succeeded in putting down this rebellion, power shifted in the process to local warlords, specifically those who had suppressed the rebellion, and internal strife replaced whatever central control had previously obtained.

When Emperor Ling died in 189, the ruthless warlord Tung Cho gained complete control over the Lo-yang area, instituting a reign of terror based on the swift and brutal murder of large numbers of people. Responding to abortive attempts at resistance, Tung Cho burned the entire city and set several million local inhabitants on a forced march to Ch'ang-an as a serf army. Those who faltered on the journey were left to die and decompose on the roadside, their bodies strewn about as silent witnesses to his power and cruelty. "Such, at any rate, is the gruesome account left behind in the written records, which allege that in this way the city of Lo-yang, which for so long had been the capital of the Han, became (in 190) a desert, where even 'the voices of cocks and dogs were not heard.'"[6]

Under such conditions, flight was a most reasonable option. Yet the place to which most fled was not to Chiao-chou in the far south, where we find Mou-tzu, but to the Hsü-chou area, east of Lo-yang. It is here that we can pick up the story of Tse Yung, who murdered the younger brother of the magistrate of Chiao-chou, as recorded in this Preface of the *Li-huo lun*. *The History of the Later Han* (*Hou Han shu*) and *The Records of the Three Kingdoms* (*San-kuo chih*) present more details on the activities of Tse Yung. They report that T'ao Ch'ien (132–94), because of his part in suppressing the Yellow Turbans, had been designated Generalissimo Pacifying the East and made the governor of Hsü-chou, to which many refugees and emigrés flocked. *The Records of the*

Three Kingdoms reports that "at this time in Hsü-chou the people were prosperous and the grain harvest plentiful. Stray people in great numbers settled there."[7] Tse Yung came at the head of several hundred followers to Hsü-chou and was appointed by T'ao Ch'ien to supervise food transport in three local commanderies. But apparently he misappropriated large quantities of food and directed the wealth gained from these stores to the building of Buddhist monasteries and temples on a grand scale, attracting large numbers to become Buddhists, and thereby avoiding tax and corvée labor. He thus gathered around himself a large group of followers.

Hsü-chou did not, however, maintain its peaceful prosperity. Ts'ao Ts'ao, who had suppressed the parallel rebellion of the "Way of the Five Bushels of Rice" in the old state of Shu, moved against T'ao Ch'ien and wreaked devastation on the entire area, so that "the men and women killed were counted in the tens of thousands, even chickens and dogs were not spared, and the river Ssu became so clogged with them that it would not flow. Thus, even those of the common people who had come in flight from the disturbances at Lo-yang and Ch'ang-an to entrust themselves to T'ao Ch'ien in rich Hsü-chou were all killed."[8]

At this point Tse Yung fled with thousands of his followers to Kuang-ling, where he was kindly received by the grand administrator, Chao Yü. Yet Tse Yung killed Chao Yü, then fled across the Yangtze to Yü-chang. It is at Yü-chang that our text reports Tse Yung killed the younger brother of the governor of Chiao-chou, who was the grand administrator at that place. The *Li-huo lun* does not report the names of either the governor of Chiao-chou or the grand administrator of Yü-chang, but the names of these officials occur separately in *The Records of the Three Kingdoms* and *The Book of the Later Han* as Chu Fu and Chu Hao, lending historical accuracy to the account in our Preface.[9] One can conclude that the author of the Preface was familiar with the history of these happenings.[10]

In the anonymous *Rectification of Unjustified Criticism* (*Cheng-wu lun*) the critic brings up the example of Tse Yung: "Again, the malinger has said, 'In the later years of the Han there was a certain Tse Yung, who joined forces under T'ao Ch'ien, the inspector of Hsü-chou. T'ao Ch'ien ordered him to take charge of [grain] transportation, but as Tse Yung considered service to the Buddha paramount, he consequently stole the officially trans-

ported [grain supplies] in order to profit himself, and put these in
[his own granaries, using the funds derived therefrom] to construct
on a grand scale Buddhist monasteries,' etc. 'In every case, as
regards those who passed by, he gave them wine and food,' etc.
'Later he was attacked by Liu Yu and slain.' etc." The Buddhist
rejoinder agrees that Tse Yung was a most cruel and unjust fellow
who violated the Buddha's precepts, and in no wise a true representative of the Buddha's teachings.[11]

The geographical setting of the *Li-huo lun* in Chiao-chih at
the extreme southern end of China also rings true.[12] In the year
113 B.C.E. the Han dynasty first sent two thousand armed men
and then sent a marine force south to unseat an autonomous
ruler of Vietnam, taking the Viet stronghold of P'an-yü and setting up nine administrative commanderies in the south, briefly encompassing even the island of Hainan.[13] *The History of the Later
Han* reports frequent visits of Roman merchants to Fu-nan (Cam-
bodia), Jih-nan (Annan), and Chiao-chih.[14] *The History of the
Liang* mentions that a Roman merchant named Ch'in-lun arrived
in southern China by way of Jih-nan and Chiao-chih in the year
226.[15] Yü Ying-shih describes the importance of Chiao-chih:

> During the decades from Wang Mang's time to the early
> years of the Later Han, in which relations between China
> and the Western Regions were generally interrupted, Sino-
> Indian overseas silk trade probably became more flourishing
> as a result of the cutting off of the overland trade route. Dur-
> ing this period, there seems to have been even some increase
> of Chinese silk in the Roman market, which, it is believed,
> was due to the more frequent use of the sea route by the In-
> dian intermediary. It may further be conjectured that the
> growth of the overseas silk trade between the east and the
> west resulted partially also from the fact that both sides
> found it desirable to avoid the Parthian monopoly. At any
> rate it is beyond doubt that in Later Han times Sino-Indian
> economic intercourse often resorted to the sea route.... In
> Later Han times, overseas trade seems to have gained much
> progress. In this respect, both Jih-nan and Chiao-chih played
> a very important role by serving as a link of intercourse be-
> tween China and the various maritime countries.... The
> prosperity of Chiao-chih (Tonkin) as a seaport during the

Later Han particularly deserves attention. Chiao-chih was known especially for the production of such curiosities as pearls, ivory, tortoise shell, incense, and so forth, from which its immense wealth derived.... It is also highly significant that toward the end of the Later Han period when the famous Shih Hsien (136–226) was Governor of Chiao-chih, the streets of Tonkin were filled with barbarian merchants. All these facts can be properly comprehended only against the commercial background of Chiao-chih at that time. I can think of no better explanation than overseas trade that can account at the same time for both the prosperity of Chiao-chih and the frequent presence of foreigners there.[16]

Mou-tzu is situated, then, not in a remote backwater of the realm, but in a prosperous, international seaport, where he would have come into contact with practitioners of the Buddhist faith. Hu Shih has examined *The Record of Wu* (*Wu chih*), which says that several hundred scholars fled to Chiao-chou at the end of the Han and provides names and information for a number of them. Fukui adds similar information, from *The Record of Shu* (*Shu chih*, i.e., Shu Han kingdom) and from *The History of Wei* (*Wei shu*), on classical scholars who fled to Chiao-chih.[17] These included several noted Buddhists. K'ang Seng-hui was born in Chiao-chih, the son of an Indian merchant whose family had come from Sogdiana to Chiao-chih, apparently for business purposes when the overland trade route was closed off. He spread Buddhism among the people in the Wu capital at Chien-yeh in 247.[18] These were the "outstanding persons" who are said in the Preface to the *Li-huo lun* to have retreated to Chiao-chih at the end of the Han.

The title of the text is given by Seng Yu as *Mou-tzu Li-huo lun*, where the character *li* (理) has replaced an original *chih* (治) because of a T'ang taboo.[19] I translate it as *Mou-tzu's Treatise on the Removal of Doubt*. Its significance, however, goes beyond the solution of discrete doubts over specific issues. It could as well be rendered as *Mou-tzu's Treatise on the Elimination of Delusion*,[20] for it treats not only the specific issues, but also the conversion of Mou-tzu's opponents from their delusion to the Path of Buddha. Perhaps it alludes to a passage from the preface to *Ho-shang Kung Commentary on the Lao Tzu*: "Ho-shang Kung bestowed on [Emperor Wen] the unadorned text of the *Tao-te ching chang-chü*, and said to the Emperor: 'If you study this thoroughly, then your doubts will be explained.'"[21]

ENGLISH TRANSLATION OF PREFACE:
MOU-TZU'S TREATISE ON THE REMOVAL OF DOUBT

Mou-tzu was well learned in the classics and their commentaries, as well as all the writings of the philosophers. There were none, large or small, that he did not cherish. He even read the [books on] military strategy, although he did not enjoy them. He had also read the books about the spirit immortals and their immortality, but he did not believe them and regarded them as vain bragging.

It happened that, after the death of Emperor Ling (189 C.E.), the world was in disorder. Since only Chiao-chou [a colonial district in the far south] remained relatively peaceful, otherworldly people[22] from the north came en masse and settled there. Many of them practiced the methods of the spirit immortals, abstaining from grains to prolong life. These methods were popular then, but Mou-tzu unceasingly refuted them by employing the Five Classics, and none among the Taoist adepts or the Magicians dared engage him in debate. He was like Mencius, who refuted Yang Chu and Mo Ti.

Sometime before this, Mou-tzu had taken his mother and retired from the world to Chiao-chih,[23] but when he reached his twenty-sixth year he returned to Ts'ang-wu and took a wife. The grand administrator[24] [of Ts'ang-wu] heard that he was devoted to study and visited him to ask that he become a public official. But [Mou-tzu's] years were just in their prime and his mind was concentrated on study. Furthermore, seeing the age in deep disorder, he had no intention of accepting the responsibility of office. Thus in the end he did not comply.

During this period all the provinces and the commanderies were suspicious of one another and their border outposts prevented free passage. The grand administrator, because of his [i.e., Mou-tzu's] wide erudition and broad understanding, [wanted to] send him to pay his respects at Ching-chou. Mou-tzu considered that, while fancy titles were easy to decline, a real mission was hard to shirk. And so he prepared himself for the journey.

But just then the governor of [Chiao-]chou [learned that] he was a highly cultured scholar living in retirement and summoned him. Again he feigned illness and excused himself. When that governor's younger brother became grand administrator of Yü-chang and was murdered by Chief Commandant Tse Yung, the governor sent Cavalry Captain Liu Yen to take troops and go to [Yü-chang]. But he was afraid that, since the outlying areas were suspicious of one another, the troops would be unable to get through. The governor then made a request of Mou-tzu: "My younger brother has been murdered by a rebel and the pain in my bones and flesh has engendered anger in my heart. I wanted to send Captain Liu to go there, but he was afraid that, being suspicious, the outlying regions would make it difficult for our men and they would not get through. Only you, sir, well skilled in both letters and tactics, have the talent to take the initiative.[25] Now, I wish you would be my chancellor and consent to go to Ling-ling and Kuei-yang to obtain passage along the open road. What do you say?"

Mou-tzu answered: "[Like a horse,] fed and nourished in your stables, I have experienced length of days. A committed scholar forgets his bodily well-being and, when the need arises, hastens to be of service."[26] Then he prepared himself to undertake the endeavor. But just then his mother died, and so he did not go after all.

Later he withdrew, thinking that, because his eloquence had made him known to [the governor], he had abruptly been given a mission, but that just then, because the age was disturbed and confused, this was not the season to reveal himself in public. Sighing, he said to himself: "Lao-tzu wrote, 'Exterminate the sage, discard the wise.'[27] If one cultivates himself and protects his essence, then the ten thousand things will not oppose his resolve, the world will not alter his serenity, the emperor will not be able to have him serve as a minister, and the princes will not win him as a confidant.[28] This is how one can be considered a noble!"

At this juncture he intensified his resolve on the Buddha Tao, both scrutinizing all the five thousand words of the Book of Lao Tzu, imbibing their dark mystery as if they were the essence of fine wine, and playing on the Five Classics as on a ch'in lute or a reed pipe. The many followers of convention condemned him, thinking that he had turned his back on the Five Classics and

gone over to heterodox ways. If he wanted to engage [them] in
disputation, that would not be [in accord with] the Way. But,
although he wanted to remain silent, he was unable. This is why
he used his time with brush and ink, bringing together and citing
the sayings of the sages and worthies to demonstrate and explain
[the Buddha Tao] to them. The title [of his work] is The Sayings
of Mou-tzu on Removing Doubt.[29]

READER-RESPONSE CRITICISM

This Preface has often been considered apart from the re-
mainder of the Li-huo lun, for it seems to give the objective background of the dialogues that follow, presenting information about
the author, Mou-tzu, and setting the stage for his apologetic treatise. The assumption is made that, since it talks about the author
Mou-tzu, it was written either by him, as an account of his life, or
perhaps by a later disciple or admirer. Yet, apart from this Preface,
we have no information on Mou-tzu at all. We do not have any
independent attestation that there ever was a flesh-and-blood
author named Mou-tzu, for he functions only within our text as
the main character, both in this Preface and in the subsequent
Dialogue. The Preface does, however, situate Mou-tzu within the
social and cultural world of an idealized Chinese scholar. It is, at
least initially, not to be read as extratextual information supplied
by an early textual critic and tacked on at the beginning of the
treatise, but as an organic part of the argument, for it provides to
the implied reader information that is necessary for understanding
and responding to the subsequent Dialogue.

It is a leap of logic to conclude from its historical accuracy
that the purpose of this Preface was to provide historical data on
a flesh-and-blood Mou-tzu. In a literary reading, the Preface's
accuracy functions to establish the verisimilitude necessary for
any reading of the subsequent Dialogue, and thus one would expect it to reflect historical conditions as accurately as possible.

The narrator of the Preface begins by depicting Mou-tzu as a
classical Chinese scholar, erudite in the expected manner. He is
explicitly compared with Mencius, who lamented that "feudal
lords do as they please; people with no official position are unin-
hibited in their expression of views, and the words of Yang Chu
and Mo Ti fill the Empire.... If the way of Yang and Mo does not

subside and the way of Confucius is not proclaimed, the people will be deceived by heresies and the path of morality will be blocked."[30] Thus, Mou-tzu, far from being unorthodox, stands in the "great" tradition of the classics and the philosophers, that is, of the Confucian classics and Mencius. He is not fond of military manuals, with their penchant for the philosophy of Legalism, but he has read them and thus is draftable for a delicate diplomatic mission during troubled times of war. He rejects *hsien* Taoism, as well as any identification of the Buddha with a *hsien* immortal. In light of the *hsien* Taoist notions behind the Yellow Turban rebellion, such a position is quite understandable.[31]

Mou-tzu is further described by the narrator as a classical scholar who both goes to Ts'ang-wu and marries in accord with the demands of filial piety and, again in good Confucian fashion, initially declines to accept the grand administrator's offer of ministerial status.[32] When that offer, however, is made more specific —that he go to pay the respects of the grand administrator of Ts'ang-wu to Ching-chou—he readies himself to undertake the task. Yet his resolve is apparently undermined by the attempts of the governor of Chiao-chou to recruit him.[33] Only when that governor presents the actual details of his request, that he proceed to Yü-chang to take care of proper arrangements for the governor's murdered younger brother, does Mou-tzu consent. Again, however, he is prevented by the constraints of filial piety, which require that he retire to mourn the death of his mother.

The outcome is that he assumes the role of a gentleman living in seclusion and is thus able to devote himself to the study of the Buddha Tao and to the collection of the sayings of the classical sages that show just how the Buddha Tao harmonizes with the classical tradition. His efforts are solitary and literary, a matter of pen and ink. There was apparently no avenue for open and public discussion, for Buddhist notions were perceived to be a negation of the Tao of China. Although he has no level playing field on which to argue for that harmony, he cannot simply remain silent. And so he composes sayings to alleviate the doubts of his critics, all of whom are represented in the Dialogue in the character of the anonymous interlocutor.

The Preface describes the personal traits of the main character of the Dialogue, establishing the context in which the implied reader is to view the main character. That is the rhetorical function of this section. To jump beyond that rhetorical purpose and conclude from its historical verisimilitude to the actual historical existence of a person called Mou-tzu would be a leap indeed. The man might well have existed, and the Preface might report actual events. The text of the *Li-huo lun* in Seng Yu's *Hung-ming chi* does give his name as Mou Yung of the Han. Nevertheless, the rhetorical strategy in the Preface, as setting the stage for the believability of the Dialogue, does not address the historical questions that concern modern scholars. In a word, it does not matter if Mou-tzu actually existed as a historical person, or if he is simply the main character of a creative work—the interplay between Buddhism and the classical Chinese tradition is unquestionably the central issue. And just as it is unwarranted to argue for the historicity of Mou-tzu from this Preface, it is likewise beside the point to characterize the text as a "forgery" concocted by a later hand and foisted on the public. The public to which the text is directed, implied in its very rhetorical structure, is not a public that focused on issues of historicity or the lack thereof.

Nevertheless, one can practice a modern, historical "misreading" of our text, trying to assess whether it does indeed reflect historical conditions and events. From the above discussion, the general conclusion must be that it does. Its author was familiar with the conditions and events around the end of the Han dynasty, even if he did write a work of creative "fiction." The description of the chaos and disorder after the death of Emperor Ling (189) does reflect actual conditions. Even the claim that "only Chiao-chou remained relatively peaceful" does seem to be accurate, if perhaps overstated.

Rather than depicting history, the placing of Mou-tzu on the very margins of Chinese culture serves as a rhetorical strategy to identify him symbolically with the main plot theme of the story: the marginality of the Buddha Tao in Chinese culture. Beyond that, at the deeper level of the discourse, it situates him at the basic crux of the narrative: the antinomy between chaos and order.

Rhetorically, even before the questioning begins, the reader is privileged with key information that will lead her to avoid the conventional mistaken view of Mou-tzu as unorthodox: he is a traditional Chinese scholar steeped in the classics of Confucianism and Taoism. This is the point of view the reader is urged to hold throughout the ensuing Dialogue. Is it believable? Yes, for Mou-tzu is located in specific historical situations and reacts to those situations as a true scholar would. The function of the Preface in this text is not, then, to offer historical information, but to impart the overriding point of view from which the text is to be read. Its verisimilitude assures, it is hoped, that the reader will assent to Mou-tzu's status as a true scholar. There is no way of knowing whether in fact Mou-tzu was a person actually living in those historical circumstances, but establishing that he was is not the intent of the narrative anyway. To argue obliquely from the Preface to the history, the most that one can say with any definite assurance is that the author knew the history of the times in which he situated the character Mou-tzu, and thus that the *Li-huo lun* does indeed reflect conditions that obtained shortly after the fall of the Later Han dynasty.

Mou-tzu's Dialogue with His Critics

WHO IS BUDDHA?

A critic asked: Where was the Buddha born? Did he have ancestors and a home place or not? Just what did he do? What did he look like?

Mou-tzu said: Rich indeed is the significance of your question! Even though I am not very bright, let me mention the main points. I have heard about the appearance of the Buddha's transformation, that when he had amassed the power of the Way for many countless aeons to a fullness unrecordable, when he was on the verge of realizing awakening, he was born in India. He borrowed his form from the wife of Śuddhodana. During a nap she dreamed that she was riding on a white elephant with six tusks.[34] Delighted, she was filled with joy and, affected [by it], conceived. On the eighth day of the fourth month, he was born from his mother's right side. When he trod the earth, he strode seven paces, lifted up his right hand, and declared, "Above or below the heavens, there is no one who excels me!" At that instant the heavens and the earth shook violently and the palace was filled with light. On that same day a blue-robed [servant girl] of

the king's household gave birth to a son and in the stable a white
horse dropped a white colt. That servant was named Chaṇḍaka
and that horse Kaṇṭhaka. The king ordered them always to attend the prince.

The prince had thirty-two major marks and eighty minor
marks. He was exceptionally tall (six chang). His body was of a
golden hue. On the top of his forehead he had the uṇīṣa. His
jaws were like those of a lion. His tongue could cover his face.
His hands held wheel [designs] with the thousand spokes. A light
from the top of his head radiated for ten thousand li. These were
his principal major marks.

When he was seventeen years old, the king presented him a
woman from a neighboring land to be his wife. But when the
prince sat down, he always moved his seat away. And when he
slept, he used a different bed. The Way of Heaven is bright indeed and its yin and yang interpenetrate. Thus [even without sexual contact], she conceived a male child, who was born after six
years.[35] His father the king greatly prized the prince and built
palaces for him. He provided for him an array both of fine women and of precious objects of amusement. But the prince did
not covet worldly pleasures. His mind dwelt on the power of the
Way.

On the eighth day of the fourth month of his nineteenth
year, in the middle of the night, he ordered Chaṇḍaka to bridle
Kaṇṭhaka and, when he was so mounted, spirits supported and
carried him in the air away from the palace. The next morning
nobody knew where he was. The king together with all his servants and the people were distraught with sorrow. They chased
him into the countryside and [when they found him] the king
said to him, "Before you were [born], I entreated the spirits until
finally you came [to me]. Now you are as [cold] as a jade tablet to
me. You were to succeed me and would have been favored with
position! Yet you leave! Why?" The prince said, "The ten thousand things are transient. Everything that exists faces demise. I
now am resolved to practice the Way and deliver [beings within]
the ten directions." Recognizing that his commitment was firm,
the king got up and went home. The prince immediately left
to meditate on the Way, and after ten years he became the
Awakened One.

[The Buddha] was born in the first month of summer (i.e.,
the fourth month), which is neither cold nor hot, when the plants
and trees flower and bloom, when one removes fox furs and

clothes oneself with light, broad-stitched cloth. Born in India, the center of heaven and earth, he was balanced and lived in harmony. In the twelve sections of the scriptures that he composed, there are 840 million chapters. The large chapters are somewhat under ten thousand words; the small chapters more than a thousand words. The Buddha taught the world and delivered the people. Thus, even after his entrance into cessation and departure on the fifteenth day of the second month, his scriptures and discipline still remain. Those able consistently to follow them also attain nonaction, for [his] blessing flows over into later generations. Those [lay followers] who uphold the five precepts and observe the six fast days each month, with one heart and mind repent their misdeeds and renew themselves. The monks uphold 250 precepts and fast every day. But these precepts are not applied to lay followers. Their ceremonies and liturgies do not differ from the classical ceremonies of antiquity. All day long and throughout the night they discuss the Way and intone the scriptures, without indulging themselves in worldly affairs. Lao-tzu says, "In his every movement a man of great virtue follows the way and the way only."[36] This [Way] is what [the monks] discuss.

Source Codes

In his opening phrase Mou-tzu signals his stance within the classical tradition. The phrase *Rich indeed is the meaning of your question* echoes the *Analects*, where Tzu-hsia exclaims, "Rich, indeed, is the meaning of these words!"[37]

This account of the Buddha appears to have been drawn from the biography of Buddha in the *T'ai-tzu jui-ying pen-ch'i ching* (T. 185), which Chih Ch'ien translated between the years 222 and 228. Maspero presents the parallel passages, which are so close that he concludes that the *Li-huo lun* has copied sections from this scripture.[38] In that case, the *Li-huo lun* could not have been written prior to the translation of this text from the Sanskrit. However, Tsukamoto holds that Chih Ch'ien's translation is "a case not of direct translation from original texts but rather of a rearrangement of notes jotted down by Chinese interested in Buddhism who heard the sermons of early missionaries, ... a collection of memorandums."[39] If Chih Ch'ien depended upon a number of already existing Chinese accounts, it is possible that the textual dependency of the *Li-huo lun* on the *T'ai-tzu jui-ying pen-ch'i ching* is not apodictic, and that the *Li-huo lun* has drawn upon a source prior to and included in that scripture.

This question is of interest in that the *Li-huo lun* refers to no specific Buddhist scriptures at all and never cites Buddhist sources to validate its argument. The Preface tells that Mou-tzu studied the Buddha Tao by analyzing *The Book of Lao Tzu*. Here in Article 1, the source for Mou-tzu's account of the Buddha, if Tsukamoto is correct, is an oral tradition disseminated by early Buddhist missionaries in their preaching of the Dharma and put into writing by Chih Ch'ien. In the Later Han dynasty, Buddhism began to be slowly received by a small number of Chinese intellectuals. As Tsukamoto explains, Chinese Buddhists did not yet understand the teachings of Buddha through examination of translated scriptures; they understood in terms of their own Taoist doctrine.[40] The only other option would have been for Chinese to abandon their culture and take on the foreign culture of Buddhist India, the stance Mou-tzu has been charged with.

Reader-Response Criticism

The allusion to the *Analects* of Confucius in Mou-tzu's initial response signals the reader that this is indeed a true Confucian scholar. The numerous subsequent allusions to Confucian and Taoist texts are by no means accidental. Rather, they lead the implied reader, a cultured and classical gentleman, to identify with Mou-tzu's stance by drawing him in with familiar allusions and citations. That implied reader must be able to recognize the Confucian allusion without any overt clue, for Mou-tzu does not identify its source. Later, however, when he quotes from *The Book of Lao Tzu*, he does identify his source, perhaps suggesting that his implied reader may not have been as familiar with that text. Confucian doctrine was indeed the state ideology, enthroned from early Han times as the political and social norm. Even after the chaos and destruction that attended the end of the Han, the Confucian classics constituted the framework for cultured thinking. Yet, by late Han times the process of incorporating the ideas of Lao-tzu within a "new" Confucianism had begun. Tsukamoto again explains succinctly:

> There arose a new form of Confucianism, the so-called 'dark learning' (*hsüan hsüeh*), which, liberated from the bonds of the by now official Confucianism, brittle and text-oriented as that was, made room for the ideas of Lao-tzu, Chuang-tzu, and the *Canon of Changes* (*Yi-ching*). The study of Lao-tzu and Chuang-tzu now became fashionable, a quest for an

awareness of human nature and the liberation of mankind was taking place, a mood of freedom of thought and study swept through the educated classes of the Middle Plain, and this intellectual mood in turn went south with the Tsin and there became intensified.[41]

Our text is situated at the beginning of this trajectory of "dark learning," piggybacking, as it were, Buddhist ideas onto the liberating words of Lao-tzu.

Mou-tzu, in presenting the story of the Buddha, steps out of his role as a character in the story to become a rather overt narrator. He reports an account of the life of Buddha designed to resonate in Chinese ears. His life of the Buddha is overlaid with Chinese notions about the power of the Way, about the interpenetration of yin and yang, and cosmic harmony. In such a context, the Buddha's celibacy can be introduced (Mou-tzu will treat the question later) and his abandonment of the world reported. In such a context, India can be identified as the center of heaven and earth, a novel notion for those who lived in the Middle Kingdom! The Buddha's father talks about the position that would have awaited the Buddha had he remained in society, much as official positions awaited Mou-tzu for the taking. Thus the Buddha's response about the transience of all things is contextualized in terms of Taoist and Confucian refusal to accept positions of public service. His awakening is reported in Chinese images of the spring awakening of flowers and trees, immune to both the heat of passion and the cold of aloofness.

Yet although the Buddha has entered cessation, Mou-tzu says nothing about the eternal Dharma body of the Buddha. Rather, he focuses only on the teaching the Buddha has left behind. The text uses the transliterated Sanskrit for the Buddha's cessation (*ni han* 泥洹), but then states that those who follow his teachings will also enter nonaction (*wu-wei* 無爲), thus equating these two terms. It is significant to observe that our text uses both terms, consciously adopting *wu-wei* as a Chinese version of *ni han*. Thus, the Chinese identification of *nirvāṇa* with nonaction (*wu-wei* 無爲) is not a matter of simple misunderstanding, but a conscious rhetorical strategy.[42]

The Buddha's vast teachings are presented as the continuing presence of Buddha himself, and the practice of those teachings is aimed at the attainment of *wu-wei*. Those practices can thus be

recommended to all who desire to attain *wu-wei*. To emphasize
this point Mou-tzu claims, perhaps ingenuously, that Buddhist
practices are no different from the classical ceremonies of antiquity. Thus to practice the Buddhist precepts is to recover the practices of antiquity. Furthermore, the practices of the Buddhist
monks are the same as those recommended by Lao-tzu.

Thus, the implied reader, a member of the Confucian literati,
is drawn to identify more strongly with Mou-tzu, the true Chinese
scholar, and assent that the Buddha is an embodiment of the Way
and that the practice of his Way is identical with the practices of
antiquity. Confucius had longed for the golden age of antiquity.
Mou-tzu shows that one can attain it by practicing the Buddha's
teaching.

ARTICLE 2.
BUDDHA AS LINKAGE TO THE WAY

*A critic asked, Why do you speak so reverently of the Bud-
dha? What does* Buddha *mean?*

Mou-tzu said, The word Buddha *is a posthumous title, like
calling the three sovereigns "divine" or the five emperors "sage."
Buddha is the original ancestor of the power of the Way, our ancestral link to spiritual understanding. The word* buddha *means
awakened. Shadowy and indistinct, by transformations in different bodies and varied forms,*[43] *'[he appears in diverse realms].
Sometimes he is present, sometimes absent. He can be small or
large, heavenly or earthly, old or young, hidden or manifest. He
can walk on fire without being burned, tread on swords without
being hurt, be mired in the mud without being defiled, encounter
misfortune without injury. When he wants to travel, he flies
through the air. When he sits, he emits light. This is what the
title* Buddha *means.*

Source Codes

On the divinity of the three sovereigns and the sageness of the five
emperors, Timotheus Pokora explains that "until Emperor Wu the Five

Emperors were esteemed not as gods but as human beings."[44] The author of the *Li-huo lun* assumes here that the normative Confucian tradition of Tung Chung-shu, who formulated Han Confucianism and the cosmic interface between Heaven and the emperor, is known and accepted by his readers.

Mou-tzu's phrase *ancestral link* (*tsung hsü* 宗緒) is said by the *P'ei-wen-yün-fu* dictionary to have been employed by two other Han dynasty authors, Yang Hsiung and Chang Heng, although I have not been able to identify the sources. The *Chuang Tzu* has a similar notion: "He who has a clear understanding of the virtue of Heaven and earth may be called the great source [*ta-pen* 大本], the great ancestor [*ta-tsung* 大宗]."[45] The *Cheng-wu lun* (Rectification of Unjustified Criticism), which is an early Chinese Buddhist apologetic text,[46] has a similar passage: "From this we can infer that the Buddha indeed was the patriarch [*tsu-tsung* 祖宗] of Wen-tzu [who begged the *Tao Te Ching* from Lao-tzu] and the primate [*yüan-shih* 元始] of all beings. How could it be that the disciple [i.e., Yin-wen-tzu] would be able to perform supranormal transformations and that the teacher [i.e., Buddha] could not?"[47]

The Buddhist layman Sun Cho (ca. 300–380) in his *Treatise Illustrating the Way* (*Yü-tao lun*) has a similar explanation of the term *buddha*: "The Sanskrit term 'buddha' is interpreted in the Chinese language as awakening. The meaning of awakening is enlightenment. In meaning it is just the same as when Mencius considered the sages to be awakened."[48] Likewise, Hsi Ch'ao in his *Essentials of the Dharma* (*Feng-fa yao*) writes: "Buddha in Chinese means awakened."[49]

Mou-tzu's description of Buddha alludes to the *Lao Tzu*, to the *Chuang Tzu*, and to the *Lieh Tzu*. Chapter 21 of the *Lao Tzu*, from which our text has just quoted in Article 1, goes on to describe the Tao: "Shadow, indistinct. Indistinct and shadowy, yet within it is an image; shadowy and indistinct." Mou-tzu alludes to these lines, complementing them in his subsequent description with ideas from the Ta-sheng chapter of the *Chuang Tzu*, which states: "Heaven and earth are the father and mother of the ten thousand things. They join to become a body; they part to become a beginning."[50] The sentence about walking on fire is drawn from the same section of the *Chuang Tzu*: "Master Lieh-tzu questioned the Barrier Keeper Yin, "The perfect man walks under water and is not hindered. He walks on fire and is not burned. He journeys above the thousand things and is not afraid. . . .'"

The *Lieh Tzu* describes the people in the country of Hua-hsü—which can be reached only by a journey of the spirit—as innocent of desire or lust and possessed of amazing abilities: "They go into the water without drowning, into fire without burning; hack them, flog them, there is no wound or pain; poke them, scratch them, there is no ache nor itch. They ride space as though walking the earth, sleep on the void as though on their beds; clouds and mist do not hinder their sight, thunder does not confuse their hearing, beauty and ugliness do not disturb their hearts, mountains and valleys do not trip their feet—for they make only journeys of the spirit."[51]

Wang Cho's *Lao-tzu p'ien-hua ching* (Scripture on the Transformations of Lao-tzu), which dates to the second century, describes the divinization of Lao-tzu in parallel terms: "Lao-tzu was at the origin of the Great Beginning, revolving in the Great Expanse. Alone and without companion, he was moving in the times of yore, before Heaven and Earth. Coming out of the hidden and returning thereto, being and nonbeing, he is the First One."[52]

A contrasting passage is found in the *Analects*: "The Master said, 'Benevolence is more vital to the common people than even fire and water. In the case of fire and water, I have seen men die by stepping on them, but I have never seen any man die by stepping on benevolence.'"[53] In his *Fa-yen* (Model Sayings) Yang Hsiung echoes this theme of fire and water in criticizing the Taoist rejection of the Confucian virtues: "Someone asked, 'Is it not Heaven that carves the multitude of forms?'[54] [Yang Hsiung] answered, 'I do not think that he carved them. How would he have obtained the strength to carve them one by one and so form them? I have accepted some things from *The Way and Its Power*, which Lao-tzu discusses. But when he flings away and rejects benevolence and righteousness, when he dispenses with and destroys ceremony and learning, I cannot agree at all! How can I bring you to understand? Only the sages can bring such understanding! Anyone else only screens off [the light of understanding]. How far-reaching, the words of the sages! If one is receptive to them, he will so enlarge [his horizon] as to see all within the four seas. But if one shuts his mind to them, he will become so narrow as not to see even what is within the walls. The words of the sages appear to be more than fire and water.'"[55]

The *Li-huo lun* also echoes Yüan Hung's *Hou Han chi* (Record of the Later Han): "His [i.e., Buddha's] transformations are unlimited, and there is no place to which he cannot go. He is therefore able, in transformation, to permeate all things and greatly to rescue a multitude of living beings."[56]

The description of the Buddha as heavenly or earthly, literally round or square, comes from the *Huai-nan Tzu*: "The King imitates Yin and Yang; his virtue stands on a par with Heaven and Earth [*t'ien ti* 天地]; his intelligence is comparable with the sun and moon; his spiritual character is like the divinities. He is similar to Heaven and Earth [they are round (*yüan* 圓) and square (*fang* 方)]."[57] The commentary of Kao Yu explains that "Round [*yüan* 圓] signifies heaven, while square [*fang* 方] signifies earth."[58]

The phrase about being "mired in the mud without being defiled" is a stock Buddhist image, reminiscent of the *Lotus Sūtra*. It is one of the few clearly Buddhist images in the text.

Reader-Response Criticism

Here Mou-tzu envisages the Buddha no longer simply as the historical Buddha of the previous article, but as a personal and cosmic embodiment of the Way. The designations he appends to the brief description of the title *Buddha* are drawn from previous descriptions of the Tao. In Article 1 Mou-tzu mentions the Buddha's *nirvāṇa*, then interprets it through a Chinese concept as nonaction (*wu-wei* 無為). Here, too, his conscious rhetorical linkage of the Buddha birth to a very Chinese notion of Tao is aimed at the implied reader, whom he is leading to associate the Buddha with the more familiar Tao. It seems quite clear that the author knows precisely what he is doing. He is not confusing Buddha and Tao, for the initial definition of the term *buddha* is clearly drawn from Buddhist sources, while the notion of the Tao is familiar from Chinese sources.

Furthermore, the ability to walk uninjured on fire here ascribed to the Buddha depicts him in terms of Chuang-tzu's and Liu An's Taoist "perfect man." We already know from the Preface that Mou-tzu places no credence in the Taoist immortal (*hsien*). It is reasonable to assume, then, that he interprets the *Chuang Tzu*, from which comes the phrase about walking unharmed on fire, not as referring to supernatural traits of the *hsien*. Indeed, this section of *Chuang Tzu* does not mention the *hsien* at all. The implied reader is assumed to be familiar with this passage, and indeed that very familiarity is the reason Mou-tzu can use it with rhetorical effect. This section of the chapter from the *Chuang Tzu* continues:

[Master Lieh-tzu asked the Barrier Keeper Yin,] "Please tell how [the perfect man] attains these [abilities]."

The Barrier Keeper said, "[He attains such abilities] because he guards his vital energy [*ch'i*]. It is not that he musters his knowledge, skill, determination, or bravery. Please sit down and I'll tell you about it. All endowed with visage, form, voices, color are all things. But how could things be distant from one another? What would lead one to conclude to any priority [among them]? They are simply forms and that's it! However, the creation of things lies in that which has no form and resides in what is not transformed. If a fellow attains this and penetrates it thoroughly, how could things come to detain him? He then abides in bounds that know no excess, hides at the limit that has no source, wanders at the end and beginning of the ten thousand things, unifies his nature, nourishes his vital energy, unifies his virtue [*te*], thereby penetrating to the creative source of things. If a fellow is like this, his heavenly protection is complete and his spirit is without fissures into which things might enter."[59]

The point of this section of the *Chuang Tzu* is that, by reaching the source whereby things arise, one harmonizes with that source, unafraid of injury and fearless in living. Mou-tzu directs the reader's attention to such a passage in the *Chuang Tzu*, not to recommend the practices of *hsien* but to encourage the attainment of *bodhi*, which is here paralleled with the attainment of the unformed source of things. He gives the etymology of the title *Buddha* (i.e., awakened) only after he has depicted Buddha as the ancestor of the Way, the immanent center of Tao. The Buddha here is not merely the historical Buddha described in Article 1; the very nature of Tao, embodied by Buddha, is described. Mou-tzu has made a rhetorical move in his interpretation of the Buddha not just as the Indian prince, but as the Tao embodied. Already in Article 1, we learned that the Buddha amassed the power of the Way for countless aeons. Thus, the reader is led to recognize the Buddha as the embodiment of the Tao that he had all along accepted. The Buddha is becoming rhetorically Chinese, and one can detect here the emergence of early notions of Buddha nature.

We know further from the Preface that Mou-tzu accepts Lao-tzu's advice about discarding knowledge, quite in disagreement with Yang Hsiung's insistence on Confucian orthodoxy mentioned above. Indeed, if Yang Hsiung's *Fa-yen*, which is structured similarly as a question-and-answer dialogue, is recognizable behind the rhetorical form of the *Li-huo lun* dialogue, then the implied reader is further alerted that the *Li-huo lun* is attempting to establish a fissure in the hermeneutical method of the *Fa-yen* for interpreting the Chinese classics, coaxing the implied reader toward a fuller acceptance of Lao-tzu and Chuang-tzu.

ARTICLE 3.
THE WAY

A critic asked: What do you mean by the Way? To what kind of Way do you refer?

Mou-tzu said: The Way (tao 道) means to lead (tao 導). It leads people toward nonaction. Push it forward and there is no ahead. Pull it back and there is no behind. Lift it up and there is no above. Press it down and there is no below. Look at it and there is no form. Listen to it and there is no sound. The four directions are vast, yet it threads its way beyond. Millimeters and centimeters are small, yet it bores its way within. This is what I mean by the Way.

Source Codes

Mou-tzu here interprets the Buddha Tao in terms of the Taoist Tao and identifies its goal with inaction. His descriptions are reminiscent of the *Lao Tzu*, "Go up to it and you will not see its head; follow behind and you will not see its rear."[60]

Yang Hsiung's *Fa-yen* has a germane passage, which discusses the Confucian virtues as the four limbs of the way: "The way serves to lead one. Its power serves to gain achievement. Benevolence serves to humanize one. Righteousness serves to straighten one. Ceremony serves to give one embodiment. [These five] are man's natural endowment. If united [in a person], he is well-integrated. If disunited, he is not."[61]

The *Huai-nan Tzu* similarly discourses on Tao: "Build it up and you cannot give it any more height of glory. Subtract from it and you cannot rob it of any virtue. Multiply it and it is the same number; detract from it and it is no fewer; hack into it and it is no thinner; slay it and it is not destroyed; dig into it and it is without depth; fill it in and it will be no shallower."[62]

Reader-Response Criticism

Lao-tzu himself became identified with the Tao, first in the *Inscription for Lao Tzu* (*Lao Tzu ming*), which is dated to 165 C.E.[63] Sun Cho's *Treatise Illustrating the Tao* says: "Buddha is the essential Tao. Tao means to lead beings. It impels and guides

[them] toward nonaction and there is nothing that is not done. Because of nonaction, because empty quietude and spontaneity leave nothing undone, it transforms the ten thousand things."[64] Mou-tzu, however, refrains from identifying Buddha directly with Tao. In Article 2, he describes Buddha as our primal link with Tao. Perhaps when he wrote, the identification of Lao-tzu with Tao was not yet widespread, and thus he was not led to Sun Cho's conclusion.

Repeating the classic etymology of the Way as "to lead," Mou-tzu identifies it with the attainment of *wu-wei*, as he has already done above. His description is consciously drawn from Chinese sources, yet he does not circumscribe it within the normative classicism, as does Yang Hsiung. Indeed, when Yang was asked, "Is there anything that you accept from Chuang Chou?" he replied, "His lessening of the desires.... But Chou nullifies the duties between rulers and ministers.... Even if he were my neighbor, still I would not take notice of him!"[65] Mou-tzu is not so begrudging as Yang Hsiung in his acceptance of Taoist categories. Yet there is no hint that Mou-tzu has misunderstood the Buddhist doctrines in terms of Taoist notions. Rather, he skillfully employs such notions to present Buddha to his Chinese readers in such a fashion that they cannot simply reject Buddha as foreign. Indeed, if a true Chinese scholar identifies the Buddha as a direct link with Tao and *wu-wei*, to reject the Buddha might be the equivalent of rejecting Tao and *wu-wei*. The implied reader is drawn to accept Mou-tzu's identifications, and to distance himself from any norms that would disallow them, no matter how classical.

ARTICLE 4.
TENSIONS BETWEEN MOU-TZU'S WAY AND
THE CHINESE CLASSICS

A critic asked: Since Confucius considered the Five Classics to be the teaching of the Way, can you respect and recite them and in all your actions follow them? It seems that the Way of which you speak is empty, confused, inconceivable, and ephemeral. How can you speak so differently from that sage?

Mou-tzu said: One shouldn't think that only the accustomed is important or that the unfamiliar is unimportant. You are misled by external appearances and forget the heart of the matter. To be engaged in affairs and yet not lose the power of the Way is like playing a stringed instrument in harmony with other instruments and yet not losing the first two notes of kung and shang. The Way of Heaven regulates the four seasons. The Way of people regulates the five constant virtues. Lao-tzu says, "There is a thing confusedly formed, born before heaven and earth.... It is capable of being the mother of the world. I do not know its name, so I style it 'the Way.'"[66] The Way in its concreteness is the source whereby at home one serves parents, whereby in ruling the country one governs the people well, whereby in "standing alone" one governs the body well. If one follows and practices it, it will fill up heaven and earth. But it is never far, even if it diminishes because one rejects or fails to employ it. Why do you not understand? What is so different [from the words of that sage]?

Source Codes

The phrase *hsü-k'ung* (empty, confused 虛空) used by the critic alludes to an expression often used by Taoist writers. The *Chuang Tzu* employs it to refer to the condition of one who lives in emptiness and isolation (*hsü k'ung* 虛空), apart from his countrymen and all alone.[67] It was taken over by Chinese Buddhists to represent *śūnyatā*, the Mahāyāna notion of the emptiness of essence. Here, in our text, it is coupled with *huang-hu*, confused or blurred, suggesting that to the author of the *Li-huo lun* the term *hsü-k'ung* had not yet become a technical term for Buddhist emptiness.

The phrase *the heart of the matter* (*chung ch'ing* 中情) seems to allude to *The Songs of the South* (*Li Sao*) where Ch'ü Yüan laments that his lord, the Fragrant One (King Huai of Ch'u) has failed to appreciate him: "But the Fragrant One refused to examine my true feelings [*chung ch'ing*]. He lent ear, instead, to slander, and raged against me."[68]

The five constant virtues mentioned by Mou-tzu are the proper relationships between prince and minister, father and son, husband and wife, elder and younger brother, and friends, traditionally defined as benevolence, righteousness, rites, wisdom, and good faith.[69]

Mou-tzu describes the Way in phrases that remind one of the *Lao Tzu*. The Way in its concreteness (*tao chih wei wu* 道之爲物) is that whereby "standing alone" (*tu-li* 獨立) one governs the body. This seems to echo the passage partially cited in our text from the *Lao Tzu* (25):

"There is a thing [*yu wu* 有物] confusedly formed, born before heaven and earth. Silent and void, it stands alone [*tu-li* 獨立] and does not change."

Mou-tzu's attitude refuses to limit the Way to the Confucian classics, and, as will be seen later, directly counters any limitation of the Tao to Chinese civilization. In so doing, he cites the phrase *it will fill up heaven and earth*, alluding to one of the most mystical passages in the *Mencius*, where Kung-sun Ch'ou questions Mencius:

"May I ask what your strong points are?"
"I have an insight into words. I am good at cultivating my flood-like ch'i."
"May I ask what this flood-like ch'i is?"
"It is difficult to explain. This is a ch'i which is, in the highest degree, vast and unyielding. Nourish it with integrity and place no obstacle in its path and it will fill the space between heaven and earth."[70]

Reader-Response Criticism

The objection is the obvious one: the Buddhist Dharma is not the teaching of the Way, but the Five Classics are. What need to speak about the empty and confused Buddhist teachings? In fact, it is alleged, Mou-tzu does not speak as do true sages. Indeed, that is the crux of his problem, for he is clearly introducing alien concepts into his understanding of the Way. This is the problem highlighted in the Preface. Mou-tzu must admit the obvious: that his speech is unfamiliar. Mou-tzu sets up the dialogue by describing the objection in such a way that it applies both to the Buddha Dharma and to the Way as described by Lao-tzu. Thus he can claim that Dharma is in harmony with the Way because it too is confusedly formed and beyond the realm of any speech, just as Lao-tzu says! He authenticates his Buddha discourse in terms of the ineffability of Tao.

The reader must here make a judgment about the validity of the alien discourse. He is led to do so by reference to accepted notions of the ineffability of Tao, familiar to anyone who has read the classical Taoist texts. If Lao-tzu only "styles" it the Way, then all speech is nothing but a styling of what cannot be expressed in any familiar terms, and Buddhist interpretations cannot be summarily dismissed.

Modern scholars often frame the question of the enculturation of Buddhism in terms of Chinese failure to appreciate the Indian dialectic of emptiness, how the emptiness of essence is identical with a bodhisattva's compassionate immersion in the dependently co-arising world. Yet, in the China that is reflected in the *Li-huo lun*, there is already a balance and harmony between the Tao (here expressed in terms of Lao-tzu's maxim) that is the cosmic Tao of Heaven, and the human Tao, the moral tradition identified with Confucius. The Indian teaching of emptiness functioned within its context as a counter to Abhidharma realism, which regarded the truth of the Dharma as a transcendent absolute. Mou-tzu was faced not with such an attempt to transcend this world to find an absolute truth, but with the orthodox Confucianism that tended to focus entirely upon this-worldly affairs. He does this by claiming not to depart from Confucius himself, and throughout the Dialogue he often appeals to the words and examples of Confucius. He need only refute the notion that the Confucian tradition is a set of fixed norms valid once and for all, apart from any changing cultural conditions.[71] He has no need as did Indian Buddhists to deconstruct a prior philosophical system that affirmed the reality of essences (*dharma-svabhāva*), but is compelled rather to demonstrate that Buddhist teaching does not lead one to abandon the world completely. His advice is that one be engaged in affairs (*li shih* 立事) without losing the Buddha Tao. The argument shows little concern that the reader will opt for the disengagement of the Neo-Taoist "dark learning" and remove himself from society altogether. Either his efforts predate the time, the Cheng-shih era (240–48), when Neo-Taoism offered the alternative of a nihilistic escape, or, more probably, he did not regard that alternative to be a serious option for his readers.[72] The need is not to recover conventional reality from the threat of a nihilistic emptiness, but rather to persuade the implied reader that, even while engaged in serving parents, ruling the country, or personal affairs, one can still adopt the Buddha teaching.

ARTICLE 5.
BUDDHIST VERBOSITY

A critic asked: What is most important is not flowery, and the best words are not ornate. Words are beautiful when concise and well chosen. Deeds are illustrious when few and carried to completion. Thus jewels and jade, being rare, are precious, while pieces of tile, being plentiful, are cheap. The sages established the texts of the Seven Classics[73] at not more than thirty thousand words, yet everything is complete in them. But the scrolls of the Buddhist scriptures are reckoned by the tens of thousands and their words by many hundreds of thousands. This is beyond the capability of any individual. I consider them troublesome and not important!

Mou-tzu said: Because of their depth and breadth, rivers and oceans differ from the rain flowing in the gutter. Because of their height and size, the five mountains differ from hillocks and mounds. If the height [of the mountains] did not exceed that of the hilly mounds, a lame goat could cross over their peaks. If the depths [of the oceans] did not exceed that of brooks and streams, a small child could bathe in their deepest pools. Race-horses[74] do not dwell in fenced pastures. Fish that swallow ships do not sport in narrow gorges. You will be disappointed if you try to find bright pearls by splitting half-inch oysters, or a phoenix's brood by searching for its nest in the brambles. This is because the small cannot contain the large.

The Buddhist scriptures presage the events of a hundred thousand generations and in retrospect lay open the basics of another ten thousand generations. Before the great simplicity had arisen and the great beginning had begun, when heaven and earth had just started to emerge, their subtlety could not be grasped and their intricacy could not be penetrated. Yet [in his scriptures] Buddha entirely fills up the exterior of their magnitude and interpenetrates the interior of their silent, obscure mystery. Since there is nothing not recorded [in them], the scriptural scrolls are reckoned by tens of thousands and their words are counted by hundreds of thousands. Their very abundance makes them complete and their vastness makes them rich. Why do you not deem them important? They are indeed important, although they are beyond the grasp of any single individual. Isn't it enough that when you approach a river to take a drink, your thirst is quenched? Why fret about the rest?

Source Codes

The objection that Buddhist rhetoric was too flowery and ornate reflects the quite distinct literary norms of Sanskrit and Chinese. Sanskrit is highly inflected, alphabetic, polysyllabic with compounds running on at times for entire lines, and elaborated in a well-developed grammar. The canons of good writing prized not only the discursive argumentation of logical reasoning, but also the use of hyperbolic metaphor and imaginative simile. By contrast, Chinese is uninflected, ideographic, terse in the extreme, and without a systematic grammar. Chinese authors draw metaphors from familiar things, especially from nature, and tend to prize concreteness and the balance of well-chosen phrases.[75] Furthermore, the literary style in Chinese was to imitate the classics, for style itself carried ideological implications. The *Wen-hsin Tiao-lung* (The Literary Mind and the Carving of Dragons) states that "the style which is defined as elegant and graceful models itself after the classical forms and adopts Confucian principles."[76] A similar complaint is found in the *Lun liu-chia yao-chih* (On Reading the Essentials of the Six Schools), which comments on Ssu-ma's *Shih chi* as follows: "The Confucians are broad-minded and keep the essentials to a minimum.... The classics and commentaries on the six arts are reckoned by the thousands and the ten thousands. Even in many generations, one cannot penetrate their teachings, in many years one cannot understand their main points."[77]

The critic's assertion that jade is prized because rare, although a commonsense assertion, runs counter to a passage from *The Record of Rites* where Confucius is asked if jade is prized because it is rare, and he responds that it is valued not because of its rarity, but because of its intrinsic qualities, seen by the ancients to reflect human virtues.[78]

Mou-tzu's reply echoes the words Mencius used to praise Confucius: "Within their species, there is the ch'i-lin among walking animals, the phoenix among flying birds, the Tai mountain among mounds and ant hills, and rivers and seas among the water flowing in gutters. The sages are of the same species as people, but they stand out from their kind and rise above their level. From the birth of humankind, there has never been one as illustrious as Confucius."[79]

The phrase about a lame goat crossing over the peak of a mountain is taken from the *Meng-tzu tsa-chi*: "Mencius said, 'If their height did not exceed hillocks and mounds, a lame goat could walk over their summit.'"[80]

The fish that swallows boats alludes to a *Lieh Tzu* passage: "I have heard that the fish which can swallow a boat does not swim in side streams, the high-flying hawk and swan do not settle in ponds and puddles. Why? Because their aims are set very high."[81] Similarly, the *Huai-nan Tzu* also states: "If you look into a running gutter, [you will find] no fish that swallows boats."[82]

Mou-tzu's description of the "great beginning" echoes the *Lieh Tzu*: "There was a great evolution, a great inception, a great beginning, and a great simplicity. The great evolution is when the energies were imperceptible, the great inception is the origin of the energies, the great beginning is the origin of forms, and the great simplicity is the origin of substances."[83]

The final sentence recalls a passage from the *Chuang Tzu*, in which Hsü Yu rejects Yao's offer of the Empire: "When the mole drinks at the river, he takes no more than a bellyful. Go home and forget the matter, my Lord."[84]

Reader-Response Criticism

The distaste for flowery and ornate rhetoric is a common theme of the philosophers. Writing around 250 B.C.E., the *Hsün Tzu* says: "Some men of the present generation cloak pernicious persuasions in beautiful language and present elegantly composed but treacherous doctrines and sow great disorder and anarchy in the world. Such men are personally insidious and ostentatious, conceited and vulgar, yet they spread through the whole world their confused ignorance of wherein lies the distinction between right and wrong and between order and anarchy."[85]

The objection presupposes that the critic is aware of the existence of a vast number of Buddhist texts, and sees the effort to study them as culturally disorientating. One does wonder how so many texts could have been known in Han times! And yet nowhere does the *Li-huo lun* show familiarity with even the most important of Buddhist texts.[86] It cites Buddhist sources only infrequently and does not evince any doctrinal sophistication. Perhaps only the existence of a large number of scriptures was known and not their doctrinal content. Any Buddhist missionary probably could have attested to the extensive Buddhist canon, even before Chinese translations were available. And it was indeed disorientating to cope with so many texts, as the subsequent history of Buddhist China demonstrates well enough. Mou-tzu's response, awash in metaphors from and allusions to the classics, defends the Buddhist scriptures, not for their brevity but for their richness and broad compass. All are important, yet one need not study every one of those many texts. Just drink until filled.

It is the implied reader, aware of the vastness of the Buddhist scriptures available to him (in what must therefore be assumed to be a cosmopolitan milieu), to whom these comments are addressed. Mou-tzu's attitude to the intra-story critic is rather condescending: he should be satisfied with what he can handle, even though he has not the capacity to master the whole. This is hardly an argument designed to convince his critic on the story level! In point of fact, the next article does present a response from the critic. Yet here Mou-tzu is speaking over the head of the critic to convince the implied reader to be unlike that objector and delve into the Buddhist scriptures. By aligning the Buddha Dharma with the Taoist Tao, Mou-tzu assures that the Dharma will not be rejected out of hand as foreign. He can assume that his readers have such high regard for the *Lao Tzu* and the *Lieh Tzu*, which he quotes in support of the Dharma, that they cannot reject it.

ARTICLE 6.
AN ATTEMPT TO TURN THE TABLES

A critic asked: Since the Buddhist scriptures are so numerous, I would like to grasp their main points and let go of the rest. Please point out only their main points and leave out the embellishments!

Mou-tzu said: That is not the way it is! The sun and moon each shine in their given realms. The twenty-eight constellations each have their proper domain. The hundred medicinal plants grow together and each heals a specific [malady]. Fox-fur garments guard against the cold, while broad-stitched linens mitigate the summer's heat. Boats and carriages take different routes, yet both can be used for a journey. Confucius himself did not consider the Five Classics to be complete, and he wrote The Spring and Autumn Annals *and* The Classic of Filial Piety *because he wanted to fully explain the practices of the Way in accord with human ideas. Therefore, although the scriptures are numerous, they revolve around one central point, just as the Seven Classics, although different, are at one in valuing the Way, virtue, benevolence, and righteousness. The many words about filial piety are meant to accommodate to human behavior. Tzu-chang and Tzu-yu both asked the same question about filial piety, yet Confucius answered them differently because he was correcting their individual shortcomings. Why reject any of the [scriptures]?*

Source Codes

The critic draws upon chapter 13 of the *Chuang Tzu*. When Confucius wanted to deposit his works with the royal house of Chou, he was

advised that he had first to see Lao Tan about it. "'Excellent!' said Confucius, and went to see Lao Tan, but Lao Tan would not give permission.
Thereupon Confucius unwrapped his Twelve Classics and began ex-
pounding them. Halfway through the exposition, Lao Tan said, 'This will
take forever! Just let me hear the gist of it!'"[87]

Mou-tzu's mention of boats and carriages may allude to the *Fa-
yen* of Yang Hsiung, which says: "Someone asked about the Way. Yang
Hsiung replied, 'The Way is like a road or a river. Carriages and boats
rush helter-skelter without ceasing day and night.' That person then
asked, '[If the Way winds around like boats and rivers,] how can one find
the straight Way and follow it?' Yang Hsiung answered, 'Even though a
road be full of curves, we can follow it since it leads to China. Even
though a river winds to and fro, we can follow it since it leads to the
sea.'"[88]

Tzu-chang and Tzu-yu, mentioned by Mou-tzu, were disciples of
Confucius. The *Analects* report: "Tzu-yu asked about being filial. The
Master said: Nowadays for a man to be filial means nothing more than
that he is able to provide his parents with food. Even hounds and horses
are, in some way, provided with food. If a man shows no reverence, what
is the difference? Tzu-hsia asked about being filial. The Master said: What
is difficult to manage is the expression on one's face. As for the young
taking on the burden when there is work to be done or letting the old
enjoy the wine and food when these are available, that hardly deserves
to be called filial."[89]

Reader-Response Criticism

The critic is not ready to take Mou-tzu's advice in the preceding article. If Mou-tzu's argument about the obscure mystery
of the Tao applies also to Lao-tzu, who only wrote the five thousand words of his famed book, then why are the Buddhist texts so
voluminous? In words from the *Chuang Tzu*, there directed to
Confucius, the critic insists on having the main points. By so
doing, he attempts to claim the Taoist tradition and turn the argument against the validity of Mou-tzu's appeal to these notions.
Mou-tzu, wily as ever, now answers by appealing to Confucian
traditions, affirming that Confucius added two further classics precisely because the "main points" needed clarification in light of
specific circumstances. The Buddhist notion of teaching as *upāya*
is here at play, for all scripture is seen as skillful means accommo-
dated to human ideas and capabilities, as witnessed in the two different replies Confucius gave to his disciples on filial piety. One
cannot simply state a general principle applicable to everyone in

every circumstance. Note that Mou-tzu does not directly take up the basic question about the validity of his appeal to Taoist notions, for he knows full well that Lao-tzu wrote no voluminous scriptures. Rather, he bases his argument on the additions Confucius allegedly made to the classics, and on Confucius's practice of answering a question in light of the questioner's circumstances.

ARTICLE 7.
LACK OF HISTORICAL PRECEDENT

A critic asked: If the Way of the Buddha is so eminently respectable and great, why did not Emperors Yao and Shun, or the Duke of Chou, or Confucius practice it? In the Seven Classics one sees no mention [of Buddhist teaching]. Since you dote over [The Book of] Poetry and [The Book of] Documents, and delight in [The Record of] Rites and [The Classic of] Music, how can you also be attracted by the Way of Buddha and be attached to heterodox practices? How can you pass over the exquisitely wise instructions of the classics and their commentaries? I wouldn't accept [Buddhist doctrine], if I were you!

Mou-tzu said: Books don't have to be in the words of K'ung-ch'iu [i.e., Confucius]. Medicines don't have to follow the prescriptions of P'ien Ch'üeh. If they harmonize with righteousness, follow them! If they cure illness, they are good! In order to sustain himself, the gentleman selects what is good from a broad spectrum.

Tzu-kung said, "How could there be such a thing as a constant teacher for the Master [Confucius]?" Yao served Yin Shou and Shun served Wu Ch'eng. Tan [i.e., the Duke of Chou] studied with Lü Wang, and Confucius with Lao Tan. Yet none of these persons appear in the Seven Classics! Although these four teachers were sages, to compare them with Buddha is like comparing a white deer with the ch'i-lin, or a martin with the phoenix. If Yao, Shun, Chou, and Confucius were partial to these [teachers], how can you reject and not study Buddha, whose major and minor bodily marks, transformations, and limitless spiritual powers are unequaled?

The Five Classics are at the service of righteousness, but there were lacunae. How can the mere absence of mention of Buddha be grounds for thinking [his doctrine] is strange and calling it into question?

Source Codes

The critic's objection appeals to the classical tradition and seems to echo Yang Hsiung's insistence on the orthodox Way in his *Fa-yen*: "Someone asked about the Way. [Yang Hsiung] replied: 'The Way is pervasive. There is nothing it does not pervade.' It was then asked, '[If it is pervasive,] does it also reach to other [peoples, i.e., barbarians]?' Yang Hsiung replied, 'That which reaches to Yao, Shun, and King Wen constitutes the true Way. That which does not reach to Yao, Shun, and King Wen is but heterodox teaching. The gentleman adheres to the true way and not to heterodox teaching.'"[90] Similarly, Tung Chung-shu had said in his *Ch'un-ch'iu Fan-lu* (Luxuriant Gems on the Spring and Autumn Annals) that "he who is in doubt about the present, let him examine ancient times. He who does not understand the future, let him look to the past."[91]

Mou-tzu also dredges up examples from the classical traditions. P'ien Ch'üeh is the semilegendary physician mentioned in many texts.[92] *The Rectification of Unjustified Criticism* has a similar passage: "Why was P'ien Ch'üeh long ago praised as a good physician? It was precisely because he gave the proper medicine suitable to the disease and [thus the sick person] did not lose his opportunity [to become well]."[93]

Tzu-kung is a disciple of Confucius. Mou-tzu's statement that Yao and Shun, respectively, served Yin Shou and Wu Ch'eng is perhaps taken from the *Hsün Tzu*: "Yao studied under Chün Ch'ou and Shun studied with Wu-ch'eng Chao." The commentary explains that Chün Ch'ou is Yin Shou.[94] Lü Wang was the teacher of Kings Wen and Wu, and thus also of Tan, the Duke of Chou, who was the principal adviser of King Wu.[95]

The sentence about Confucius is cited from the *Analects* 19:22: "Kung-sun Ch'ao of Wei asked Tzu-kung, 'from whom did Chung-ni learn?' Tzu-kung said, 'The way of King Wen and King Wu has not yet fallen to the ground but is still to be found in men. There is no man who does not have something of the way in him. Superior men have got hold of what is of major significance while inferior men have got hold of what is of minor significance. From whom, then, does the Master not learn? Equally, how could there be such a thing as a constant teacher for him?'"[96]

Mou-tzu's assertion that Confucius studied with Lao Tan is taken from *The Record of Rites*, where Lao Tan instructs Confucius on the proper procedure for interrupting a funeral procession during an eclipse.[97]

According to the *Hou Han shu*,[98] the Seven Classics are *The Odes*, *The Documents*, *The Record of Rites*, *The Classic of Music*, *The Classic of Changes*, *The Spring and Autumn Annals*, and the *Analects* of Confucius. The discussion begins with reference to these seven, but toward the end Mou-tzu mentions only five classics that teach righteousness. Yang Hsiung in his *Fa-yen* likewise cites only five classics: *The Book of Documents*, *The Classic of Changes*, *The Classic of Odes*, *The Rites*, and *The Spring and Autumn Annals*.[99] In fact, the canon of the classics was not agreed upon. Different authors arranged the classics differently, sometimes dividing one text into separate classics, sometimes adding a text, such as *The Classic of Music*, Confucius's *Analects*, or the *Mencius*.[100] Mou-tzu's reading is the traditional one, that Confucius added *The Classic of Filial Piety* and the *Tso Chuan*, as mentioned in the previous Article.

Reader-Response Criticism

Mou-tzu has claimed that the Buddha Tao is in fact a reclamation of the Tao of antiquity. The obvious objection is then: Why do not the sage figures from antiquity even mention the Buddha? Mou-tzu mounts a frontal attack on the normative sufficiency of the classics, intended to lead the reader to recognize that a literal adherence to the classics can serve as no sure guide, for there are omissions even in the classics. Rather, the point is whether or not a teaching—here, Buddhism—harmonizes with the values taught in antiquity. The critic had mentioned the classics and their commentaries. Mou-tzu proceeds to cite examples from those very texts to bolster his argument, showing that the sages themselves, who are the classical paradigms of the normative story of Chinese culture, sought out and studied under nonclassical teachers. He even cites the legendary example of Confucius studying under Lao-tzu. The reader then is justified in following the Buddha Tao, even though Buddha is never mentioned in the Classics.

ARTICLE 8.
THE FOREIGNNESS OF BUDDHA'S BODY

A critic asked: The Buddha had thirty-two major marks and eighty minor marks. Why was he so different from the rest of men? Such extravagant descriptions are not true!

Mou-tzu said: The proverb says that "to nearsighted people many things appear strange." They see a camel and think it is a horse with a swollen back! Yao's eyebrows were of eight colors. Shun's eyes had two pupils apiece. Kao Yao had a horse's snout. King Wen had four nipples. Each of Yu's ears had three orifices. The Duke of Chou was humpbacked. Fu I had a dragon's nose. The top of Confucius's head was concave. Lao-tzu had sun lumps and moon marks [on either side of his forehead],[101] *his nose had a double bone, his palms were traced with shihs [the character for ten 十], and his feet were marked with two wus [the character for five 五]. Were these not different from the rest of men? Why should you call into question the Buddha's major and minor marks?*

Source Codes

Mou-tzu draws from classical sources to cite examples of Chinese sages with strange and unusual physical characteristics. Among other sources,[102] Wang Ch'ung in his *Lun Heng* critiques the popular physiognomy of his time—that one could read spiritual qualities by means of bodily characteristics. In a passage that is close to that of the *Li-huo lun*, he reports the popular belief: "According to tradition Huang Ti had a dragon face, Chuan Hsi was marked with the character wu on his brow, Ti Ku had a double tooth, Yao's eyebrows had eight colors, Shun's eyes were double pupils, Yü's ears three orifices, T'ang had double elbows, Wen Wang four nipples, Wu Wang's spine was curved backwards. Chou Kung was inclined to stoop forward, Kao Yao had a horse's mouth, Confucius' arms were turned backwards. These twelve sages either held the position of emperors and kings, or they aided their sovereigns, being anxious for the welfare of the people. All the world knows this, and the scholars speak of it."[103]

A similar account of physical abnormalities found in worthy and sagacious figures is found in the *Hsün Tzu*, which also argues against the practice of physiognomy.[104]

Reader-Response Criticism

At the end of Article 7, Mou-tzu refers to the Buddha's major and minor marks. There the reference is somewhat out of place, for the issue is not his physical characteristics. The implied author seems to have been setting the stage for the question here discussed: the description of the Buddha's physical characteristics as reported in the scriptures. In their Indian context, such characteristics were indications of exalted status, yet to the Chinese they must have seemed strange and foreign. Mou-tzu domesticates that strangeness by citing parallel examples from Chinese antiquity, for many of the revered sages also had remarkable physical characteristics. The argument in the Chinese texts is focused on questions of physiognomy, the practice of judging inner character, and foretelling a person's future, from physical traits. Mou-tzu simply borrows the references and turns them to his purpose of aligning the Buddha, even with his unusual physical characteristics, with the sages already described in the Chinese literature as themselves somewhat unusual in appearance.[105]

ARTICLE 9.
FILIAL PIETY AND BUDDHIST PRACTICE

A critic asked: In the words of The Classic of Filial Piety, *"Since body, limbs, hair, and skin are received from one's parents, do not dare to harm them." Tseng-tzu, when about to die, said, "Uncover my hands and my feet." But the monks shave their heads! Why do they go against the sage's words and fail to follow the way of the filial son? How can you, sir, who love to discuss right and wrong, to weigh the crooked and the straight, reverse yourself and approve [such a practice]?*

Mou-tzu said: Certainly it is not good to revile the sages and the worthies. To miss the mark in adjudicating is not wise. How could what is not good or not wise plant the seeds of virtue? When virtue is not planted, one becomes a companion of the unprincipled and insincere. But is the discussion [about filial piety] so simple? A long time ago the Ch'i people crossed a large river in a boat and it happened that their father fell into the water. His sons rolled up their sleeves, seized his head, and turned him upside down, forcing the water out of his mouth, thus bringing their father back to life. Now, to seize one's father's head and turn him upside down is certainly not very filial. Yet they could have done nothing better to save their father's life. If they had folded their hands and practiced the norm of filial sons, their father's life would have been lost in the waters.

Confucius once said, "A man good enough as a partner in the pursuit of the Way … need not be good enough as a partner in the exercise of moral discretion." This is what we call acting in a timely fashion.

The Classic of Filial Piety states that "the former kings had perfect virtue and were intent upon the Way." Yet T'ai Po cut his hair and marked his body. Thus, because he followed the customs of Wu and Yüeh, he went contrary to the principle [of filial piety about not harming] body, limbs, hair, or skin. But Confucius nevertheless praised him, saying that "he can be said to be of the highest virtue." Chung-ni did not revile him because of his short hair! From this it can be seen that if one has great virtue, one should not cling to minor matters.

The monks renounce their homes and possessions, forego having wives and children, do not listen to music nor leer at beautiful women. This could be termed the perfection of the virtue of yielding. How does this go against the words of the sages or fail to harmonize with filial piety!

Yü Jang swallowed charcoal and painted his body. Nieh Chang peeled [the skin] off his face and inflicted punishment on himself. Po Chi walked on fire. And Kao Hsing mutilated her appearance. Yet a gentleman would consider them brave and righteous. I have never heard anyone ridicule them for injuring themselves or taking their own lives. If you compare the monks with their shaven heads and cut hair with these four, they are not so very different!

Source Codes

After citing the famous passage from The Classic of Filial Piety, the critic alludes to the following section in the Analects: "When he was seriously ill Tseng-tzu summoned his disciples and said, 'Take a look at my hands. Take a look at my feet. The Odes say, "In fear and trembling, as if approaching an abyss, as if walking on thin ice." Only now am I sure of being spared [the risk of mutilating my body], my young friends!'"[106] The point is that the norms of filial piety entailed the obligation to preserve one's body intact as a gift from one's parents.

Mou-tzu's story about the people of Ch'i finds a parallel in a passage from the Huai-nan Tzu that argues that the norms of filial piety must be applied in accord with the exigencies of concrete circumstances: "Filial service demands a pleasant countenance, a humble demeanor and an orderly deportment from the son, when he stops to tie the gaiter and the shoe of the father; but when one's father is drowning, the son may pull the father out by the hair, to save him."[107]

The passage from the *Analects* quoted in our text reads in full: "The Master said, 'A man good enough to be a partner in one's studies need not be good enough to be a partner in the pursuit of the Way; a man good enough to be a partner in the pursuit of the Way need not be good enough to be a partner in a common stand; a person good enough to be a partner in the pursuit of a common stand need not be good enough to be a partner in the exercise of moral discretion.'"[108] The point is that one must practice moral discretion in applying classical norms to concrete cases.

The *Classic of Filial Piety* (*K'ai-tsung ming-i*) reports: "Confucius sat. Tseng Tzu attended upon [him]. The Master said, 'The former kings had perfect virtue and were intent upon the Way. Thereby they were in harmony with all under heaven. The people followed [them] and lived in peace. There was no resentment between superiors and inferiors.'"

T'ai Po and Yü Chung were the elder brothers of Chi Li, the father of King Wen of Chou. Learning that their father wanted to leave power to Chi Li, whose son would become King Wen of Chou, they retired to live among the Man barbarians in Wu and Yüeh, where they conformed themselves to the indigenous customs, "tatooing themselves and cutting their hair."[109] Their acquiescence in the wishes of their father thus led to the enthronement of King Wen, the sage founder of the Chou dynasty. Confucius praised their action, saying, "Surely T'ai Po can be said to be of the highest virtue. Three times he abdicated his right to rule over the Empire, and yet he left behind nothing the common people could acclaim."[110]

Yü Jang twice attempted to assassinate the Viscount of Chao to carry out his duty of avenging the death of his master, the Earl of Chih, whom the viscount had slain. The first attempt failed. Then "Yü Jang swallowed charcoal and varnished his body, so that he got ulcers and nobody recognized him."[111] After his second failed attempt, he implored the viscount to allow him to pass his sword through the viscount's garment, thus fulfilling his duty to avenge his master before being executed.

Nieh Chang, another accepted example of a "filial assassin," after fulfilling his appointed killing of a minister of the state of Han, mutilated his face, plucked out his eyes, and died after disemboweling himself, all in order to avoid being recognized and implicating his sister in the deed.[112]

Po Chi is identified by Pelliot with the woman in *The Spring and Autumn Annals* who died in a palace fire rather than violate the norm that women should not leave unescorted from their chambers: "In the fifth month on chia-wu, there was a fire in [the palace of] Sung, [in which] the eldest daughter [of our Duke Ch'ing, who had been married to Duke Kung] of Sung, died." The *Tso Chuan* comments: "Someone

called out in the great temple of Sung, 'Ah! Ah! On chia-wu there occurred a great fire in Sung, when Duke [Ch'ing's] eldest daughter who
had been married to the ruler of Sung, died;—through her wailing for the
instructress of the harem."[113]

Kao Hsing was a maiden of Liang who discouraged an unwanted
princely suitor by cutting off her nose to maintain her chastity. The
prince was impressed by her deed and named her "Sublime Action."[114]
All these classical examples show that at times those who injured their
bodies were still models of filial practice.

Reader-Response Criticism

The Confucian virtue of filial piety entailed the care and nur-
ture of one's own body as a gift from one's parents. Thus the dying
Tzu-kung uncovered his hands and feet to witness to the fact that
he had managed to keep his body intact until the end. Such care
was a recognized value among Chinese readers, so Mou-tzu must
account for the apparent divergence from this norm by Buddhist
monks, who in shaving their hair would seem to violate the in-
junction of *The Classic of Filial Piety* not to harm their hair.
Again he makes his point by citing counterexamples from the
classical tradition. To stick to the literal word means to miss the
mark, to fail to be adequate to the exercise of moral discretion recommended by Confucius. The reader is led to acknowledge that
the monks do not in fact violate filial piety any more than did
the individuals cited as examples from antiquity.

ARTICLE 10.
BUDDHIST CELIBACY AND FILIAL PIETY

*A critic asked: The highest happiness is an unbroken line
of posterity. The most unfilial conduct is to lack posterity. [But]
the monks reject women and children, renounce wealth and
goods, and often for their whole lives do not marry. Why do they
go against the filial conduct that bestows happiness? There is
nothing wonderful in their experiencing hardship, and nothing
remarkable in their holding themselves aloof!*

---

*Mou-tzu said: What is long on the left must be short on the
right. What is large in front must be short behind. Meng Kung-
ch'uo was chief officer of the Ch'ao and Wei families [of Ch'in].*

His excellence was not such, however, that he could have been a high officer of T'eng or Hsüeh.

Wives, children, property, and possessions are the nonessential things of this world. Purification and nonaction are the mysteries of the Way. Lao-tzu said, "Your name or your person, which is dearer? Your person or your goods, which is worth more?"[115]

Mou-tzu continued to explain: When we inspect the customs handed down from the Three Dynasties [of antiquity], we observe in the way and method of the Confucians and Mohists, that they recite The Book of Poetry *and* The Book of Documents, *practice propriety and moderation, revere benevolence and righteousness, and look toward purification. The fame and praise for these instructions, handed down by our fellow countrymen, is widespread. [But,] this is the mode of conduct of the average student. [By contrast,] he who practices limpidity has nothing to regret.*

If you had the pearl of the Marquis of Sui right in front, but a raging tiger right behind, would you not, upon seeing that tiger, run away and not dare reach out for the pearl? This would be because you valued life above profit.

Hsü Yu perched in the nest of a tree. [Po] Yi and [Shu] Ch'i starved on [Mount] Shou-yang. When Confucius eulogized their worthiness, he said, "They sought benevolence and attained it." I have never heard them blamed for not having posterity or possessions!

Monks cultivate the virtue of the Way, employing it to replace the pleasures of this fleeting world. They revert to purity and eminence, thereby replacing the joys of women and children. If this is not wonderful, then what is? If this is not remarkable, then what is?

Source Codes

The critic refers to the *Mencius:* "There are three ways of being a bad son. The most serious is to have no heir."[116] In his response, Mou-tzu refers to Ch'ao and Wei, two of the great families in the state of Ch'in, and to T'ang and Hsüeh, two small states. The *Analects* report: "Meng Kung-ch'uo would be more than adequate as steward to great noble families like Ch'ao or Wei, but he would not be suitable as Counselor even in a small state like T'ang or Hsüeh."[117]

The added response of Mou-tzu appears to be a later redaction of the text, perhaps because a later reader thought the argument not sufficiently clarified. The allusion to the average person recalls the words of the *Lao Tzu*: "When the best student hears about the way, he practices it assiduously; when the average student hears about the way, it seems to him one moment here and gone the next...."[118]

Mou-tzu's mention of limpidity (*t'ien-t'an* 恬惔) is a reference to a passage from the *Chuang Tzu* that describes the contrast between different scholars and the sage:

To be constrained in will, lofty in action, aloof from the world, apart from its customs, elevated in discourse, sullen and critical, indignation his whole concern—such is the life favored by the scholar in his mountain valley, the man who condemns the world, the worn and haggard one who means to end it all with a plunge into the deep. To discourse on benevolence, righteousness, loyalty, and good faith, to be courteous, temperate, modest, and deferential, moral training his whole concern—this is the life favored by the scholar who seeks to bring the world to order, the man who teaches and instructs, who at home and abroad lives for learning. To talk of great accomplishments, win a great name, define the etiquette of ruler and subject, regulate the position of superior and inferior, the ordering of state his only concern—this is the life favored by the scholar of court and council, the bringer of accomplishment, the annexer of territory. To repair to thickets and ponds, living idly in the wilderness, angling for fish in solitary places, inaction his only concern—this is the life favored by the scholar of the rivers and seas, the man who withdraws from the world, the unhurried idler. To pant, to puff, to hail, to spit, to spit out the old breath and draw in the new, practicing bear-hangings and bird-stretchings, longevity his only concern—such is the life favored by the scholar who practices Induction, the man who nourishes his body, who hopes to live to be as old as P'eng-tsu. But to attain loftiness without constraining the will; to achieve moral training without benevolence and righteousness, good order without accomplishments and fame, leisure without river and seas, long life without Induction; to lose everything and yet possess everything, at ease in the illimitable, where all good things come to attend—this is the Way of Heaven and earth, the virtue of the sage. So it is said, Limpidity [*t'ien-tan* 恬澹], silence, emptiness, inaction—these are the level of Heaven and earth, the substance of the Way and its Virtue.[119]

On the pearl of the Marquis of Sui, the *Chuang Tzu* reports: "Now suppose there were a man who took the priceless pearl of the Marquis of

Sui and used it as a pellet to shoot at a sparrow a thousand yards up in the air—the world would certainly laugh at him."[120] Kao Yu's commentary to the *Huai-nan Tzu* also reports: "The Marquis of Sui came upon a large serpent, which was bruised and cut, and healed its wounds with medicinal herbs. Later on, the serpent emerged from the Chiang [River] holding a fine pearl in its mouth, and offered it to the Marquis as a reward; whence its name, 'the pearl of the Marquis of Sui.'"[121]

The legendary Emperor Yao wanted to cede the throne to Hsü Yu, but Hsü Yu declined and fled, saying, "You govern the world and the world is already well governed. Now, if I take your place, will I be doing it for a name? But name is only the guest of reality—will I be doing it because I can play the part of a guest? When the tailor bird builds her nest in the deep woods, she uses no more than one branch."[122] This passage is perhaps the basis for the story that Hsü Yu himself nested in the tree.[123]

The *Chuang Tzu* also reports on "two gentlemen who lived in Ku-chu named Po Yi and Shu Ch'i. When offered governmental offices, they too fled: "The two gentlemen thereupon went north as far as Mount Shou-yang, where eventually they died of starvation."[124] They were the sons of the prince of Ku-chu. When their princely father attempted to leave the throne to the younger Shu Ch'i when he died, the latter fled the realm, because he did not want to offend his elder brother. Upon the fall of the Yin dynasty, these two refused to serve the Chou, choosing instead starvation on Mount Shou-yang.[125] Confucius praised them a number of times in the *Analects*: "[Tzu-kung] went in and said, 'What sort of men were Po Yi and Shu Ch'i?' 'They were excellent men of old.' 'Did they have any complaints?' 'They sought benevolence and got it... .'"[126] The *Huai-nan Tzu* similarly holds them in high esteem: "It was not that Po I and Shu Ch'i were not able to receive emoluments and bear office so that they might bring forth their merit. Though this was so, they took pleasure in departing from the generation and [engaging in] lofty practices to cut [themselves] off from the multitude—thus they made no [official] endeavors."[127]

Reader-Response Criticism

Celibacy was not a recognized value in classical China, for it ended one's family lineage and thus offended against filial piety. This Buddhist practice seemed clearly to offend the classical norms. Mou-tzu has to respond to such a rejection of normative behavior. He does so by citing Lao-tzu, implying for the reader, who is to make the connection, that the celibate monk is following Lao-tzu's advice to prize one's person over the possession of a family or one's family name. Thus, the reader is to conclude that monks follow a more excellent path, above the capability of lesser

men, just as Meng Kung-ch'uo was unequal to the higher task of
being a counselor even in a small state.

The additional response has perhaps been added by a later
scribe, who was not confident the reader could make the appropriate connections. He invites the reader to explicate the difference
between the average practices of the Confucians and Mohists,
and the higher practice of the monks, focused on the prize of limpidity. Examples from antiquity that counter that average practice
are adduced to extol the monks' quest for transcendence in returning to the original Way of true sages.

ARTICLE 11.
MORE COMPLAINTS ABOUT MONKISH BEHAVIOR

*A critic asked: The Yellow Emperor attired himself in gar-
ments and designed ornaments for them. The Viscount of Chi
disclosed the Great Plan, and considered a proper demeanor to
be the most important of the five proper actions. Confucius
authored* The Classic of Filial Piety *and deemed proper dress to
be the first of the three virtues. He also spoke about "[the gentle-
man] with his robe and cap adjusted properly and dignified in his
gaze." Yüan Hsien, although poor, did not remove his bark cap.
And Tzu-lu, even in distress, did not forget to tie his cap strings.*

*But the monks shave the hair off their heads and don red-
colored robes.*[128] *When they encounter some personage, they do
not observe the proper obeisance, nor do they have the proper demeanor of yielding the right of way. Why do they violate the rules
for demeanor and dress? Why do they denigrate the adornments
of the court officials?*

---

*Mou-tzu said: Lao-tzu states that "a man of the highest
value does not keep to virtue and that is why he has virtue. A
man of the lowest virtue never strays from virtue and that is why
he is without virtue."*[129] *During the times of the Three Emperors,
people ate raw meat, wore skins, lived in the trees, or lodged
in caves.*[130] *Thus they revered a natural simplicity. Why then do
we now need those ostentatious and embroidered caps, and wrap-
around fur adornments? Those people are said to have had virtue,*

straightforward sincerity,[131] *and nonaction. The monks' conduct is just like their conduct!*

Someone said: According to your words, such persons as the Yellow Emperor, the Emperors Yao and Shun, the Duke of Chou, and Confucius are to be rejected as inadequate models!

Mou-tzu said: He who sees the whole picture will not be confused. He who listening understands will not be in doubt. Yao, Shun, Chou, and Confucius practiced worldly affairs, while Buddha and Lao-tzu set their minds on nonaction. Chung-ni [Confucius] roosted in over seventy countries, but Hsü Yu heard there was to be an abdication of the throne [for his sake] and washed out his ears in the river. The Way of the gentleman is sometimes to go out, sometimes to stay home, sometimes to keep silent, sometimes to speak out. He is not to exaggerate his feelings nor defile his nature. Thus the nobility of the Way lies in how one employs it. What is all this business about rejecting [their worldly application of the Way]?

Source Codes

The critic's objection draws upon the traditional account that the Yellow Emperor was the inventor of ceremonial garb. *The Annals of the Bamboo Books* states that the Yellow Emperor "invented the cap with pendants and the robes to match."[132] *The Classic of Filial Peity (Ch'ung ta-fu)* states: "They did not dare dress other than in the clothing patterned by the former emperors. They did not dare utter words other than those of the former emperors. They did not dare follow virtue other than that of the former emperors. For this reason, if it was not the right pattern, they did not speak. If it was not the right way, they did not act. From their mouths came no exceptional words and from their persons no exceptional conduct. Even though their words filled the world, their speech was not blameworthy. Even though their conduct filled the world, it was not odious. These three [i.e., clothing, words, and conduct] constitute a single whole." *The Book of Changes* also notes: "The Yellow Emperor, Yao, and Shun allowed the upper and lower garments to hang down and the world was in order. They probably took this from the hexagrams of the creative and the receptive."[133] Wilhelm comments that "allowing their garments to hang down was later taken to mean that the Yellow Emperor, Yao, and Shun sat quietly without stirring, and as a result of their inaction, things automatically righted themsleves."

The Great Plan (*hung fan*) is book 4 of the *Documents*, which recounts the advice of the Viscount of Chi of the Shang dynasty. Imprisoned under the last Yin ruler, he was freed by King Wu of Chou, upon whose request he composed his Great Plan.[134] The five proper actions are described by this Great Plan as "demeanor, respectfulness, seeing, hearing, and thinking."[135]

Confucius, upon being asked by Tzu-chang about the meaning of "being awe-inspiring without appearing fierce," one of the five excellent practices needed for governance, answered: "The gentleman, with his robe and cap adjusted properly and dignified in his gaze, has a presence which inspires people who see him with awe. Is not this being awe-inspiring without appearing fierce?"[136]

Yüan Hsien, a poor disciple of Confucius famed for his indifference to his poverty, still managed to don a rustic bark cap when meeting colleagues. Tzu-kung was the most affluent of Confucius's disciples. The *Chuang Tzu* reports:

> Yüan Hsien lived in the state of Lu, in a tiny house that was hardly more than four walls. It was thatched with growing weeds, had a broken door made of woven brambles and branches of mulberry for the doorposts; jars with the bottoms out, hung with pieces of coarse cloth for protection from the weather, served as windows for its two rooms. The roof leaked and the floor was damp, but Yüan Hsien sat up in a dignified manner, played his lute, and sang. Tzu-kung, wearing an inner robe of royal blue and an outer one of white, and riding in a grand carriage, whose top was too tall to get through the entrance to the lane, came to call on Yüan Hsien. Yüan Hsien, wearing a bark cap and slippers with no heels, and carrying a goosefoot staff, came to the gate to greet him. 'Goodness!' exclaimed Tzu-kung. 'What distress you are in, Sir!' Yüan Hsien replied, 'I have heard that if one lacks wealth, that is called poverty; and if one studies but cannot put into practice what he has learned, that is called distress. I am poor, but I am not in distress!' Tzu-kung backed off a few paces with a look of embarrassment. Yüan Hsien laughed and said, 'To act out of worldly ambition, to band with others in cliquish friendships, to study in order to show off to others, to teach in order to please one's own pride, to mask one's evil deeds behind benevolence and righteousness, to deck oneself out with carriages and horses—I could never bear to do such things.'[137]

The *Tso Chuan* recounts of Tzu-lu, a disciple of Confucius, that when he was attacked with swords by two enemies, the strings of his cap were also severed, but he responded, "The gentleman, even at the point of death, does not let his cap fall to the ground." He then tied them together and died.[138]

Mou-tzu alludes to a passage from the *Analects*: "Wei-sheng Mu said to Confucius, 'Ch'iu, why are you so restless? Are you, perhaps, trying to practice flattery?' Confucius answered, 'I am not so impertinent as to practice flattery. It is just that I so detest inflexibility.' "[139] Legge translates *hsi hsi* (栖栖) not as "restless," but, more literally, as "roosting,"[140] which I take to mean strutting about and making a lot of noise.

Hsü Yu, the sage mentioned by Mou-tzu in the previous article, is again mentioned as a counterexample. He is described by the *Chuang Tzu*: "Yao wanted to cede the throne to Hsü Yu. 'When the sun and moon have already come out,' he said, 'it's a waste of light to go on burning the torches, isn't it? When the seasonal rains are falling, it's a waste of water to go on irrigating the fields. If you took the throne, the world would be well ordered. I go on occupying it, but all I can see are my failings. I beg to turn the world over to you.' Hsü Yu said, 'You govern the world and the world is already well governed. Now if I took your place, would I be doing it for a name? But name is only the guest of reality— will I be doing it so I can play the part of a guest? When the tailor bird builds her nest in the deep woods, she uses no more than one branch. When the mole drinks at the water, he takes no more than one bellyful. Go home and forget the matter, my lord. I have no use for the rulership of the world!' "[141]

Another counterexample is afforded by the *Chuang Tzu*: "A man of Sung who sold ceremonial hats made a trip to Yüeh, but the Yüeh people cut their hair short and tattoo their bodies and had no use for such things."[142]

Reader-Response Criticism

The questions continue to focus on specific issues that jar the cultural sensitivities of the Chinese literati, and how these matters can be understood in light of the classical tradition. Buddhist monks obviously do not follow the normative behavior for a *chün-tzu*, that model of a Confucian gentleman, as is so clearly pointed out by the critic. The reader is aware of the truth of this criticism, and Mou-tzu does not attempt to alter the description of the monk's behavior.

Indeed, complaints about the monks may have been common. *The History of the Later Han* reports a similar criticism:

"Moreover, the monks should all be of the highest integrity and uprighteousness: their capabilities should be of the best.... At present the monks are very numerous. Some are troublemakers and avoid state service."[143]

In response, Mou-tzu calls Lao-tzu to witness that the monks follow the greater simplicity, such as characterized the people of old, that is, the people of the golden age to which Confucius looked with such nostalgia. Indeed, the critic's mention of Yüan Hsien as a model of Confucian orthodoxy is perhaps crafted ironically by the implied author to foreshadow Mou-tzu's reply, for in context in the *Chuang Tzu* Yüan Hsien seems to be parodying the proper behavior of Tzu-kung.

The second exchange, perhaps added at a later time, both makes more incisive the objections and makes more explicit Mou-tzu's reply. Indeed, Mou-tzu is claiming that the Confucian sages are not adequate models, but his grounds for so doing are to be found in the recognized Taoist practice of *wu-wei*, as the obverse of worldly practice. To set one's mind on *wu-wei* is to abandon such worldly practice. The reader is quite ready to admit that the Way is practiced differently according to circumstances, for this too is taught by Confucius. Thus both Lao-tzu and the Buddha are identified with an alternate practice of the Way. There is, then, no need to reject either the worldly models of Confucius and the ancient sages or the otherworldly practice of either Lao-tzu or the Buddha. The Buddha is riding Lao-tzu into the center of Chinese cultural acceptance.

ARTICLE 12.
LIFE AFTER DEATH

A critic asked: The Buddha teaching says that after death people must be reborn. I just cannot believe this opinion!

———————

Mou-tzu said: When a person is on the point of death, his family ascends to the roof to call him. But after he is dead, whom are they calling?

———————

Someone said: They are calling to his heavenly soul [hun] [to rejoin] his earthly soul [p'o].

Mou-tzu said: If that spirit returns, he lives; if it does not, then to what spirit are they calling?

[Someone] said: Then, it must be the spirit of the dead [kuei-shen] [that does not come back].[144]

Mou-tzu said: Isn't this because his earthly spirit [p'o-shen] certainly is not extinguished? Only the body withers and decays. The body is like the roots and the leaves of the five grains, while the descending spirit is like the seeds and kernels. The roots and leaves are born and so inevitably die. But how would the seeds and kernels have a final dissolution? When one attains the Way, the body perishes indeed. Lao-tzu said, "The reason I have great trouble is that I have a body. When I no longer have a body, what trouble have I?"[145] Again he said, "To abandon the body when the task is over is the way of heaven."[146]

Someone said: Those who seek the Way die, those who do not seek the Way also die. What's the difference?

Mou-tzu said: You exemplify the saying, "Lacking even one day's goodness, yet you want the praise of an entire lifetime!"[147] Even though they die, the spirits of those who attain the Way return to fortunate abodes.[148] But when those who do evil die, their spirits meet with certain misery. The fool is unclear about affairs already completed, while the wise prepares beforehand for things that have not even arisen. The Way is to the negation of the Way as gold is to weeds. Good is to evil as white is to black.[149] When these are clearly different, how can you say what's the difference?

Source Codes

Yü Ying-shih explains the ritual mentioned by Mou-tzu as follows:
"In Han China there was an important death ritual called *fu*, 'The Summons of the Soul.' It was the first of a series of rituals to be performed
to the newly dead. Although this *fu* ritual, as variously reported in the
Chou-li, the *I-li*, and the *Li-chi*, is a highly complex one, it may nevertheless be briefly described. As soon as a person dies, a 'summoner' (*fu-che*),
normally a member of the family, climbs from the east eaves to the top of
the roof with a set of clothes belonging to the deceased, and calls him by
name aloud—'O! Thou so-and-so, come back!' After the call has been repeated three times, the summoner throws down the clothes, which are
received by another person on the ground. Afterwards the summoner descends from the west eaves. Thus the ritual of *fu* is completed. According
to the Han commentator Cheng Hsuan (127–200) the purpose of the *fu*
ritual is 'to summon the *hun* soul of the dead back to reunite with its
p'o soul' (*chao-hun fu-p'o*). In fact the ritual is predicated on the belief
that when the *hun* separates from the *p'o* and leaves the human body,
life comes to an end. However, at the moment when death first occurs,
the living cannot bear to believe that their beloved one has really left
them for good. The living must first assume that the departure of the
hun soul is only temporary. It is possible, then, that if the departed soul
can be summoned back the dead may be brought back to life. A person
can be pronounced dead only when the *fu* ritual has failed to achieve its
purpose, after which the body of the dead will be placed on the bed in his
or her own chamber and covered with a burial shroud called *lu* or *fu*."
Such a ritual is depicted in one of the paintings found in tomb number 1
at Ma-wang-tui.[150]

The term *p'o* (魄), originally signifying the "white light" or soul of
the changing phases of the moon, came to be associated with the life or
death of a person. To this was joined the notion of the *hun* (魂), probably
of a southern origin, associated with light *ch'i*, the breath of life. At death
the *hun*, being light and ethereal, ascends to the heavens, while the *p'o*,
associated with the heavier bodily *ch'i*, descends to the earth. "We have
seen that it was a general belief in Han China that the *hun* owes its existence to the refined *ch'i* from heaven while the *p'o*, being always associated with the body, is composed of coarse *ch'i* from earth."[151]

The *Tso Chuan* offers an explanation of the relationships between
these two souls: "When man is born, that which is first created is called
the *p'o* and, when the *p'o* has been formed, its positive part (*yang*) becomes *hun* or conscious spirit. In case a man is materially well and abundantly supported, then his *hun* and *p'o* grow very strong, and therefore
produce spirituality and intelligence. Even the *hun* and *p'o* of an ordinary
man or woman, having encountered violent death, can attach themselves

to other people to cause extraordinary troubles. ... The stuff Po-yu [whose ghost was causing trouble] was made of was copious and rich, and his family great and powerful. Is it not natural that, having met with a violent death, he should be able to become a ghost?"[152]

The Record of Rites says: "When one dies, they went upon the housetop, and called out his name in a prolonged note, saying, 'Come back, So and So.' After this they filled the mouth (of the dead) with uncooked rice, and (set forth as offerings to him) packets of raw flesh. Thus they looked up to heaven (whither the spirit was gone), and buried (the body) in the earth. The body and the animal soul (*hun*) go downwards; and the intelligent spirit (*p'o*) is on high. Thus (also) the dead are placed with their heads to the north, while the living look to the south. In all these matters the earliest practice is followed."[153]

The *Huai-nan Tzu* says: "Though the form dies the spirit does not, because that which can undergo no change supplies and responds to that which is subject to change, and to the myriad fluctuations and thousand changes which never come to an end."[154]

Sometimes there was a distinction drawn between the ascending spirit (*hun* 魂), identified with *yang*, and the descending spirit (*p'o* 魄), identified with *yin*, as mentioned above in the citation from *The Record of Rites*. *The Record of Rites* has another passage: "The energy of the *hun* returns to the heavens, while the *p'o* of the physical form returns to the earth."[155] The *K'ung-tzu chia-yü* says that "The energy of the *hun* returns to the heavens and is called the spirit (*shen* 神)."[156] It is difficult to decipher the exact sense of the usage of the terms in the *Li-huo lun*, for differences of opinion abounded. Commenting on the Taoist notion of physical immortality, Maspero writes: "If the Taoists in their search for longevity, conceived it not as a spiritual but as a material immortality, it was not as a deliberate choice between different possible solutions but because for them it was the only possible solution. The Graeco-Roman world early adopted the habit of setting Spirit and Matter in opposition to one another, and the religious form of this was the conception of a spiritual soul attached to a material body. But the Chinese never separated Spirit and Matter, and for them the world was a continuum passing from the void at one end to the grossest matter at the other; hence 'soul' never took up this antithetical character in relation to matter. Moreover, there were too many souls in a man for any one of them to counter-balance, as it were, the body; there were two groups of souls, three upper ones (*hun*) and seven lower ones (*p'o*), and if there were differences of opinion about what became of them in the other world, it was agreed that they separated at death. In life as in death, these multiple souls were rather ill-defined and vague; after death, when the dim little troop of spirits had dispersed, how could they possibly be re-assembled into a unity? The body, on the contrary, was a unity, and served as a home for these as well as other spirits. Thus it was only by a perpetuation of the body, in some form or other, that one could conceive of a continuation of the living personality as a whole."[157]

The notion of karmic recompense for past deeds and transmigration to future realms in accord with those deeds was evidently a strange and somewhat troubling idea for some. The *Hou Han chi* says that "princes and nobles, once they consider the limits of death, rebirth, and retribution, in every case succumb to panic."[158]

Mou-tzu's citation of the passage from the *Lao Tzu* recalls An Shih-kao's translation of *anātman* (no-self) as *fei-shen* (非身), not of the body, thus suggesting that the author of the *Li-huo lun* was familiar with these early translations of Buddhist scriptures by An Shih-kao, who arrived in Lo-yang in 148 C.E. In Chen Hui's *Commentary on the Yin-ch'ih-ju ching*, which was translated by An Shih-kao, we read: "Though young now, it (i.e., the body) will become empty when it is finally completed; emptied once more, this is called emptiness. The body is of the four great elements, but each of these will return to the origin. As they are never ours, it is called not-mine (fei-shen: literally not-of-the-body, the current Chinese for no-soul)."[159]

The second objection leveled, perhaps by a later critic, echoes a passage from Yang Chu: "In life the myriad creatures all differ from each other, but in death they are reduced to a single uniformity. In life they may be virtuous or degenerate, honorable or despicable: that is how they differ from each other. But in death they will stink and rot and decompose: that is how they are all equal to each other.... Perhaps it may be ten years or perhaps a hundred years ... they will all nevertheless die. They may be virtuous or sage, or they may be evil and degenerate; quite regardless they will die. In life they may be Yao or Shun; in death they will only be rotting bones. In life they may be [the tyrants] Chieh or Chou; in death they too will be rotting bones. In being rotting bones they are all alike. Who, then, will be able to distinguish their [former] differences?"[160]

Mou-tzu's proverb, "Lacking even one day's goodness, yet you want the praise of an entire lifetime!" perhaps imitates the *Chuang Tzu's* parody of the Lord of the River, who seeing his flooded domain become so grand, "began to wag his head and roll his eyes. Peering far off in the direction of Jo, he sighed and said, 'The common saying has it, "He heard the Way a mere hundred times but thinks he's better than anyone else." It applies to me.'"[161]

Reader-Response Criticism

This is the very first attempt that the *Li-huo lun* makes to defend a Buddhist doctrine. Yet even here the rhetorical structure of the text does not move simply to support Buddhist ideas against

Chinese criticism, for the section operates not only to argue for the reality of transmigration but also to set the stage for the next article, which returns the discussion to the central issue of classical hermeneutics. Here, Mou-tzu does not have much to say in regard to the classical tradition, quoting only the *Lao Tzu*, twice.

In support of the Buddhist doctrine of transmigration, Mou-tzu appeals to Chinese beliefs in the afterlife of the soul, recounting folk practices of calling upon the spirit of the dead. The classic reader can see that Buddhist notions of an afterlife are not entirely strange to Chinese culture, unless he also wants to reject Lao-tzu, who talks about retiring from his body, with the implication—to be made by the reader—that one is then united with the Way.[162]

The modern reader is prone to see in such an interchange a Chinese misunderstanding of Buddhist doctrine. It is sometimes asserted that, since the Buddhists teach a doctrine of no-self (*anātman*), any affirmation of a soul is contrary to Buddhist doctrine. T'ang Yung-t'ung, the well-respected Chinese scholar, citing this passage from the *Li-huo lun*, concludes that "from the very beginning the Chinese failed to comprehend the deep meaning of Buddhism [as to the nonexistence of the *ātman*]. . . . Buddhism spoke about the endless cycle of transmigration. Because of this, the doctrine that the soul does not perish, but is carried on as a result of karma, became a current belief [among the Chinese]."[163] Yet if the rhetorical strategy of the *Mou-tzu Li-huo lun* is any indication, the point is to graft Buddhist doctrine onto Chinese cultural ideas. Scattered, perhaps unsophisticated, Chinese notions of a soul or spirit here become the mediating vehicle for Buddhist doctrine. Thus, the notion of transmigrating souls is a rhetorical strategy to effect such a mediation.[164] Indeed, it would have been surprising if the Chinese had been able to relate to the Indian context, where the Buddhist notion of *anātman* was in major part directed toward earlier Indian notions of a permanent self (*ātman-svabhāva*).

This article is also rather unique for the *Li-huo lun* in that the conversation goes back and forth between Mou-tzu and perhaps a number of different critics. The objector is not merely the defender of the classical tradition, but people who want to question any notion of an "afterlife," any notion of future recompense. Nevertheless, the issue is immediately brought back into the overall focus of the *Li-huo lun* on the issue of classical hermeneutics.

ARTICLE 13.
VAIN TALK ABOUT SPIRITS

A critic asked: Confucius says: "You are not able even to
serve man. How can you serve the spirits?" These are the recorded words of the sage.[165] But nowadays the Buddhists blurt
out opinions about the realities of life, death, and the affairs of
the spirits. This dangerous course is against the clear words of
the sage! One who treads the Way must indeed abide tranquilly
in emptiness and return his attention to basic simplicity. Why
then do they discourse on life and death, thereby dissipating
their resolve? Why speak of the various deeds of the spirits?

_____

Mou-tzu said: Your words exemplify viewing things from the
outside, with no awareness of what is within. When Confucius
was ill, Tzu-lu did not ask him a lot of questions [about the
spirits], for he cut him off. [But] The Classic of Filial Piety [which
was written by Confucius] says, "He prepares the ancestral temple,
so that the spirits may receive them. In the spring and autumn,
he sacrifices to them and remembers them at the proper seasons."
It continues, "When alive, he serves them by love and respect.
When dead, he serves them by grief and sorrow."[166] Is this not
teaching men to serve the spirits and know about life and death?
When the Duke of Chou asked for orders for the sake of King
Wen he said, "Having many talents and arts, Tan is [i.e., I am]
able to serve the spirits." Is this not similar to the descriptions
of the destinies of the wheel of transmigration in the Buddhist
scriptures? Lao-tzu said, "When you know the mother, go on to
know the child. After you have known the child, go back to holding fast to the mother, and to the end of your days you will not
meet with danger."[167] Again he said, "Use the light, but return
to its brilliance. Bring not misfortune upon yourself!"[168] This relates to the transmigratory passage to the abodes of fortune or
misfortune.
      The essence of the perfect Way is to value quiet and silence.
How can you say that the Buddhists love to indulge in words?
Only when someone comes to ask questions, then I am forced to
use words. Like a bell or a drum, [my words] have no voice until,
when struck by a baton, they make their sounds.

Source Codes

The critic refers to a passage from the *Analects*: "Chi-lu asked how the spirits of the dead and the gods should be served. The Master said, 'You are not able even to serve man. How can you serve the spirits?' 'May I ask about death?' 'You do not understand even life. How can you understand death?'"[169] This agnostic attitude of Confucius toward spirits is seen in another passage: "Fan Ch'ih asked about wisdom. The Master said, 'To work for the things the common people have a right to and to keep one's distance from the gods and spirits while showing them reverence can perhaps be called wisdom.'"[170]

The critic seems to parallel the words of *The History of the Later Han*: "The [Buddhists] are skilled at making wide-sweeping talk on a grand scale. What they seek is within the body, but what they state plainly is beyond the reach of sight and sound. Worldlings take them to be vain and deceptive. Yet, since they reduce themselves to the dark and the subtle, to the profound and the far-removed, they are difficult to appropriate and plumb."[171]

The critic's phrase, "One who treads the Way must indeed abide tranquilly in emptiness and return his attention to basic simplicity," recalls a similar phrase from *The History of the Han*: "Abiding tranquilly in pure emptiness, he returns to the natural."[172]

Mou-tzu's reference to Confucius and Tzu-lu is from the *Analects*: "The Master was seriously ill. Tzu-lu asked permission to offer a prayer. The Master said, 'Was such a thing ever done?' Tzu-lu said, 'Yes, it was. The prayer offered was as follows: Pray thus to the gods above and below.' The Master said, 'In that case, I have long been offering my prayers.'"[173] This is one of the passages from the *Analects* that lead some to conclude that Confucius's attitude was not altogether against belief in spirits.

Similarly, *The Book of Documents* reports that when King Wu was ill, his brother, the Duke of Chou (i.e., Tan) prayed that he be taken in place of the king: "Let me, Tan, be a substitute for his person. I have been lovingly obedient to my father; I am possessed of many abilities and arts which fit me to serve the spirits."[174]

Reader-Response Criticism

The classical Confucian tradition, as represented by the critic's quotation from the *Analects*, stresses the this-worldly governance of human affairs, bracketing otherworldly concerns. The critic claims for his position not only such a Confucian distancing from the spirits, but also the maxims of Lao-tzu about emptiness, silence, and simplicity, seeing in them a proper disregard for the spirits, about which we can know but little for certain.

Mou-tzu has been using Taoist themes as the insertion point for Buddhist doctrines. Now he appeals to the Confucian traditions, claiming that Confucius's restraint of his disciple Tzu-lu signifies not a disbelief in spirits, but simply an absence of discourse on the subject. That absence is made up for in his *Classic of Filial Piety*, with its explicit affirmation of serving the spirits, and by the example of the Duke of Chou, who clearly says that he is able to serve the spirits. Mou-tzu further counters his critic by quoting the *Lao Tzu*, so as to lead the reader to conclude that the mother is like the karmic source of actions, while the child represents future destinies that result from those actions. If one would avoid the misfortune of being reborn into evil destinies, then hold fast to the mother, that is, see that your actions are the source of good destinies, not evil ones.

Mou-tzu further argues that Buddhist discourse is not an indulgence in vain words, but arises only from the exigencies of the moment, thus repeating the classical Confucian view that "a reasonable solution is one that takes into account not only the abstract principle of right (*i*), but one that gives due weight to the extenuating circumstances,"[175] which view parallels the classical Mahāyāna theme of all speech as *upāya*.

ARTICLE 14.
ETHNOCENTRISM

A critic commented: Confucius said, "Barbarian tribes with their rulers are inferior to Chinese states without them."[176] *Mencius reviled Ch'en Hsiang for switching to the study of Hsü Hsing's methods, saying, "I have heard of using China [as the standard] to transform the barbarians, but I have never heard of using the barbarians [as the standard to transform China]."*[177] *When you were young, you studied the Way of Yao, Shun, Chou, and Confucius. But now, rejecting them, you are switching to the study of barbarian methods. Are you not deluded?*

Mou-tzu said: You are prattling on about a time before I had understood the Great Way. I grant that you see the [outer] beauty of the ceremonies and rules, but you are in the dark about the essence of the Way and its virtue. You squint in the light of torches and candles, but never gaze at the sun in its heavenly abode. Those things that Confucius said were meant to reform his age. The saying of Meng-k'o [i.e., Mencius] was uttered in abhorrence at the obsession [of Ch'en Hsiang]. Yet formerly, Confucius wanted to live among the nine barbarian [tribes] of the east. He did say, "Once a gentleman settles among them, what uncouthness will there be?"[178]

But Chung-ni was not employed in Lu or Wei,[179] *and Mencius was not utilized in Ch'i or Liang. [Not being used even in China], how then could they have gained official employment among the barbarians?*

Emperor Yü came from the western Ch'iang tribes, and yet clearly he was broad-minded and wise. Ku Sou was the father of Emperor Shun [and thus ethnically Chinese], and yet he was obstinate and unprincipled. Yu Yü was born in the land of the I, and yet he was set up in the overlordship by [Duke Mu of] Ch'in. Kuan [Shu-hsien] and Ts'ai [Shu-tou, the younger brothers of the Duke of Chou] were from the [Chinese] lands of the Ho and Ko rivers, yet they were slanderers.

The Tso Chuan *states, "The north star is in the middle of the heavens, and to the north of human beings." Looking at it from this perspective, the Han country is certainly not in the middle of the heavens. As the Buddhist scriptures say, all kinds of living beings, whether above or below or at any point around, converge around Buddha. It is for this reason that I constantly respect and study these [scriptures]. But why must I reject the Way of Yao, Shun, Chou, and Confucius? Pearls*[180] *and jade do not harm one another! Crystal and amber do not oppose one another! You say that other people are confused, when it is you yourself who is confused!*

Source Codes

Quoting Confucius and Mencius, the critic presents a standard version of Chinese ethnocentrism. The *Mencius* reports: "There was a man by the name of Hsü Hsing who preached the teachings of Shen Nung. He came from T'eng to Ch'u, went up to the gate and told Duke Wen, 'I, a man from distant parts, have heard that you, my Lord, practice benevolent government. I wish to be given a place to live and become one of your disciples.'" Ch'en Hsiang became delighted with his teachings and "so abjured what he had learned before and became a follower of Hsü

Hsing." Mencius criticizes Ch'en Hsiang for attempting himself to make everything he uses and recommending that a ruler share the work of tilling in the fields. Rather, the *Mencius* states: "There are those who use their minds and those who use their muscles. The former rule; the latter are ruled. Those who rule are supported by those who are ruled."[181] The state of Ch'u, where this episode took place, was regarded as a semibarbaric land, and Hsü Hsing a practitioner of foreign, heterodox teachings.

A similar passage is found in the *Fa-yen*: "Someone asked, 'Can the ceremonies [of the barbarians] on the eight borderlands be understood as truly ceremony, and their music as truly music?' [Yang Hsiung] replied, 'Measure them by the central realm.' The questioner asked again, 'What do you mean by the central realm?' [Yang Hsiung] answered, 'By the central realm I mean that country in which there is governance based on the five teachings, supported by the seven taxes, and which lies in the center of heaven and earth. Are those beyond this [really] human? When the sages governed the world, they consolidated it by means of ceremony and music. To lack these is to be as wild birds. To differ from them is to be a Mo barbarian!'"[182]

Mou-tzu's references to Emperor Yü and Yu Yü recall *The Records of the Grand Historian*, which reports on Emperor Yü, the last of the predynastic rulers, and Yu Yü, who, although from a Chinese family of the state of Chin, was born among the barbarians and employed by Duke Mu of Ch'in as an advisor on barbarian affairs.[183]

As explained by Burton Watson, "Yu Yü's ancestors came from the state of Chin; he himself had been born among the barbarians but could speak the language of Chin. The barbarian king sent him to the court of Duke Mu of Ch'in, who questioned him closely on the customs, lands, and military strength of the barbarians. Duke Mu later succeeded in arousing enmity between the barbarian ruler and Yu Yü, and the latter finally fled to Ch'in and became the Duke's adviser on barbarian affairs."[184] For his service Duke Mu allowed him to establish himself as ruler of the western barbarians.

The Book of Documents reports that when Emperor Yao was searching for a successor, it was reported to him that "there is a certain man among the lower people called Shun of Yu. The Emperor said, 'Yes, I have heard of him. What is his character?' His Eminence said, 'He is the son of Ku. His father was obstinately unprincipled; his step-mother was insincere; his [half-brother] Hsiang was arrogant. He has been able, however, by his filial piety to live in harmony with them, and to lead them gradually to self-government, so that they no longer proceed to great wickedness.' The Emperor said, 'I will try him!'"[185]

Kuan Shu-hsien and Ts'ai Shu-tou were two younger brothers of King Wu of Chou. When the king died, they plotted against their young nephew, who turned to the famed Duke of Chou, another brother of King Wu. Kuan and Ts'ai had slandered the Duke of Chou, claiming that his authority as the mentor of King Ch'eng Wu was unwelcomed by King Wu.[186] The outcome was that Kuan Shu-hsien was executed and Ts'ai Shu-tou exiled.[187]

The sentence Mou-tzu quotes from the *Tso Chuan* is apparently not found there.[188] But it does call to mind a passage from the *Analects*: "'The Master said, 'The rule of virtue can be compared to the Pole Star [i.e., the North Star] which commands the homage of the multitude of stars without leaving its place.'"[189]

Reader-Response Criticism

The very name for China (*chung-kuo*) means the middle kingdom, reflecting the cultural perspective of a cultured and civilized land surrounded by less-cultured, less-civilized tribes. It is that cultural ethnocentrism to which the critic appeals, for heretofore Chinese scholars had seldom if ever encountered the high culture of another land. Does this not itself invalidate any claim for the superiority of the foreign Buddhist doctrine? Mou-tzu replies by challenging this cultural and geographical ethnocentrism, claiming that the Chinese standards of Confucius and Mencius were case-specific and not to be raised as a universal standard for all later contact with things not Chinese. He again offers counterexamples for the reader to ponder, coaxing forth the conclusion that the Buddha Tao is indeed superior. The Chinese perception of being culturally at the very center of the world is refuted by considering the North Star, which although truly in the middle of the heavens appears to humans to be off up to the north. So China appears to be the center of culture, but is itself off on the margin. Article 1 explicitly states that India is "the center of Heaven and earth." Furthermore, the sentence alludes to the passage cited above from the *Tso Chuan* about the North Star and then substitutes the Buddha as the center around which all converge, just as the many stars all assemble and do homage to the North Star.

ARTICLE 15.
THE PRIMACY OF THE FAMILY

A critic asked: Now it is certainly not kind to use one's father's goods to give alms to beggars on the road. It is not benevolent to sacrifice one's life for another while one's parents are still alive. But the Buddhist scriptures state that the Prince Sudāna distributed his father's goods to strangers. And the pre-

cious elephant of that land he gave as a gift to enemies. He even gave his own wife and children to others. But to respect others rather than one's own parents is to rebel against propriety. To love others rather than one's own parents is to rebel against virtue. Sudāna was neither filial nor benevolent, and yet you Buddhists revere him! Is this not strange?

Mou-tzu said: According to the Five Classics the proper thing to do is to take the eldest son of the legal wife as heir. Yet King T'ai, seeing Ch'ang's firmness of character, made the youngest son heir. Thus he completed the work of the Duke of Chou and brought about peace.

The right thing to do when taking a wife is to inform one's parents. Yet Shun married without telling [his parents] and established the great relationship [of husband and wife].

 An upright scholar must be invited to serve. An illustrious minister waits to be summoned. Yet Yi Yin sought to attend T'ang with his pots, and Ning Ch'i knocked on the horns [of his ox] to get the attention of the Duke of Ch'i. As a result T'ang won the throne and the Duke of Ch'i gained hegemony!

According to the proprieties there should be no intimate contact between men and women. But if one's sister-in-law is drowning, to grab her by the hand is to act with discretion in accord with the exigency of the moment. If you saw the whole, you would not be trapped in the minutiae. How could a great man be bound by the ordinary [rules]? Sudāna saw the impermanence of this world and understood that goods are not themselves precious. Thus he followed his inclination to give in order to attain the Great Way. His father's realm received blessings and its enemies were unable to encroach. When he became the Buddha, his entire family attained deliverance. If this is not filial piety, what is? If this is not benevolence, what is?

Source Codes

The example of Prince Sudāna (Hsu-ta-na) is taken from the *Vessantara Jātaka*, and recounts one of the former lives of the Buddha. The story tells of Vessantara, the princely son of King Sanjaya of Sivi, committed from birth to giving to others. When eight years old, unsatisfied with giving away his royal goods, and wanting to give something not given to him by another, he said, "If one should ask my heart, I would cut open my breast, and tear it out, and give it; if one ask my eyes, I would pluck out my eyes and give them; if one should ask my flesh, I would cut off all the flesh of my body and give it." Such a wish stands in stark contrast to the admonition of *The Classic of Filial Piety* that one may not harm one's body, limbs, hair, or skin, as cited by the critic in Article 9. Prince Vessantara, however, gives constantly and without respite. He had been raised with a precious white elephant, who caused the rains to fall on the land and the realm to prosper. The neighboring kingdom of Lakinga was suffering from a drought and sent brahmin emissaries to ask for the rain-bringing elephant, which Vessantara immediately gave to them, whereupon they contemptuously rode out of the city mounted on the elephant. The prince thereby incurred the anger of his own people, who regarded the elephant as a potent force not only for rain making, but also for warfare. They demanded that the prince be banished into the jungles at the foot of the Himalayas. Together with his wife Maddi and his son Jali and daughter Kanhajina, he settled in a hermitage deep in the forest. There he was sought out by Jujaka, a cruel and avaricious brahmin who asked for his two lovely children because he needed servants. True to form, the prince granted the request and gave his children away. The children, however, "hearing these harsh words, slunk behind the hut, and away they ran from behind the hut, and hid close to a clump of bushes. Even there they seemed to see themselves caught by Jujaka: trembling, they could not keep still anywhere, but ran hither and thither, until they came to the bank of the square lake; where, wrapping the bark garments tightly about them, they plunged into the water and stood there concealed, their heads hidden under the lily leaves." Yet their charitable father called them out and, not wanting to quarrel with him, they submitted and were led away by Jujaka, who treated them cruelly, tying them up and beating them, until they managed to escape and run back home. "Where he struck them, the skin was cut, the blood ran, when struck they staggered against each other back to back. But in a rugged place the man stumbled and fell: with their tender hands the children slipped off the light bond, and ran away weeping to the Great Being." Yet, suppressing his paternal affection in favor of the perfection of giving, Vessantara stilled his anger and returned his children to Jujaka. Maddi was of course upset when she learned of the donation of her children, but finally understood how noble was the deed. Here the god Sakka, fearful that Vessantara would give his wife Maddi to some vile creature, comes himself in the guise of a brahmin to ask for her. Vessantara gives her away, thereby realizing the perfect fulfillment of his commitment to giving. Sakka then returns Maddi to Vessantara, and his children are both protected by divine beings and at length restored to their parents, who once again are restored to their royal thrones in Sivi.[190] The critic refers to the prince not as Vessantara, but as Hsu-ta-na, Sudāna, follow-

ing Chinese versions of the account. Mochizuki gives various forms of
this name,[191] which perhaps was an attempt to play on the Sanskrit, *su*
(well) *dāna* (giving). The name Sudāna, or a variant thereof, appears in
many Chinese texts.[192]

The critic sees Sudāna as an example of the untoward behavior
mentioned in *The Classic of Filial Piety*: "One who loves others rather
than his parents rebels against virtue. One who respects others rather
than his parents rebels against propriety. When he should be obedient,
he is disobedient. The people find no model in him."[193]

Among the counterexamples Mou-tzu adduces from the classical
tradition is the story of King T'ai of Chou, who "in order that King Wen
might come to the throne, ... desired his third son (Wen's father, whose
tzu was Ch'ang) to be his successor. That meant, however, passing over
two older sons. These sons, knowing their father's wish, left the court
and went to live among the barbarians. Confucius apparently refers to
this tradition in *Analects*, 8.1. There is a more certain reference to it in
the *Tso Chuan*, 124::125 (Min I). The elaborated tradition is given in the
Shih-chi, 4.8–9, 31.2–4; *Mémoires historiques*, I. 215–16, IV. 1–2."[194] In
The Records of the Grand Historian, it was Chi Li the third son of King
T'ai who was chosen to be the successor.[195]

The rule about informing one's parent of a marriage is found in
The Book of Poetry.[196] The Emperor Shun is a clear exception to this rule.
The *Huai-nan Tzu* states: "Shun, however, married without telling his
people about it. This indeed was not permissible from the point of view of
propriety."[197] The *Mencius* reports that: "Wan Chang asked, 'The Book
of Odes* says, "How does one take a wife? By first telling one's parents
about it!"'"[198]

The Records of the Grand Historian report that Yi Yin found favor
with T'ang, the founder of the Yin dynasty, by means of his culinary
skills, that is, with his pots and pans.[199] The *Chuang Tzu* reports that Yi
Yin helped T'ang plot his campaign against Chieh to gain the throne.[200]
The *Mencius*, however, disputes this tradition: "I have heard that Yi Yin
attracted the attention of T'ang by the way of Yao and Shun, but I have
never heard that he did it by his culinary abilities."[201] The *Mencius* describes him both as accepting a request from the Emperor T'ang,[202] and
as going five times to T'ang and five times to Chieh seeking office.[203]
For Mencius, Yi Yin was the paragon of a responsible minister.[204] Our
only knowledge of Yi Yin came from such references to him in early
literature, until his essay on "Nine Rulers" was found among the texts
discovered at Ma-wang-tui in 1974.[205]

The *Huai-nan Tzu* reports that Ning Ch'i desired to procure an official post from Duke Huan of Ch'i but, unable to get an interview, worked
as a merchant with his ox-drawn cart full of goods. One day at the city
gates, when Duke Huan appeared, Ning Ch'i seized the opportunity and
began to sing and tap the ox's horns, thus impressing the duke, receiving

an interview, and at last being appointed to a post, wherein he assisted the duke to become overlord.[206]

The reference to saving one's sister-in-law is from the *Mencius*: "Ch'un-yü K'un said, 'Is it prescribed by the rites that, in giving and receiving, man and woman should not touch each other?' 'It is,' said Mencius. 'When one's sister-in-law is drowning, does one stretch out a hand to help her?' 'Not to help a sister-in-law who is drowning is to be a brute. It is prescribed by the rites that, in giving and receiving, man and woman should not touch each other, but in stretching out a helping hand to the drowning sister-in-law, one uses one's discretion.'"[207]

Reader-Response Criticism

The classical reader understood benevolence, filial piety, and all the virtues within the overarching context of the extended family. The four relationships center on the family. If relationships between younger brother and elder brother, husband and wife, children and parents are in order, then so will be the relationship between subject and ruler. The well-ordering of the ideal Confucian society is grounded on the well-ordered family, and examples from the classics abound to illustrate the point.

Mou-tzu must broaden the perspective. He has just attempted to elicit the consent of the reader to see beyond the confines of Chinese ethnocentrism. Here he argues that one must see beyond the confines of one's personal family. Although one must first inform one's parents about a marriage, Shun did not do so, because, as Mencius explains, "he would not have been allowed to marry if he had told them. A man and a woman living together is the most important of human relationships. If he had told his parents, he would have had to put aside the most important of human relationships and this would result in bitterness against his parents. That is why he did not tell them."[208] Mou-tzu offers this example not only to show that outward observance and inward realization can at times differ, but to suggest that the rule itself is narrow. What it deems to be benevolence within one's family circle may turn out to be unfilial.

In the case of the drowning sister-in-law, Mou-tzu argues that one must not blindly follow universal principles, but take into account the particular context of the case—one must use discretion, for that is the source of moral authority. "Significantly, the word used by Mencius to refer to this discretionary process is quan 權, which originally meant: (n) a scale, (v) to weigh. By extension, the word takes on the meaning of 'authority.' The one who is able to balance the various concerns is the person who has the authority, the power, to effect order. The pragmatic, coherent character of the project is brought out by an additional connotation of quan: exigency, as opposed to regularity (jing 經)."[209]

The critic could have argued that the examples Mou-tzu adduces are exceptions to the general rule, which are well recognized in the classical Confucian tradition, as Mencius makes clear. Yet there is no uptake on Mou-tzu's argument here, for it is actually aimed not at the intra-story critic, but at the implied reader, that he might conclude that there are precedents in the classical tradition itself for a Buddhist reading of the classics, and for the Buddhist practice of leaving family and joining the saṃgha.

ARTICLE 16.
THE DEPRAVITIES OF BUDDHISTS

A critic asked: The Way of Buddha venerates nonaction and takes delight in giving. He who upholds these rules is like a person who upon approaching a chasm should be very cautious. But the monks are addicted to their wine and spirits. Some support wives and children. They buy cheap and sell at an excessive profit. All they do is trick and cheat people. This is the great hypocrisy of the world and yet the Way of Buddha terms them nonaction!

Mou-tzu said: Kung Shu could give people axes and marking lines, but he could not make them skillful. The sage can bestow the Way upon men, but he cannot make them follow and practice it. Kao Yao can punish thieves but cannot make greedy fellows into Po Yis and Shu Ch'is. The five punishments can chastise violators but cannot make evil people into Tsengs and Mins. Yao was not able to change Tan Chu, and the Duke of Chou could instruct neither Kuan nor Ts'ai. Was the teaching of T'ang [i.e., Emperor Yao] not clear? Was the Way of Chou not complete? Do those [teachings] have anything in common with evil people? Although one may have studied and understood the Seven Clas-

sics, still he can be misled by bribes and lust. Is this because the six [classical] arts are depraved and debauched? Ho-po, although the spirit [of the Yellow River], cannot drown people on solid ground. The whirlwind, although violent, cannot raise dust from a deep pool. We must lament that men cannot follow him, but how can you say that the Way of Buddha is evil?

Source Codes

In his advice about approaching nonaction, the critic alludes to *The Classic of Poetry*: "We should be apprehensive and careful as if we were on the brink of a deep gulf, as if we were treading on thin ice."[210] His phrase "support wives and children" seems to recall the *Mencius*.[211] He also alludes to the *Tao Te Ching*: "When cleverness emerges, there is great hypocrisy."[212]

Mou-tzu mentions Kung Shu, the most famous craftsman in Chinese classical memory. A possible reference is found in the *Mencius*: "Even if you had the eyes of Li Lou and the skill of Kung-shu Tzu, you could not draw squares or circles without a carpenter's square or a pair of compasses."[213]

Kao Yao was a famous minister under Emperor Shun, said to have been the first to introduce laws for the repression of crime.[214] *The Book of Documents* reports: "The Emperor said, 'Kao Yao, the barbarous tribes disturb our bright great land. There are also robbers, murderers, insurgents, and traitors. It is yours, as the minister of crime, to employ the five punishments for the treatment of offenses, for the infliction of which there are the three appointed places; and the five banishments, with their several places of detention, for which three locations are assigned. Perform your duties with intelligence and you will secure a sincere submission.'"[215] Po Yi and Shu Ch'i were the two sages mentioned in Article 10 who starved on Mount Shou-yang rather than accept office.

The Tseng and Min referred to by Mou-tzu are Tseng-tzu (Ts'an) and Min Tzu-chien, two virtuous disciples of Confucius. "Traditionally, filial duty is firmly associated with the name of Tseng Tzu (Ts'an)."[216] Min Tzu-chien "was highly thought of by Confucius, and is said to have been a very good son (11:5). He once made a remark which prompted Confucius to comment, 'Either this man does not speak or he says something to the point' (11:14). His refusal to take office with the Chi Family (6:9) shows that he was a man of principle."[217]

Tan Chu was the unworthy son of Emperor Yao, passed over to make room for Shun. *The Book of Documents* reports: "Do not be like the haughty Tan Chu, who found his pleasure only in indolence and dissipation, and pursued a proud oppression. Day and night, without ceasing, he was thus. He would make boats go where there was no water. He introduced licentious associates into his family. The consequence was that he brought the honors of his House to an end."[218]

Kuan Shu-hsien and Ts'ai Shu-tou, treated in Article 14, were the rebellious brothers of King Wu of Chou. T'ang refers to the sage emperor Yao. Ho-po is the spirit-deity of the Yellow River.[219]

Reader-Response Criticism

The critic's objection bespeaks a time when Buddhist monks were already an accepted and noted presence in literati circles, which is a bit jarring in the context of late Han, since the establishment of the Buddhist saṃgha is often dated to post-Han times. Yet, earlier communities did apparently exist. Chang Heng (78–139), in his description of the enticing and bewitching dancing girls of the Han capital of Ch'ang-an, remarks, "Even if one were as sternly upright as old Liu Hsia-hui or a Buddhist Śramana, one could not but be captivated."[220] The monks have, according to the critic in the Li-huo lun, acquired enough power to support wives and children and to engage in buying and selling. Nor does Mou-tzu deny the charge. The historical situation assumed by their dialogue is not that of a new religious tradition just introduced into China, but that of a somewhat established and recognizable tradition with its inevitable shadow side of inauthentic practice. There is evidence of a Buddhist community in the middle of the second century at Lo-yang, under the guidance of Yen Fou-t'iao.[221] Furthermore, the same Tse Yung who is reported in the Preface to have killed the younger brother of the magistrate of Chiao-chou, and who was thus a contemporary of the Li-huo lun's Mou-tzu, is reported by The History of the Later Han to have built Buddhist monasteries and to have recruited thousands of followers who were housed in his monasteries and to whom scriptures were read.[222]

The Rectification of Unjustified Criticism, which probably dates from the early fourth century, and which also criticized the Buddhism of Tse Yung,[223] has a similar critique of such behavior: "Again, the malinger has said, 'The monks collect contributions from the common people and construct on a grand scale stūpas and monasteries; ornamenting and adorning these, they extravagantly spend funds and waste materials on expenditures which are of no benefit.'"[224]

Mou-tzu's response is that failure to follow the Buddha Tao

does not invalidate that Tao, and he offers examples that show the same in regard to classical norms and practices. The argument indeed reflects social conditions, not necessarily those of Mou-tzu, who remains a character in the narrative discourse, but of the implied author, who assumes his classical readers are familiar with the false practices of some Buddhist monks.

ARTICLE 17.
BUDDHIST EXTRAVAGANCE

A critic asked: Confucius said that "extravagance means ostentation, frugality means shabbiness. I would rather be shabby than ostentatious."[225] *Cho Sun said that "frugality is a respected virtue, while exaggeration is the worst vice." Yet the Buddhists gain notoriety from emptying all their possessions in giving. They exhaust their goods in giving to others in order to gain fame. How can this bring them happiness?*

Mou-tzu said: That was one time, this is another. The words of Chung-ni [i.e., Confucius] raged against the extravagance and absence of propriety [of his time]. The speech of Cho Sun lampoons the carved pillars of Duke Chuang. Neither prohibits giving!

When Shun [originally] ploughed Mount Li, his benefit did not reach [even] a lone hamlet. When Duke T'ai [for the first time] butchered the cows, the boon did not extend to [even] his own wife and children. [But] when these [practices] were [later] employed, benefits flowed out into the eight wildernesses and boons were granted to the four seas. With abundant possessions and many goods, one should treasure the ability to give. In hardship and dire poverty, one should treasure the following of the Way. Hsü Yu did not covet the four seas and Po Yi was not attached to the realm. Yü Ch'ing ceded a fief of ten thousand families to alleviate the distress of the poor. Such was their commitment! Hsi Fu-chi saved his old village through the kindness of one meal. Hsüan Meng saved his life because of one bowl of rice given without forethought.[226]

Such hidden giving arises without premeditation, yet the manifest results shine bright like clear, glistening sunshine. Even

greater are the merits of those who pour out their household pos-
sessions to realize their good intentions! They are as exalted as
Mounts Sung and T'ai, as far-reaching as the great rivers and the
seas! Those who cherish goodness are rewarded with happiness.
Those who embrace evil are recompensed by sufferings. No one
plants rice and harvests wheat. No one inflicts sorrow and finds
happiness.

Source Codes

The *Tso Chuan* reports the same opinion about frugality and exaggeration as does the critic, but attributes it not to Cho Sun, but to the
officer Yü Sun, who remonstrated against the carved pillars in Duke
Huang's temple, saying, "Your subject has heard that frugality is a respected virtue, while extravagance is the worst vice."[227] Contrary to the
rule that the pillars on an ancestral temple should be painted in a very
dark color, Duke Huang painted them bright red, both to dazzle his
young wife, the daughter of his father's murderer, and to propitiate his
father's spirit for her presence.

Mou-tzu's initial remark, "That was one time, this is another,"
copies directly from the *Mencius*.[228] Mou-tzu talks about the pillars of
Duke Yen, but the *Tso Chuan* refers to the pillars of Huang. It appears
that because *Huang* was part of the personal name of the Emperor Ming
(58–76 C.E.), there was a taboo against its use, the character *Yen* being
substituted, but being pronounced *Chuang*. Thus below it is transcribed
as "Huang."[229]

The tradition of the Emperor Shun ploughing Mount Li and thus
benefiting many is given in *The Records of the Grand Historian*.[230] Mencius also describes Shun as follows: The great Shun, "from the time when
he ploughed and sowed, exercised the potter's art, and was a fisherman,
to the time when he became emperor, ... was continually learning from
others."[231]

The biography of Duke T'ai, who is mentioned as Lü Wang in
Article 7, in chapter 34 of *The Records of the Grand Historian*, does not
mention any butchering of cows, but the legend is contained in other Han
works.[232] The So Yin Commentary on *The Records of the Grand Historian* reports that "Ch'iao Chou (200–270 C.E.) says: 'Lü Wang always
butchered cows at Chao-ko and sold rice at Meng-chin.' "[233]

Yü Ch'ing is the author of *The Spring and Autumn [Annals] of
Master Yü (Yü-shih ch'un-ch'iu)* and a court official of Prince Hsiao-
ch'eng of Chao in the third century B.C.E. Although he had attained
wealth and position, he abandoned it all for the sake of his friend Wei
Ch'i.

Mou-tzu's mention of dire poverty (*lü-k'ung* 屢空) alludes to the
Analects: "The Master said, 'Hui is perhaps difficult to improve upon; he

allows himself constantly to be in dire poverty (*lü-k'ung* 屢空). Ssu refuses to accept his lot and indulges in money making, and is frequently right in his conjectures.'"[234]

Hsi Fu-chi was an officer of Ts'ao. Chung-erh of Chi, because of political problems at home, fled to Ts'ao but was not well received. Hsi Fu-chi, to make him well-disposed toward Ts'ao, sent him a bowl of food with a precious jade ring in the bottom. Chung-erh accepted the food but returned the ring. Later when Chung-erh had become duke of Chin and was devastating Ts'ao, he remembered Hsi Fu-chi's kindness and spared his village.[235]

Hsüan Meng (i.e., Chao Tun) became a target of assassination plots because he was criticized by his master, Duke Ling of Chin. He always escaped because he was warned by a man whom he had once saved from starvation.[236]

The last paragraph seems to echo the *Huai-nan Tzu:* "One whose virtue is hidden will certainly have a manifest reward. One whose practice is hidden will certainly have an illustrious reputation."[237]

Reader-Response Criticism

The criticism is directed toward the Buddhist practice of giving (*dānapāramitā*). It presupposes a common awareness of Buddhists rich enough to make a display of their virtue. Mou-tzu does not say that his critic's descriptions are inaccurate. Rather, he argues that the critic's citations from the classics are to be seen in their proper contexts, and not woodenly applied to all acts of giving. He recites a number of examples to demonstrate that, in his interpretation of the classics, giving is also prized, even when practiced inadvertently. Thus, even more to be praised than these are Buddhists who abandon their goods with explicit good intentions.

The critic could well have pressed his point: that despite the doctrinal idealization of giving, the Buddhists give only out of a desire for ostentation and fame. But there is again no uptake here, for Mou-tzu's remarks are directed over the critic's head to the implied classical reader, who is to conclude that, even if some are ostentatious, true giving is nevertheless to be practiced.

ARTICLE 18.
ANALOGIES AND LITERALNESS

A critic asked: In one's actions nothing is better than being straightforward. In one's speech, nothing is better than being direct. *Lao-tzu rejected flowery, ornate words and prized plain, simple speech. But the words of the Buddhist scriptures do not clearly indicate what they are about, engrossing themselves instead in extravagant analogies. Analogy, however, is not necessary for the Way. To pretend that different things are analogous is not the best procedure. Although the phrases [of the Buddhist scriptures] be many and their words extensive, yet, like a cartload of jade fragments, they cannot be considered real gems!*

Mou-tzu said: One's speech can be direct about things with which everyone is already familiar. But it is difficult to speak straightforwardly about things that one person understands and another does not. A person who has never seen a lin *might ask one who has, "What is it like?" The one who has seen it could reply, "A* lin *is like a* lin!" *The one who has never seen it would then reply, "If I had seen a* lin, *I wouldn't have asked you about it. How can I understand when you say a* lin *is like a* lin?" *The one who has seen it then would reply, "A* lin *has the body of a stag, the tail of an ox, the hooves of a deer, and the back of a horse." Then the questioner would immediately understand.*

Confucius said, "Is it not like a gentleman not to take offense when others fail to appreciate your abilities?"[238] *And Lao-tzu said, "Is not the space between heaven and earth like a bellows?"*[239] *Again he said, "The way is to the world as rivers and seas are to rivulets and streams."*[240] *Aren't these statements flowery and ornate? The* Analects *say, "The rule of virtue can be compared to the pole star."*[241] *[Here Confucius] compares man with the heavens! Tzu-hsia said, "The former is as clearly distinguishable from the latter as are grasses from trees."*[242] *The three hundred items of* The Book of Odes *arrange things according to their similarity. From the prognostications of the philosophers to the hidden teachings of the sages, none fail to employ analogies and adduce comparisons. Why then do you single out the scriptures related by Buddha for blame and point out their analogies and comparisons?*

Source Codes

Mou-tzu's reply recalls a story about the famous sophist Hui Shih in the *Shuo-yüan*: "Someone said to the King of Liang, 'Hui Tzu is very good at using analogies when putting forth his views. If your Majesty could stop him from using analogies he will be at a loss what to say.' The King said, 'Very well. I will do that.' The following day when he received Hui Tzu the King said to him, 'If you have anything to say, I wish you would say it plainly and not resort to analogies.' Hui Tzu said, 'Suppose there is a man who does not know what a *tan* is, and you say to him, "A *tan* is like a *tan*," would he understand?' The King said, 'No.' 'Then were you to say to him, "A *tan* is like a bow, but has strips of bamboo in place of the string," would he understand?' The King said, 'Yes, he would.' Hui Tzu said, 'A man who explains necessarily makes intelligible that which is not known by comparing it with what is known. Now your Majesty says, "Do not use analogies." This would make the task impossible.'"[243]

Reader-Response Criticism

The Buddhist scriptures seem to be very alien in style to the questioner, and he latches on to their constant use of analogies and metaphors as the source of this unfamiliarity, wishing to be told plainly and literally what they are saying. Indeed, the objection was evidently a frequent one, for in the "Notice of the Western Regions" of *The History of the Later Han* (*Hou Han shu*), Fan Yeh (d. 445) criticizes the Buddhist scriptures, saying: "Yet, for love of grandeur without restraint, for outlandish deception without surcease, even Tsou Yen's eloquence in discoursing on Heaven and Chuang Chou's parable of the snail's feelers are not equal to one-ten-thousandth part [of the outlandish rhetoric of the Buddhist scriptures]."[244] The deeper issue, however, relates to the hermeneutic employed by Mou-tzu, who constantly sees the classical narratives as analogies for Buddhist notions or practice.

But the question is something of a setup, for the use of analogy was not only accepted literary practice, but had already been argued in the classical literature, as shown in the above story about Hui Shih. For example, *The Literary Mind and the Carving of Dragons* praises Ch'ü Yüan's use of metaphor in his *Li Sao*: "When he uses dragons as a metaphorical expression for men of virtue, and clouds and rainbows as metaphorical expressions for sycophants, he is adopting the devices of metaphor and moral allegory."[245] Metaphors, similes, and analogies abound in the classical literature, so much so that D. C. Lau has written an article on how to understand the many analogies used by Mencius. Lau cites the Mohist description of analogy: "Analogy is to put forth another thing in order to illumine this thing. Parallel is to set [two] propositions side by side and show that they will both do."[246] A few further examples can be adduced.[247] Wang Ch'ung recommends that one interpret metaphors intelligently, but not that they be abandoned. Speaking of ghosts and funeral sacrifices, which he argues should be kept simple, he says: "To attain this aim [of adjudicating between opinions about the dead] there must first be a holy heart and a sage mind, and then experience and analogies are to be resorted to. If anyone in his reasoning does not use the greatest care and discernment, taking his evidence indiscriminately from without, and thus establishing right and wrong, he believes in what he has heard or seen from others, and does not test it in his mind. That would be reasoning with eyes and ears, and not with the heart and intellect."[248] The Han formulator of Confucian doctrine, Tung Chung-shu, has similar advice, for his "ontology is based upon several premises, viz. to recognize the principle of the thing [*ch'iu wu chih li* 求物之理] which may in its turn be used for foreseeing and the forming of analogies and finally be formulated by means of a suitable name."[249] Thus, the employment of analogies and similes should render the Buddhist literature no more unfamiliar than the classical literature.[250]

Yet the point is not just the use of analogy. The implied author is directing the implied reader to adopt not only an analogical interpretative strategy, but specifically a reading of the Chinese classics from a Buddhist viewpoint—seeking therein analogues of Buddhist notions. The method of matching concepts (*ko-yi*) is often attributed to Chu Fa-ya, who lived in the fourth century.[251] Yet the practice of reading Chinese culture through Buddhist eyes and expressing one's understanding of Buddhist teachings through Chinese notions was part and parcel of the enculturation of Buddhism in China from its very inception. There is, I think, truth to Liebenthal's observation that "all world-understanding begins with a basic observation handed down in a basic simile. These similes are the material in analogy to which world patterns are built. The initial process becomes unconscious, the standards derived from the original pattern appear as evident...."[252] What the *Li-huo lun* is all about is a recasting of such basic cultural assumptions, a reformulation of the common patterns of Chinese culture. It is this against which the critic objects, not simply the use of analogy. Mou-tzu's answer that one should not single out the Buddhist scriptures for special blame is then rather ingenuous. What he is in fact doing is grafting a foreign set of interpretative assumptions onto the trunk of the classical tradition at points where it most easily fits and parallels similar developments within that tradition. It is this use of analogy that the implied author recommends to his readers.

ARTICLE 19.
RENUNCIATION

A critic asked: Among the men of this world there are none who do not love riches and honor, hating poverty and meanness. There are none who do not take joy in pleasure and ease, shrinking from work and weariness. The Yellow Emperor considered the five delicate foods to be the best for nurturing his nature. Of Confucius it was said: "He did not eat his fill of polished rice nor did he eat his fill of finely minced meat!"[253] Yet the monks wear red robes, eat only once a day, shut off their six senses, and cut themselves off from the world. How is all this of any good?

Mou-tzu said: [In the words of Confucius,] "wealth and high station are what men desire but unless I got them in the right way I would not remain in them. Poverty and low station are what men dislike, but even if I did not get them in the right way I would not try to escape from them."[254] Lao-tzu said, "The five colors make men's eyes blind; the five notes make his ears deaf; the five tastes injure his palate; riding and hunting make his mind go wild with excitement; goods hard to come by serve to hinder his progress. Hence the sage is for the belly, not for the eyes."[255] Are these words just lies? Liu Hsia Hui did not alter his behavior for employment with three dukes. Tuan-kan Mu did not sell himself for the wealth of Wen of Wei. Hsü Yu and Ch'ao Fu perched in the trees and lived there; and they are considered to have been much more contented than those who lived under the Emperor's roof! Po Yi and Shu Ch'i were dying of hunger at Shou-yang, and yet they are reckoned to have been more sated than [Kings] Wen and Wu. For each of these it was enough to develop his character. How could this not be of any good?

Source Codes

The critic's comment seems to allude to *The Scripture in Forty-Two Articles*, Article 3 of which states: "The Buddha said, 'Those who, shaving their heads and faces, become monks and who receive instruction in the Way, should surrender all worldly possessions and be contented with whatever they obtain by begging. One meal a day and one lodging under a tree, and neither should be repeated. For what makes one stupid and irrational is attachments and the passions."[256]

Liu Hsia Hui, referred to by Mou-tzu, is the posthumous name for Chan Ch'in, governor of the Lu-hsia district of Lu shortly before the time of Confucius. He is famous for having lost his position three times. Mencius says of him that "Liu Hsia Hui would not have compromised his integrity for the sake of three ducal offices."[257]

Tuan-kan Mu steadfastly refused office, although offered such by Lord Wen of Wei. Again Mencius says that "Tuan-kan Mu climbed over the wall to avoid a meeting [with the Lord of Wei]."[258]

Hsü Yu is the legendary recluse mentioned in the *Chuang Tzu*, for which see the story cited in the source codes for Article 10.

Ch'ao Fu was another recluse who fled office. It is recounted that when Hsü Yu was offered the throne, he washed out his ears in a stream, but Ch'ao Fu was so untainted that he would not even let his calves drink the water thus defiled.[259]

The stories about Po Yi and Shu Ch'i are treated in Article 10.

Reader-Response Criticism

No moderately intelligent critic could have asked such an ingenuous question, for the classical literature abounds in examples of sages and worthies who turned their backs on riches and honors in order to develop their inner natures. The words the critic uses to introduce his objection cannot but have reminded the *Li-huo lun*'s readers of the passage from Confucius that Mou-tzu cites in his reply. Even the final phrase of the objection, that the monks shut off their six senses and cut themselves off from the world, resonates with a passage from the *Lao Tzu*: "Block the openings; shut the doors."[260] The answer is presaged even in the presentation of the critic's objection.

The author of the *Li-huo lun* has raised this question to stress that Buddhist monks do indeed practice sobriety and asceticism and are not all as profligate as suggested in Article 16. Even the critic's quotation from Confucius is ambiguous. Although it says that he did eat polished rice and minced meat, it also says he refrained from eating his fill.

ARTICLE 20.
MIXING TRADITIONS

A critic asked: If the Buddhist scriptures are profound, mysterious, and unexcelled in beauty, why do you not discuss them at court and explain them to our ruler and father? Why do you just talk about their [teaching] in the privacy of your home and share them with your friends? Why bother about the study of [the Chinese] classics and commentaries or reading of the philosophers?

Mou-tzu said: Not having attained the source, you question its course! Would you arrange the sacrificial vessels at the door of the ramparts? Would you send up the military banners and flags from the ancestral hall of the palace? Would you put on fox fur to welcome the summer? Or wear light linens to greet the winter? These things are not without their value, but [such use] is unreasonable and untimely. Hence, I use the methods of Confucius. I enter through the door of Shang Yang. I take in hand the speeches of Mencius. I visit the abode of Su Ch'in and Chang Yi, although their merits are not a tenth of an inch and their faults come in feet and meters! Lao-tzu said, "When the best student hears about the way, he practices it assiduously. When the average student hears about the way, it seems to him one moment there and gone the next. When the worst student hears about the way, he laughs out loud."²⁶¹ Because I fear that boisterous laughter [of inferior students], I do not go about discussing [the Buddhist scriptures at court]. As for reading [the classics and commentaries], when one is thirsty, it is not necessary to go to the Chiang and Ho rivers, but only to drink some water from a well or spring. Do not these quench thirst? In such fashion I concern myself also with the classics and commentaries.

Source Codes

The phrase *ruler and father* used by the critic is found in the *Tso Chuan*, under the fifth year of Duke Hsi, where Ch'ung Erh says: "The command of my ruler and father is not to be opposed."²⁶² *The History of the Former Han* says: "To respect and comfort one's ruler and father is the utmost of loyalty and filial piety."²⁶³

Mou-tzu's phrase *arranging sacrificial vessels at the door of the ramparts* alludes perhaps to the *Analects*: "Duke Ling of Wei asked Confucius about military formations. Confucius answered, 'I have, indeed, heard something about sacrificial vessels, but I have never studied the manner of commanding troops.' The next day he departed."[264]

Shang Yang was an early Legalist thinker and reformer of the state of Ch'in. "Though Ch'in was ... in culture and political organization so different from the rest of China, there occurred in 361 B.C. an event that was to throw it into the direct orbit of Chinese politics, make of it a great state, and lead ultimately to its supremacy over the other states of China. This was the arrival in Ch'in of the notable statesman, Shang Yang, who soon gained the confidence of the Ch'in ruler. Under his regime a new division of the land, new forms of taxation, and other economic reforms were introduced."[265] Chang Yi and Shu Ch'in were wandering strategists during the Warring States period, both of whom studied under Kuei-ku Tzu. Chang Yi was an advisor to the Ch'in state. He died before 309 B.C.E.[266]

Reader-Response Criticism

The critic's objection is to Mou-tzu's divided allegiance, for he belongs to two interpretative communities, one Buddhist and one classically Chinese. Why not simply choose between them and devote oneself to Buddhist practices in the privacy of one's own quarters? On the other hand, if one wants to spread Buddhist teaching, why not go straight to the court and announce its truth? The question tries to place Chinese Buddhists on the horns of a dilemma, to force them to choose one community or the other.

Mou-tzu's rather indirect answer cites examples of what is appropriate to time and circumstance, to wit, what is appropriate for such a Buddhist in the Chinese cultural matrix in which he lived. In point of fact, of course, cultured Chinese did not have the option of simply becoming Buddhist. That is why they had to enculturate the Buddha Tao through the Chinese traditions. Mou-tzu quotes Lao-tzu to show that the capacities of people differ, arguing by implication that he does not preach at the court because there one finds only inferior students. The implication is that even "our ruler and father," which must refer to the emperor himself, is an inferior student. This argues not only that the *Li-huo lun* was written and circulated far from the center of court power, but that the emperor envisaged was not only regarded by the *Li-huo lun's* readers as hardly an embodiment of virtue, but was so far removed that our author had no fear of being charged with the crime of lèse-majesté—perhaps because nobody knew who he was.

The final sentences sound condescending toward the classics. The Preface mentioned that Mou-tzu had read the military manuals, although he did not like them. Here, the Dialogue picks up the theme, mentioning a few ancient personages associated with political and military affairs. Yet the final argument that Mou-tzu reads the Chinese books only when he needs a bit of an intellectual drink seems not quite to the point, for the entire text focuses not on Buddhist scriptures, but on a Buddhist reading of the Chinese classical literature.

ARTICLE 21.
EMPEROR MING'S DREAM

A critic asked: How did the land of Han first come to hear about the Buddha Tao?

―――――――――

Mou-tzu said: Once in a dream the Emperor Hsiao Ming saw a spirit man whose body shone like the rays of the sun and who flew in front of the palace. It made him very happy, and the very next day he closely questioned his assembled ministers as to who that spirit might be. A man of insight, Fu Yi, said, "Your servant has heard that in India there is one named Buddha who has attained the Tao. He moves through the open sky by flying. His body shines like the rays of the sun. It must have been this spirit." Then the Exalted One understood. He sent the Envoy Chang Ch'ien, the Palace Guard Ch'in Ching, the Disciple of the Erudite Wang Tsun, altogether eighty people to the Great Yüeh-chih in order to copy The Scripture in Forty-Two Articles, *which he then stored in the fourteenth cubicle of the Stone Chamber at Lan-t'ai [in Lo-yang]. He built a monastery to Buddha outside the Hsi-yung gate of Lo-yang.²⁶⁷ On its walls were painted a thousand chariots and ten thousand riders who were all circumambulating his stūpa three times. Moreover, he had an image of the Buddha placed on the Ch'ing-ching tower, in the Southern Palace, and on the Kai-yang wall gate. It was at this time that the Emperor Ming was having his tomb constructed in prepara-*

tion for his death. That tomb was called "The Illustrious Integrity of Purity." On its peak he placed a likeness of Buddha. During this period the realm prospered, the people were at peace, and barbarians respected righteousness. This is why the practitioners [of the Buddha Tao] have so multiplied.

Source Codes

Henri Maspero is of the opinion that this account is based on the preface to *The Scripture in Forty-Two Articles,* some form of which existed during Han times. Its account, as translated by Leon Hurvitz reads: "In former times, Emperor Hsiao-Ming of the Han at night in a dream saw a superhuman man, his body of a golden hue, the nape of his neck bathed in sunlight, flying in front of the palace. Delighted at heart and much rejoicing, the next day he asked his assembled ministers who this god might be. There was an accomplished man, one Fu Yi, who said, 'Your servant has heard that in India there is one who has got the Way, whose name is Fo [*but*], who moves lightly and can fly. Surely it is that god!' Thereupon, His Majesty, understanding, straightway dispatched emissaries: Chang Ch'ien, the *yü lin chung lang chiang,* Ch'in Ching, the *po shih ti tzu,* Wang Tsun; and others, twelve in all. When they arrived in the land of the Great Yüeh-chih, they copied the Buddhist *Scripture in Forty-Two Articles,* contained in fourteen stone containers. [When they got back to China,] they erected a stūpa-temple [over it], and thereupon the religion [*tao fa*] spread abroad, and in all places there was erection of Buddhist temples. Of distant persons who submitted to conversion and who begged to become [the Buddha's] servants and handmaidens the number cannot be calculated. The interior of the realm became pure and tranquil, and beings possessing consciousness received the gracious gift of kindness and something in which they could put their faith. Till this very day it has not ceased to be so."[268]

Yüan Hung (328–97) in his *Record of the Later Han* (*Hou Han chi*) remarks that "once in the past, Emperor Ming, having dreamt of a golden man great and tall, the light of the sun and moon issuing from the nape of his neck, questioned his ministers about this. When a certain person said that in the west there was a superhuman being named *Fo* [*but*], whose form was great and tall, [the emperor] inquired into the latter's Way and methods, and had them brought to China, and had copies of his images made."[269]

The account did not go unchallenged. The *Kuang Hung-ming chi* records a Taoist critique: "*The Classic of Converting the Barbarians* (a Taoist critique by Wang Fou) records: 'The Bodhisattva Kāśyapa said, Five hundred years after the extinction of the Tathāgata, I will come east to confer the Way upon Han P'ing-tzu and [then] in broad daylight I will return to the Heavens. Then, in two-hundred years, I will confer the Way upon Chang Ling. Then in another two hundred years I will confer the Way upon Chien P'ing-tzu. In yet another two hundred years I will confer the Way upon a thousand households. Thereafter, toward its end, the Han shall be wayward and not respect my Way, until the seventh year of Yung-p'ing (64) in the year *chia-tzu*, when the night stars shall appear during daylight in the western quarter [of the sky]. During that night Emperor Ming will dream of a spirit-man, six chang in height, his head surrounded by sunlight. He shall question his assembled ministers and Fu Yi shall say: In the west a royal prince has realized awakening. He is called Buddha. Then the Emperor Ming sent Chang Ch'ien and others to follow the [Yellow] River to its source and passing through thirty-six king-doms, they reached Śrāvasti. Since the Buddha had [long] since entered cessation, they copied 6,500 words of [his] scriptures. Then, in the eigh-teenth year of Yung-p'ing (75), they returned.' Now, I find this ridiculous. *The History of the Han* says that 'Chang Ling lived in the Later Han dur-ing the reign of Emperor Shun (126–145 C.E.).' He learned about foreign parts in Szechuan and entered the Kunming Mountains for the sake of his covetous designs. We reckon seven generations between Emperor Shun and Emperor Ming. It stands to reason that [Chang Ling] could not be pres-ent some hundred years before Emperor Ming [and still be sent on the jour-ney by him]. Moreover, it also says that Emperor Ming sent Chang Ch'ien to follow the [Yellow] River to its source. This too is erroneous. According to *The History of the Han*, Chang Ch'ien followed the [Yellow] River to its source under Emperor Wu of the Former Han. How then he could once again follow it under Emperor Ming, I cannot fathom! Was Ch'ien a long-lived immortal? Who generation after generation received the same mis-sion? What a pain! I ridicule these erroneous records!"[270] The *Li-huo lun* version does not mention Chang Ling, but its reference to Chang Ch'ien is clearly anachronistic. In point of fact, Chang Ch'ien made his journey to Bactria during the second century B.C.E., while Emperor Ming died in 76 C.E. Later versions of the account properly omit any reference to him in connection with Emperor Ming. Ch'in Ching is reported by the *Wei Lüeh*, a third-century record, to have been sent by Emperor Ai to Yüeh-chih in 2 B.C.E.[271] Nothing at all is known about Wang Tsun. Maspero concludes that the account is not historical at all, but simply a legendary story.[272]

Lan-t'ai was the library and archives during the Han dynasty. Its "Stone Chamber" is mentioned in *The History of the Later Han.*[273] Michael Loewe reports that "two depositories of documents within the city were said to have been built by a statesman who had played a vital role in founding the dynasty and acted as its principal servant of state until his death in 193 B.C. In the civil wars which had preceded the foun-dation of the Han house, this statesman had taken steps to preserve intact the records of the previous administration, with the result that the new government could start its work with the help of its predecessor's maps, and, possibly, its tax returns. These records were deposited in a stone-built chamber that still stored such documents a century or two later."[274]

Reader-Response Criticism

The legendary account is straightforward, supplying information to both the critic and the reader. It grounds the Buddha Tao in Chinese culture, and attributes to Buddha the prosperity the sages promise to those who follow the Way, whether Taoist or Confucian.

Scholarly discussion has centered on the historicity of this passage and its import for determining the date and authenticity of the *Li-huo lun*. It seems to be mainly legend and probably depends on *The Scripture in Forty-Two Articles*, which was brought to China as early as 70 C.E. Since no Sanskrit version exists, some have thought it to be not a direct translation but a compilation from sources available in China.[275] From a Reader-Response perspective, however, these questions fade from view, and Mou-tzu here becomes the narrator of a story about the initial enculturation of Buddha in China, showing how it resulted in the now-lost prosperity and peace of the early years of the Later Han. The critic withdraws almost completely into the background, and the narrator speaks directly to the implied reader, telling within the story another story about how the Buddha Dharma first came to China. His implied reader is presented not with a historically accurate version of past events, but with a more important etiological myth that presents in legendary terms the arrival and enculturation of Buddhism in the not too distant past. The account is true not in its particulars, but in the process of enculturation it represents.

ARTICLE 22.
MORE ABOUT SILENCE AND SPEECH

A critic asks: Lao-tzu said, "One who knows does not speak; one who speaks does not know."[276] *He also said, "Great eloquence seems tongue-tied; great skill seems awkward."*[277] *The gentleman is sparing in his speech, but carries through in his actions.*[278] *If the monks have the true Way, why do they not practice it privately? Why are they always chattering about truth and falsity and debating about right and wrong! I consider all this the ruin of virtue!*

Mou-tzu said: What would you think of someone who, facing the prospect of famine in the spring, stops eating in the fall! Or someone who dons doubled furs in May because November is going to be cold! Such early planning cannot but be stupid! Lao-tzu's maxim refers only to those who have realized the Way. What do those who have not realized the Way know about it! One word from the Great Way, and heaven and earth rejoice! Is that not great eloquence! But, [you say,] doesn't Lao-tzu say that to retire when the task is complete is the Way of Heaven![279] *If a person has so retired, he cannot speak at all. But since the monks have not yet realized the Way, how can they not speak! Indeed, Lao himself spoke! If he had not spoken, then how did he narrate the Five Thousand Words [i.e., his* Tao Te Ching*]! It is acceptable to know and not speak. But only a fool is able neither to know nor to speak. He who is able to speak but unable to act becomes the teacher of a country. He who is able to act but unable to speak becomes an official of a country. But he who is able both to speak and to act becomes the jewel of a country. Each of these three has his proper contribution to make. How is this the ruin of virtue! I think the ruin is the inability either to speak or to act.*

Source Codes

The critic alludes to the *Analects*: "The gentleman is ashamed of his words outstripping his deed."[280] The phrase *the ruin of virtue* is drawn from the *Analects* also: "The village worthy is the ruin of virtue."[287] Mou-tzu alludes to the *Hsün Tzu*: "A person who both can speak and act is the jewel of a country. A person who cannot speak, but can act can be a useful instrument of a country. A person who can speak, but cannot act can be useful to a country. A person who can speak well but acts badly is the bewitcher of a country. One who well governs the country respects such jewels, cherishes such useful instruments, employs those who can be of use, and removes such bewitchers."[282]

Reader-Response Criticism

The question of Article 21 is pressed: Why not simply be a Buddhist privately without trying to engage in discourse with the classical community of literati? The critic raises the point by questioning the need for speech in following the Way. Yet the objection is easily answered, for even those who recommend silence, such as Lao-tzu, clearly spoke in making that recommendation. The reader himself is engaged in a language event in the very reading of this text.

However, a deeper issue is involved, for the critic is trying to wrest Lao-tzu away from Mou-tzu in order to turn him against Buddhist notions. But the Tao, both Taoist and Confucian, is the mediating structure that Mou-tzu has adopted for enculturating Buddhism in China, and he cannot allow the critic to use it against him.

ARTICLE 23.
RHETORIC AND ENGAGEMENT

A critic asked: According to your words, one has only to study disputation and be well trained at interpretation! How then can he govern his nature and follow the virtue of the Way?

Mou-tzu said: What is so hard to understand? Words and discussions have their appropriate times. Chu Yuan spoke when the Way was present to rectify the realm, but when it was not he furled up [his knowledge] and kept it in his heart. Confucius said of Ning Wu Tzu: "He was intelligent when the Way prevailed in the country, but stupid when it did not." Again Confucius said, "To fail to speak to a man who is capable of benefiting is to let one's words go to waste. To speak to a man who is incapable of benefiting is to let one's words go to waste."[283] *Thus intelligence and stupidity have their seasons. Discussion and interpretation each have their proper significance. When faced with [the need to] to express [our] interpretation [of the classics], why should we desist?*

Source Codes

The critic seems to allude to ideas from the *Analects* and the *Tao Te Ching*. The *Analects* recommend simplicity of language: "The Master said, 'It is enough that the language one uses gets the point across.'"[284] The *Tao Te Ching* encourages the practice of nonaction, declaring that when "one practices nonaction, there will be nothing not well governed."[285]

Chu Yuan is Ch'ü Po-yü, a counselor in the state of Wei, about whom the *Analects* say: "How gentlemanly Ch'ü Po-yü is! When the Way prevails in the state he takes office, but when the Way falls into disuse in the state he allows himself to be furled and put away safely."[286]

Ning Wu Tzu also was a counselor in the state of Wei, mentioned often in the *Tso Chuan* for his gentlemanly character. The *Analects* report of him: "The Master said, 'Ning Wu Tzu was intelligent when the Way prevailed in the state, but stupid when it did not. Others may equal his intelligence but they cannot equal his stupidity.'"[287]

Reader-Response Criticism

Established orthodox traditions tend to regard themselves as beyond the need for further interpretation, aloof from mere human opinions. It is thus that such traditions assume the normative character of classical or scriptural authority. As Tsukamoto writes,

> The governing, i.e., the literate class, highly educated through the medium of 'classical learning,' were subject to severe restrictions from the classics on their thinking, their speech, their actions, indeed on everything, and came to believe that it was only by close reliance on the classics that one could speak, write, and act properly. Even after the collapse of the Han, this classical learning, the scholarship premised on the assumption of the supreme authority of the Confucian classics that had achieved such a firm position under the Han, long provided a framework for China's thought process.[288]

This assumption underlies the critic's objection, for he is somewhat loath to enter into the interpretative fray to which Mou-tzu invites him. Just accepting that invitation, even before any points of argumentation are stated or won, demotes the classics from their august position beyond further interpretation, to a much more human level, perhaps recording the events and values of the past, but always requiring reinterpretation in light of the present. Of course, during the late Han and after, the normative fabric of the classical values was rent, both from the social upheavals that seemed to render them irrelevant, and from the development of the Neo-Taoist synthesis of the "dark learning" then in vogue. In such a context, Mou-tzu can easily present his case that a Buddhist hermeneutic may claim a legitimacy equal to any Neo-Taoist interpretation.

Again this objection is hardly one that would be raised in an actual debate. Mou-tzu could as well argue that the critic should focus on following the virtue of the Way and retire from the discussion. The implied author, through his character Mou-tzu, speaks to his implied classical readers, presenting the pattern of both engaging in speech and withdrawing into silence.

After Han times the practice of "pure talking" (ch'ing-t'an), a style of repartee and pleasant conversation, was adopted by the Neo-Taoist romantics who eschewed politically dangerous "pure criticism" (ch'ing-i) of the governing powers.[289] Such a practice of disengaged discourse was more than merely an affected style of argumentation, for it constituted an entire way of life, eschewing both Confucian formalism and engagement in trying to right the ills of that chaotic era. According to the Confucians, the famed Seven Sages of the Bamboo Grove "all revered and exalted the void and non-action, and disregarded the rites and laws."[290] Perhaps the critic's accusation that Mou-tzu recommends only studying disputation and being well-versed in interpretation points to an early Buddhist version of "pure talking, for he had fled the chaos of the times to the safe haven of Chiao-chou."[291] Yet Mou-tzu will have none of it, asserting that speech and silence have their seasons, and ending his response with a commitment to continue recommending his hermeneutical approach to the Chinese tradition.

ARTICLE 24.
A DIRECT CRITIQUE OF THE BUDDHIST STYLE
AND DOCTRINE

A critic asked: You say that the Way of Buddha is to be greatly honored and cherished, and that nonaction is tranquil peace. But so many of the scholars of this world revile and ridicule that teaching. They say its discourse is vague and difficult to put into practice, and that it is hard to have faith in emptiness and nothingness [hsü wu]!

Mou-tzu said: The best flavors are not discernible to common tastes. The best music is not appreciated by untrained ears. You could play "The Pool of Heaven" [of the Yellow Emperor], perform the "Great Chapter" [of Emperor Yao], play the Hsiao Chao music [of Emperor Shun], or chant the nine [classical] airs, but nobody could keep up with you. Yet if you pluck the chords of Cheng and Wei or sing popular tunes, then without hesitation everyone will clap their hands [in rhythm with you]. Thus Seng Yü said, "A visitor sang in Ying, [the capital of Ch'u,] and performed the Hsia-li song. A thousand people sang along with him. But when he drew out the shang note and reached the chiao note, no one could follow him." Everybody likes sensual tunes, but few are familiar with the classical pieces. Because he had tunnel vision, Han Fei spoke ill of Yao and Shun. Because he split hairs, Chieh Yü reviled Confucius. These people occupied themselves with the minutiae and neglected the important. To hear a pure shang note and mistake it for a chiao note is not the fault of the musician. It is because the listener does not have a good ear. If someone looks at Master Ho's jade and calls it a stone, it is not because the jade is inferior in quality but because the beholder has poor eyesight. The spirit snake can reconstitute itself after having been cut up, but it cannot stop people from cutting it up! The numinous tortoise could give dreams to [King] Yüan of Sung, but could not avoid Yü Chü's net. The great Way is nonaction, imperceptible to common people. It is not precious because it is praised, nor cheap because it is reviled. Whether one employs it or not depends upon Heaven. Whether one practices it or not depends upon the times. Whether it is believed or not depends on one's destiny.

Source Codes

The critic's characterization of Buddhist teaching as "ridiculously vague and difficult to employ [難用]" perhaps alludes to the story about Hui Tzu's gourd in the *Chuang Tzu*:

Hui Tzu said to Chuang Tzu, 'The king of Wei gave me some seeds of a huge gourd. I planted them, and when they grew up, the fruit was big enough to hold five piculs. I tried using it for a water container, but it was so heavy that I couldn't lift it. I split it in half to make dippers, but they were so large and unwieldy that I couldn't dip them into anything. It's not that the gourds weren't fantastically big—but I decided they were of no use [無用] and so I smashed them to pieces.[292]

Mou-tzu begins with an allusion to the *Lao Tzu*: "The Way in its passage through the mouth is without flavor. It cannot be seen; it cannot be heard; yet it cannot be exhausted by use."[293]

The objection of the critic echoes that of Yüan Hung in his *Record of the Later Han*, who, after giving the account of the dream of Emperor Ming, continues:

Its scriptures, numbering in the thousands of myriads, have emptiness and nothingness [*hsü wu*] as their main principle. Encompassing both the gross and the subtle, there is nothing they do not purify. They are skilled at making wide-sweeping talk on a grand scale. What they seek is within the body, but what they state plainly is beyond the reach of sight and sound. Men of the world take them to be vain and deceptive [*hsü tan*]. Yet, since they reduce themselves to the dark and the subtle, to the profound and the far-removed, they are difficult to appropriate and plumb. Therefore princes and nobles, once they consider the limits of death, rebirth, and retribution, in every case succumb to panic.[294]

The music called "The Pool of Heaven" is the traditional music of the Yellow Emperor.[295] The "Great Chapter" is the traditional music of Emperor Yao. The invention of the flute (*hsiao*) is attributed to the Emperor Shun, and his music called the Hsiao Chao.[296] In the *Analects*, Confucius criticizes the music of Cheng as wanton: "as for music, adopt the *shao* and the *wu* [i.e., the music of Emperor Shun and King Wu]. Banish the tunes of Cheng and keep plausible men at a distance. The tunes of Cheng are wanton and plausible men are dangerous."[297] The distrust of popular airs continued. As Doeringer explains,

From the very beginning of his reign, Emperor Ai had shown particular interest in the classical purity of the arts. In 7 B.C., his first year on the throne, he had promulgated a special edict suppressing the activities of the Music Bureau (*Yüeh Fu*), a state agency created over a century before by Emperor Wu to collect folk songs that could be adapted to court music and dynastic hymns. Emperor Ai appears to have objected to this office because it was popularizing improper music. 'As the notes of Cheng were immoderate and brought disorder to music,' he proclaimed, 'they were something which the sage kings banned. So let the melodies of the Music Bureau be abolished.' By condemning the songs of the Music Bureau as impure, linking them as he did with the music of the old state of Cheng which Confucius had castigated for its departure from classical models, Emperor Ai probably cast suspicion over all contemporary music and art lacking a classical source.[298]

Yang Hsiung's *Explaining Away Difficulties* (*Chieh Nan*) has a similar passage:

So let non-action be the governor, and stillness and silence be the rule. The greatest flavor must be rarefied, and the greatest tone attenuated; the greatest way a winding path. The subtlest sounds, therefore, cannot be combined for the ears of the common man.... Now, if a zither player pulls the strings high and plays rapid glissandos in pursuit of animation and passion, the audience, though it might be unprepared, will accompany him. But if he tries to present on its behalf such classical pieces as the 'Hsien Ch'ih,' the 'Six Stalks,' the 'Rhapsody for Panpipes,' or the 'Nine Refrains,' no one would keep in tune.[299]

Seng Yü, nephew of the famed poet Ch'u Yuan, is one of the authors of *The Elegies of Ch'u*. Mou-tzu here summarizes the story found in *The Spring and Autumn Annals* and in chapter 45 of the *Wen-hsüan*.

Han Fei was the famous Legalist philosopher, who argued for law-and-order measures. In his *Han Fei Tzu*, he writes: "And so today if there were someone who lauded the ways of Yao, Shun, T'ang, Wu and Yü to the present generation, he would be laughed at by the modern sages. Hence the Sage does not aim at practicing antiquity, and does not model himself upon what is considered to be permanently correct. He discusses the affairs of his own age, and prepares for them accordingly."[300] Pelliot notes that in section 36 of his work Han Fei says that Yao and Shun were not perfect.[301]

Chieh Yü is the strange sage mentioned in the *Analects*: "Chieh Yü, the madman of Ch'u, went past Confucius, singing, 'Phoenix, oh phoenix, how your virtue has declined! What is past is beyond help, what is yet to come is not yet lost. Give up, give up! Perilous is the lot of those in office today.' Confucius got down from his carriage with the intention of speaking with him, but the madman avoided him by hurrying on, and in the end Confucius was unable to speak to him."[302]

The story about the jade of Master Ho can be found in the *Han Fei Tzu* account of Pien Ho, who offered a precious jewel to Ling Li of Chou. The king took it to a jeweler, who identified it as a fake. Thereupon he

had Pien Ho's right foot cut off. When King Wu took the throne, Pien Ho again presented his jewel, but, the verdict being the same, he lost his left foot. When King Wen took over, the mutilated Pien Ho, weeping tears of blood, told his sad tale. And when King Wen had the jewel examined, it was recognized as authentic.[303]
The *Huai-nan Tzu* is the source for two stories alluded to by Mou-tzu. "The spirit snake is able to be cut up and then to rejoin itself together again, but it cannot stop people from cutting it up. The spirit tortoise could give dreams to King Yüan, but he was unable to get out of the fisherman's trap." Kao Yao's commentary says: "King Yüan of Sung at night dreamed that he saw the spirit tortoise, but he could not catch it. A fisherman, Yü Chü, while fishing, captured it and offered it to King Yüan. King Yüan flayed it to divine the future. This is why the text says that it could give dreams to King Yüan but was unable to get itself out of the fisherman's net."[304]

Reader-Response Criticism

Mou-tzu sets up the critic's objection in such a way as to identify the vague explanations of classical Taoism with the Buddhist teaching of emptiness. The critic is again put in the position of negating both, while the implied reader is led to affirm both.

Mou-tzu's answer asserts the excellence of what is noble and valued over what is ignoble and common. It is directed over the head of the critic, whose criticism is never directly addressed, to the reader, who unlike the faulty narratee, is urged to see himself as a cultured gentleman able to appreciate the fine style and content of the Buddhist scriptures, to have eyes to see and ears to hear. One who does not so listen and hear is characterized as lacking the requisite karmic history, despite the fact that the times are appropriate for belief in the Buddha Tao.

The last sentence speaks merely of fate in a situation where Mou-tzu could have, and one would expect he would have, mentioned the Buddhist doctrine of *karma*. Yet our text is consistent in confining itself to accepted Chinese notions without introducing Buddhist doctrinal ideas.

ARTICLE 25.
BUDDHISM AS A READING GRID FOR THE CLASSICS

A critic challenged: You use the classics and commentaries to explain the Buddha's teachings. Your words are rich and your meaning clear. Your style is splendid and your speech elegant. But you attain nothing and there is no truth to what you say! It is all rhetoric!

Mou-tzu said: It's not just rhetoric. It's just that I have no doubts, because of the breadth of my perspective.

A critic asked: How is it that you have such a breadth of perspective?

Mou-tzu said: It is because of the Buddhist scriptures. When I had not yet understood these scriptures, I was more profoundly doubtful than you! Although I read the Five Classics, they impressed me as flowers that had not yet matured their fruit. But when I understood the words of the Buddhist scriptures and examined the essentials of the Lao Tzu, *I was able to maintain a tranquil nature and gaze at the operations of nonaction. When I reflected upon the events of this world, it was as if I were looking over the edge of Heaven Well [Pass] to espy the gorges and valleys [below], as if I had climbed Mounts Sung and T'ai and was overlooking hillocks and anthills. The Five Classics are the five flavors [and give a taste of things]. The Buddha Tao is the five grains [and give the substance]. After I had heard the Way, it was as if the clouds had opened and I saw the shining sun. It was as if a flaming torch had entered a dark room.*

Source Codes

Mou-tzu's initial response about not having doubts recalls Mencius's treatment of the heart that cannot be perturbed: "Kung-sun Ch'ou asked [Mencius], 'If you, Master, were raised to a position above the Ministers in Ch'i and were able to put the Way into practice, ... would it cause any stirring in your heart?' 'No,' said Mencius, 'My heart has not been stirred since the age of forty [*pu tung hsin* 不動心].'"[305]

The Classic of Mountains and Rivers (*Shan-hai Ching*) reports that "above what one can see of the mountains is a well, called Heaven Well."[306]

Mou-tzu's mention of Mount T'ai and of mounds and anthills alludes again to the *Mencius*, which, in praising Confucius, waxes eloquent: "Is it only among men that it is so? There is the ch'i-lin among animals, the phoenix among birds, the T'ai mountain among mounds and anthills, and rivers and seas among rain pools. [Though different in degree,] they are the same in kind. So the sages among mankind are also the same in kind. But they stand out among their fellows, and rise above the level, and from the birth of mankind until now, there has never been one so complete as Confucius."[307]

The last sentence of Mou-tzu's response recalls a passage from *The Scripture in Forty-Two Articles*: "The Buddha said, 'Seeing the Way is like going into a dark room with a torch; the darkness instantly departs, while the light alone remains....'"[308] The metaphor about the sun shining through the clouds is a frequent metaphor in many Buddhist texts. In India it frequently is found in texts with a Tathāgatagarbha orientation. In China it becomes a central Ch'an image.[309]

Reader-Response Criticism

This dialogue is the central point of the entire text, for the critic spells out Mou-tzu's rhetorical strategy in clear terms: he employs the Chinese classical literature in explicating Buddhist notions. The critic begrudgingly admits that Mou-tzu has performed his task well, in a splendid and elegant style, arguing for his Buddhist hermeneutic of the tradition in the light of traditional models and examples. Indeed, Mou-tzu has enunciated his Buddhist faith in terms of the consensual background of Chinese culture. For such persuasion "to be effective, then, the audience must identify with the speaker's position, and in turn the speaker must appeal to the opinions of the audience."[310] The process is described by Kenneth Burke: "You persuade a man only insofar as you can talk his language by speech, gesture, tonality, order, image, attitude, ideas, *identifying* your ways with his."[311]

The implied author through his Mou-tzu character here promises the implied reader that he too will gain broader perspectives and tranquillity of mind. While recommending that one employ the classics and commentaries to explain Buddhist teaching, in fact Mou-tzu has been employing his Buddhist perspective as a reading grid for these Chinese classics and commentaries with the purpose of bringing them to full perfection. The *Li-huo lun* is not, then, a straightforward apologetic for Buddhist teachings, but rather an attempt to present a Buddhist hermeneutic of the

Chinese classics, thereby creating an entry into Buddhism for literate Chinese. The Chinese classics have only a taste of the truth, while the Buddhist scriptures, whose teachings are hardly ever defended here, constitute the kernels of the truth. The issue is not the truth of those scriptures, for that is assumed by Mou-tzu throughout. The real question being addressed here is whether one converted to the Buddha Tao can still remain within the interpretative community of the Chinese literati. Throughout the Dialogue, the character Mou-tzu has frequently been addressing himself not to his narratee—who frequently fails to follow up on his own arguments—but over the head of that story-level character to the implied reader—a Chinese gentleman who like Mou-tzu himself is familiar with the classics and interested in, if critical of, the Buddha Tao.

ARTICLE 26.
CULTURAL BOUNDARIES

A critic asked: You say that the Buddhist scriptures are like the rivers and seas, that their style is like brocade and embroidery. Why then do you not use these Buddhist scriptures in reply to my questions? Why do you prefer to quote The Book of Poetry *and* The Book of Documents? *And thus make different things appear to be the same?*

Mou-tzu said: A thirsty person does not need a great river or a sea to take a drink. A hungry person does not need the Ao Granary to satisfy himself. The Way has been established for the wise; discussions are incisive for the accomplished. Books have been handed down for the intelligent; affairs are clear for the insightful. I quote these things because you are familiar with their meaning. If I spoke only the words of the Buddhist scriptures and confined my discussion to the main points of nonaction, it would be like speaking to the blind about the five colors or playing the five notes for the deaf. Although he was skillful, Shih K'uang could not strum a ch'in that had no strings. Fox or badger furs, although warm, cannot make the dead warm! Kung-ming Yi practiced playing the motif in the pure chiao key for his cow, but she just continued grazing as before. It wasn't that she didn't hear, but that her ears couldn't appreciate the notes. Instead, she thought she was surrounded by the buzzing of mosquitoes and gnats. But when she heard the cry of her lost calf, immediately she would wag her tail, pick up her ears, run over, and attend to him. This is the sole reason why I employ The Book of Poetry *and* The Book of Documents *[in my discussions with you].*

Source Codes

The Ao Granary was established by the state of Chin and located at Yung-yang in Honan, alongside the Yellow River. The *Huai-nan Tzu* says: "Suppose the Ao Granary were put at the service of a man and a river of water were given to him, he would eat when hungry and drink when thirsty from these supplies. Still he can only take a peckful of grain and a ladleful of water into his stomach."[312]

Shih K'uang was a famous musician of the fifth century B.C.E. The *Mencius* offers a related passage: "Even if you had the acute ears of Shih K'uang, you could not adjust the pitch of the five notes correctly without the six pipes."[313]

Kung-ming Yi is mentioned a number of times in the *Mencius*. Kung-ming Yi is mentioned in the *Chan-kuo Ts'e*, the *Li Chi*, and the *K'ung-tzu chia-yü*, although not the story about his unappreciative cow.[314]

Reader-Response Criticism

Continuing the discussion begun in the previous article, the critic reveals a desire to seal off the traditions, to keep the Chinese classics apart from the Buddhist scriptures. Underlying his story-level objection is the basic discourse-level issue: Can one be Buddhist and still culturally Chinese? The issue is an urgent one, for the normative value of Chinese cultural patterns is the bulwark against a descent into the social and personal chaos that so threatened the age and indeed threatens every age. The critic wants Mou-tzu to engage in "straight-up" apologetic, to argue the truth of Buddhist claims vis-à-vis the truth of the Chinese traditions. And that is precisely what the implied author never has Mou-tzu do, for if the point is to persuade, any such attempts would only emphasize the foreignness of Buddhism.

A precedent for Mou-tzu's strategy is found in "The Old Fisherman" chapter of the *Chuang Tzu*, where Confucius encounters the strange old fellow, is intrigued by his cryptic sayings, and begs to be instructed.

> Confucius bowed twice and then, straightening up, said, "Ever since childhood I have cultivated learning, until at last I have reached the age of sixty-nine. But I have never yet succeeded in hearing the Perfect Teaching. Dare I do anything, then, but wait with an open mind?" "Creatures follow their own kind, a voice will answer to the voice that is like itself," said the stranger; "this has been the rule of Heaven since time began. With your permission, therefore, I will set aside for the moment my own ways and try applying myself to the things that you are concerned about."[315]

This is precisely the method the *Li-huo lun* follows, not citing Buddhist sources, but confining its story-level dialogue to what concerns its implied readers.

That does not, however, mean that those readers were altogether unfamiliar with the Buddhist scriptures. Before Buddhism could become any kind of cultural option to Chinese people, there had to be available some scriptures that were understandable to them.[316] Both Mou-tzu and his critic are aware of such scriptures, although Mou-tzu never cites them directly. The assumption of the text is that the implied reader is more familiar with the Buddhist scriptures than is the narratee critic. Otherwise, the insulting retort of Mou-tzu, that he uses the classics because his critic is familiar only with them, would hardly be likely to achieve its rhetorical effect. The implied reader, by contrast, is urged to examine those scriptures and to see how the Chinese classics conform to the higher meaning of the Buddhist scriptures. Mou-tzu's explanation to the narratee critic adopts the notion of *upāya*, but uses it as a device to distance him—a blind, deaf, and dumb hearer—from the better-informed implied reader. Such a strategy is hardly skillful if one sees the dialogue as an actual encounter. Yet rhetorically the implied author is indeed skillfully employing his character/narrator Mou-tzu to address the reader and to distance that reader from the critic by painting the latter as obtuse. The last sentence of Mou-tzu's response even compares him to a cow!

In fact, if the issue at discourse level is the validity of a culturally Chinese Buddhism, then the implied author cannot base his argument on the Buddhist scriptures alone, for all that would accomplish is an abstract and noncontextual demonstration of the doctrines of the Buddha Tao. And this is not his point. Rather, the argument is over the interpretation of the traditions of the Chinese classics, whether the normative readings handed down from Han times are the only valid interpretation of these texts, or whether a Chinese Buddhist can employ Buddhist thought as a hermeneutical method for reading the classics. All along, the constant allusions to and citations from classical figures are aimed at fissuring that normative structure, already under the strain of increasing irrelevancy to the social chaos of the times and drowning in pedantry and nostalgia for the past. It is into that fissure that the Buddha Tao can move, establishing patterns for the enculturation of Buddhism in China.

ARTICLE 27.
ORTHODOXY

A critic asked: Once when I was in the capital, I went to the Tung Kuan Library and strolled through the Hall of Great Learning. I observed what the eminent professors were examining and heard what the Confucian scholars were discussing. But never did I hear that in their studies they regarded the Buddha Tao to be precious or thought themselves at any disadvantage because it was superior. Why are you so addicted to it? When you have lost direction, change your path! If your course comes to a dead end, turn back to the ancients! How can you fail to consider this, eh?

Mou-tzu said: Long familiar with changing [my path], I cannot be instructed through deceptions! Having penetrated to the Tao, I cannot be alarmed by anomalies. Having inquired into rhetoric, I cannot be thrown into doubt by words. Since I have attained righteousness, I cannot be swayed by profit. Lao-tzu said that fame damages the person and profit defiles one's conduct. Again he said that [people] devise tricks in order to be powerful, but emptiness and nothingness are themselves valued. To observe closely the proprieties of the home, to regulate every ordinary encounter, to move in at every opening, to worry only about the present—this is all the conduct of the worst student, and is rejected by the average student. How much more is the vastness of the perfect Tao and the sphere of action of the highest sage![317] *[This sage] is as far-reaching as the heavens and as profound as the seas. He is not like the student who peeks over the wall, or even the distinguished sage [whose walls] are several feet high, [i.e., Confucius]. In accord with their proper [capabilities, those Confucian scholars] see [only] its [i.e., Tao's] outer wall, while I have gazed upon its inner chambers. They gather the flowers, while I obtain the fruit. They strive for its preparatory stages, while I cherish its unity. You say, "Change your path!" I invite [you] to tread it! As for the sources of [worldly] calamity and prosperity, you do not know what course they take!*

Source Codes

The Tung Kuan was one of the buildings of the Imperial Library of the Later Han at Lo-yang. It became the bastion of orthodox Han scholarship. Pan Ku and Fu Yi, who figured in the account of Emperor Ming's dream in Article 21, worked at organizing books there. The Hall of Great Learning was established in 29 C.E., outside of the Kai-yang Gate of the city. It was "the most prestigious seat of learning of the time, established to disseminate and unify Confucian ideas."[318] Fairbank writes about the Han academy: "An ... important innovation was the creation in 124 B.C., at the suggestion of both Tung Chung-shu and Kung-sun Hung, of a sort of imperial university, at which fifty appointed officials, destined for government service, were to study under the Erudites.... Details are lacking about this university, but it is said to have grown to 3000 students in the second half of the first century B.C. and to 30,000 students under the Later Han dynasty."[319]

The two sentences Mou-tzu cites from the *Lao Tzu* appear to be direct citations, introduced by "Lao-tzu said." Yet neither of these maxims appears in the text of the *Lao Tzu*, either in the received texts or in the recently discovered Ma-wang-tui texts.[320] Perhaps they are not meant as direct citations, but as summary statements of Lao-tzu's thinking. Mou-tzu's phrase "Fame [*ming* 名] damages one's person" reflects chapter 44 of the *Lao Tzu*: "Fame [*ming* 名] or your person, which is dearer?"[321] Mou-tzu's phrase "Profit [*li* 利] defiles one's conduct" repeats the idea of chapter 7 of the *Lao Tzu*:

Therefore the Sage puts himself in the background and yet finds himself in the foreground; puts self-concern out of [his mind], yet

finds self-concern in the fore; puts self-concern out of [his mind],
yet finds that his self-concern is preserved. Is it not because he has
no self-interest that he is therefore able to realize his self-interest?

Also, chapter 19 says, "Eliminate craftiness, throw away profit [*li* 利],
then we will have no robbers and thieves."[322] Mou-tzu's phrase *Men
devise tricks in order to be powerful* finds a faint echo in chapter 52:
"Meddle in affairs, and till the end of your life your will not be spared,"
or again, chapter 81: "Therefore, the Way of Heaven is to benefit [*li* 利]
and not cause any harm; the Way of Man is to act on behalf of others
and not to compete with them."[323] Mou-tzu's phrase, "But emptiness
[*hsü* 虛] and nothingness [*wu* 無] are themselves valued [*kuei* 貴],"
echoes chapter 4: "The Way is empty; yet when you use it, you never
need fill it again. Like an abyss! It seems to be the ancestor of the ten
thousand things," or perhaps chapter 5: "The space between Heaven and
Earth—is it not like a bellows? It is empty [*hsü* 虛] and yet not depleted,"
or chapter 14: "Boundless, formless! It cannot be named, and returns to
the state of no-thing" [*wu wu* 無物]," or chapter 62 on the Tao: "Therefore it is the most valued thing [*kuei* 貴] in the world."[324] Mou-tzu's
phrase, that men *devise tricks in order to be powerful*, perhaps refers to
chapter 18: "When cleverness emerges, there is great hypocrisy," or chapter 58, "When the state is crafty and cunning."[325] Mou-tzu perhaps is
merely paraphrasing such ideas found scattered throughout the text of
the *Lao Tzu*.

Mou-tzu's reference to peeking over the wall and gazing upon the
inner chambers alludes to the *Analects* (19:23): "Shu-sun Wu-shu said to
the Counsellors at court, 'Tzu-kung is superior to Chung-ni.' This was
reported to Tzu-kung by Tzu-fu Ching-po. Tzu-kung said, 'Let us take
outer walls as an analogy. My walls are shoulder high so that it is possible to peer over them and see the beauty of the house. But the Master's
walls are twenty or thirty feet high so that, unless one gains admittance
through the gate, one cannot see the magnificence of the ancestral temples or the sumptuousness of the official buildings. Since those who gain
admittance through the gate are, shall we say, few, is it any wonder that
the gentleman should have spoken as he did?"

Mou-tzu's proclamation that he will tread the Path perhaps alludes
to Hexagram 10, Treading, from *The Book of Changes*: "The recluse
treads his path peacefully. Righteous persistence will bring good fortune." The commentary explains: "The recluse is a fortunate man because he cleaves to the middle path and does not allow himself to be
confused."[326]

The last sentence echoes the *Lao Tzu*: "It is on disaster that good
fortune perches; it is beneath good fortune that disaster crowds. Who
knows the limit?"[327]

Reader-Response Criticism

The scene is set at the heart of Han orthodoxy, in the center of the Confucian academy at Lo-yang. The fact that Buddhism is not received there is sufficient proof for the critic of Buddhism's lack of value. The critic enlists the best minds of the land to bolster his hold on and interpretation of the classical tradition. That classicism "presupposes an immutable order underlying the world that provides structure, harmony and meaning to all things, be they ever as humble as blades of grass or as majestic as kings and empires."[328]

By any calculation the period after the fall of the Han dynasty was not one in which the Academy at Lo-yang commanded respect, which may suggest that the *Li-huo lun's* reference to that academy is a rhetorical move, showing the critic as hopelessly outdated in the eyes of the implied readers.[329] During the final days of the Later Han, Lo-yang—the capital chosen by Emperor Kuang Wu at the beginning of that dynasty after Chang-an and its environs had been ravaged by rebels—was itself sacked in 189 by General Tung Cho, who terrorized the city, finally setting it ablaze and leaving it a desert where "even the voices of cocks and dogs were not heard."[330] As Étienne Balazs explains,

> The Chinese world at that time was nothing but desolation. A desolation total and universal. Everything was in ruins: villages destroyed, the countryside devastated, the population robbed, burned out of their homes, and massacred. As a consequence there was general panic and constant anguish, an immense state of disorder with brigands and soldiers, disasters and refugees. From such chaos emerged a few small islands of relative security where the more fortunate land owners came together.[331]

According to the Preface, Mou-tzu himself is to be numbered among such refugees, seeking such an island of relative security. Many scholars in fact fled to Chiao-chou and constituted an active community of literati in that area.[332]

The Confucian reaction to these conditions was to focus solely upon symptoms rather than causes; this did nothing but encourage the demise of the realm.[333] The august Imperial Academy simply ceased to function as the bastion and nursery of orthodoxy.

The examination system, which had been designed to promote persons to office on the basis of their cultural accomplishments, was impossible to implement under such conditions. Power was usurped by the great families and warlords, and advancement took place through the System of Nine Categories, according to which governmental functionaries were graded in nine ranks without any regard for Confucian learning or any examination process, solely at the recommendation of some powerful dignitary or other.[334] Furthermore, in the far south, where Mou-tzu was located, Lo-yang no longer served as the capital, for the Han dynasty was approaching its final demise and the realm was split into the Three Kingdoms—Wei, Wu, and Shu Han. In this context the critic's reference to the Imperial Academy at Lo-yang may perhaps witness to the continuing symbolic importance of the academy for cultural continuity. Yet it may indeed have sounded strange to the readers of the Li-huo lun, for it was already a largely discredited institution. The advice of Tung Chung-shu, the Han Confucian, that "he who does not understand the future, let him look to the past,"[335] could not have been received but as a piquant bit of irony. And that, I think, was exactly the intent of the implied author of the Li-huo lun, for the passage is directed on the discourse level to the implied reader, aware of the nostalgic appeal to a somewhat beleaguered institution, and aimed to dethrone the orthodox reading of the classics. The author uses Mou-tzu, his narrator, to counter orthodox wisdom in the eyes of his implied readers. The point is made even before Mou-tzu begins to respond that he has himself experienced such changes in his life that he cannot be deceived. Those very changes have rendered the old values questionable and the old methods inappropriate, no matter how normative they might once have been, and thus Mou-tzu has converted to the Buddhist teachings.

Mou-tzu's collection of passages from the Lao Tzu are perhaps invented or, more likely, expressive of his reading of that text. What is offered by Mou-tzu is not merely a look over the wall at the wealth of the official buildings, which everybody knows have long since been razed to the ground, but a gaze into the inner chambers of the perfect Tao. Mou-tzu shoots barbs at the Confucian scholars, describing them as those who only peek over the wall of Tao. Even Confucius, whose "walls were several feet high," is not the equal of the true sage, whose vastness is heaven-like and whose depth is sea-like. They are only at the beginning stages of the Tao, gathering its flowers, while Mou-tzu abides in its oneness, maintaining its fruit. And that is the fruit of Buddhist practice, which goes beyond the fruitless flowers of the classics.

The final sentence addresses the issue of good and bad fortune and is perhaps aimed at the sad changes in society that led to the fall of the Han. The orthodox Confucians had engaged in practices of prognostication, trying to predict, and thus somehow control, the future by reading the signs of the cosmic times. As Tsukamoto explains, "Under the Later Han, classical learning, which was the official doctrine of the State, became linked with belief in prognostication, which ... was rife in society. The classics were interpreted by resort to a form of astrology alleged to have been devised by Confucius and to the warp books (*wei shu*), which placed a supernatural construction on those classics. It thus became the fashion to conduct Confucian studies, created by a man who rejected the supernatural, in terms of *yin-yang*, *ch'an wei*, and the five elements."[336] The mere mention of the official scholars at the capital in those days might have implied such practices.

Note also that, in accord with the usual practice of the *Li-huo lun*, no mention is made here of the Buddhist doctrine of karma, according to which fortune and misfortune are the results of past actions. Our text consistently confines itself to the task of interpreting the Chinese classical texts and practices without reference to any Buddhist doctrinal notions that are not directly called into question.

ARTICLE 28.
REALITY AND CRITICISM

A critic asked: With flowery, ornate language you praise and laud the acts of the Buddha and acclaim his virtues by means of the words of the classics and commentaries. In their loftiness, [you tell us,] those [acts and virtues] surpass the clouds in the blue [sky] and in their breadth, they go beyond the borders of the earth! Have you not gone far beyond the actual [Buddha] and his true reality? My criticisms have pierced your pustules and your sickness!

Mou-tzu said: My goodness! My praises are like a grain of dust alongside Sung or T'ai mountain. I merely collect the morning dew and cast it into the rivers and seas. Your slanders are like trying with a gourd cup to lower [the waters of] those rivers and seas, like pushing a plow in an attempt to cut down the K'un-lun mountains, like sticking up your hand to screen off the rays of the sun, or like taking up a clump of earth to stop the rushing flow of the Yellow River. My praises cannot make Buddha more lofty, and your insults cannot make him any less!

Source Codes

There are no codes cited or alluded to in the passage, for the dialogue turns not to interpreting the classics but instead to a rather frontal and ungentlemanly attack on Mou-tzu.

Reader-Response Criticism

The dialogue here has all but abandoned allusions to the classical literature and focuses on the central interpretative strategy of our text: reading the classics with a Buddhist template. The critic's objection against the usage Mou-tzu makes of the classics and the commentaries is rather caustic, declaring that Mou-tzu's claims for Buddha are outlandish, and implying that his very person is disgusting, sick, and filled with pustules.

In reply, Mou-tzu merely asserts that his descriptions of Buddha can neither increase nor decrease the latter's virtue and stature. Over the head of the critic, however, the implied author is demonstrating to the implied reader just how unyielding the critic is, to be so attached to an orthodoxy now outmoded and already under serious question. Article 27 identified orthodoxy with what happens at the court in Lo-yang, and it was precisely that Lo-yang court that failed to uphold the classical pattern of governing and allowed the realm to sink into chaos and disorder. Increasingly, the critic comes across as a narrow-minded and carping fellow. The point of the discourse is that, recognizing this, the implied reader will distance himself even farther from that critic's orthodoxy and make room for hearing the Buddha Tao.

ARTICLE 29.
REJECTION OF HSIEN PRACTICE

A critic asked: Are the records about Wang Ch'iao and Ch'ih Sung and the eight immortals[337] *and the references to prolonging life in the 170 chapters of* The Spirit Book *in agreement with the [Buddhist] scriptures?*

Mou-tzu said: To compare such [records and books with the Buddhist scriptures] is like comparing the five tyrants to the five emperors, like comparing Yang Huo with Chung-ni [i.e., Confucius]. To compare their form with the Buddhist scriptures is like comparing mounds and anthills to Mount Hua or Mount Heng, or brooks and drainage ditches with the great rivers and seas. To compare their literary style is like comparing a tiger hide with lambskin, or mottled hemp with fine embroidery. There are ninety-six different teachings, but none are more respectable than the Buddha Tao. When one listens to books about the immortals, they fill the ear. But when one seeks their actual effect, it is like grasping the wind and catching the shadows. This is why they are not included in the Great Way, nor valued by nonaction. How could they be in agreement [with the Buddhist scriptures]?

Source Codes

Legend reports that Wang Ch'iao was noted for his magical powers, especially his ability to travel on the backs of a pair of ducks. He is also described as riding off on a crane to become an immortal.[338]

Ch'ih Sung was the legendary master of wind and rain during the time of Shen Nung.[339] At a later time he became the mentor of Chang Liang, who, under his influence, undertook a regime of fasting to lighten his body and attain immortality.[340] Both are paradigms for the Taoist *hsien,* or immortal.

The Spirit Book (*Shen shu*) is one of the first works of religious Taoism and was popular during the second century C.E.[341] It appears to be identical with the *T'ai-p'ing ching,* which was the scripture of the Yellow Turbans.[342] Hsiang K'ai is reported to have come to remonstrate with Emperor Huan (r. 147–68 C.E.) for sacrificing to the Yellow Emperor, Lao-tzu, and Buddha. During his discourse he mentioned that "at an earlier date Yü Chi had presented to the court of Emperor Shun

(r. 126–44) *The Book of the Pure Acceptance of Grand Tranquillity* (*T'ai p'ing ch'ing ling shu*), which he boasted he got from a god. This book of allegedly divine origin, one that prescribed recipes for healing sickness, extinguishing calamity, and inviting good fortune, all on the basis of the doctrines of *yin yang* and the five elements, the words of shamans, protective amulets, mystical phrases and the like, was in due course supplemented, developing into that important Taoist classic, *The Classic of Grand Tranquillity* (*T'ai p'ing ching*)."[343]

Yang Huo, mentioned by Mou-tzu, is traditionally identified with Yang Hu, who belonged to one of the great families of Lu and is reported in the *Analects* to have treated Confucius with a lack of courtesy by presenting him with a piglet and urging him to get engaged in public affairs.[344] Yang Huo is also discussed in the *Mencius*, where Yang Huo's present becomes a more respectable "steamed piglet," and his actions motivated by a desire to observe the proprieties.[345]

Mou-tzu's reference to tiger hide and lambskin is an allusion to the *Analects*: "Chi Tzu-ch'eng said, 'The important thing about the gentleman is the stuff he is made of. What does he need refinement for?' Tzu-kung commented, 'It is a pity that the gentleman should have spoken so about the gentleman. "A team of horses cannot keep up with one's tongue." The stuff is not different from refinement; refinement is not different from the stuff. The pelt of a tiger or a leopard, shorn of hair, is no different from that of a dog or a sheep!' "[346]

Mou-tzu's phrase *they fill the ear* again echoes the *Analects*: "The master said, 'When Chih, the Master Musician, begins to play, and when the *Kuan chü* comes to an end, how the sound fills the ear!' "[347]

The phrase *the ninety-six teachings* comes from the Indian Buddhist reckoning of heterodox teachings. The *Aṅguttaranikāya* reports: "I have exhaustively examined the significance of the ninety-six kinds of heterodox teachings and they cannot compare with the significance of the teaching of the Tathāgata."[348]

Reader-Response Criticism

Ever since the appearance of popular Taoist religion, particularly that identified with the Celestial Master Sect in 150 C.E., the usual escape from rigid orthodoxy had taken the form of *hsien* Taoism. This was not, however, confined to the common people. Indeed, royalty and nobles, with their wealth and rank, were the most avidly engaged in trying to lengthen their life spans.[349] Mou-tzu's critic, influenced by the vogue among literate gentlemen for various methods of "nourishing life," here begins to show some uncertainty in regard to the normative patterns of classical Confucian thought. Tsukamoto Zenryū describes Confucianism at the end of the Former Han as follows:

In sum, Confucianism, by now converted into official state doctrine as the culmination of a process begun under the Former Han, was attended by many evils, at the same time that political and ethical theories holding Confucianism in the highest esteem, rooted in the Confucian classics (*ching*) and based on the theories of these classics, were permeating society and fixing the social order. Also, having forfeited its freedom as a philological, exegetical form of dry learning, it lost whatever charm it might have had for men of letters. This was an era in which those very intellectuals who had been trained in Confucianism, while adopting a Confucian stance in their public lives, in their private lives had recourse to faith in sylphs, magic, and the like. It was at such a time as this, be it noted, that the passage of Buddhism began.[350]

Hsi K'ang (223–62), a Taoist thinker who rejected Confucian values and positions, affirmed the existence of the immortals, although he thought they were a separate species of human beings: "Although immortals are not seen with the eyes, nonetheless they are cited in books and records and [their lives] are narrated in the former histories. When we compare these and discuss it, their existence becomes certain."[351]

Scholars have often seen the reception of Buddhism into China as molded by such *hsien* notions. There is evidence that the Buddha himself was regarded as a numinous *hsien*. Again Tsukamoto writes,

The foreign religion was received as a *hsien*, magical teaching on the model of the Yellow Emperor and Lao-tzu, while the golden Buddha-images were the recipients of sacrifice, as if they were immortal sylphs able to grant wishes and answer prayers, and the foreign monks for their part, were feared and venerated as beings of supernatural power who in the manner of Yü Chi and Chang Chüeh [i.e., *hsien* Taoist sages], could enter into direct communication with the gods. Yet the Buddhism received into China, without coming to terms in some way with China's traditions, above all with the classically based doctrines such as Confucianism and the *tao chia* [i.e., Taoist religious practitioners of the *hsien* variety] and traditional popular beliefs, as well as with Taoism, which originated as a development out of these, could never have become a Chinese religion.[352]

Hurvitz states the case most succinctly: "For the early Chinese Buddhists, there can be no doubt that the Buddha and the Chinese Sage (*sheng*) or immortal (*hsien*) were one and the same."[353]

Our text, however, does not follow this pattern, for it rejects outright the practices of *hsien* Taoism, including them in the ninety-six heretical teachings. Mou-tzu, we are told in the Preface, does not put his faith in the practices of the *hsien* immortals. Thus, the classical tradition that Mou-tzu reclaims as the propaedeutic for Buddhist teaching does not include popular, *hsien* Taoism. Scholars at times argue that one should not differentiate too rigidly between classical, philosophical Taoism and popular *hsien* Taoism, for they share a unified tradition. Indeed, one can discern *hsien* elements in the *Lao Tzu* and the *Chuang Tzu*. And yet Mou-tzu clearly does make a definite distinction between the two, disallowing that *hsien* practices (including, as we shall see, specific dietary practices) should be included within the Way, either of classical Taoism or of Buddhism.

This point is fairly important, for the rhetorical strategy of the *Li-huo lun's* author is to graft the new branch of the Buddha Tao onto the trunk of classical Chinese culture, which is represented for him by the Confucian classics and the works of classical Taoism. The latter means for him in particular the *Lao Tzu*, which he does not regard as teaching *hsien* practices at all.[354] For Mou-tzu, *hsien* texts enjoy neither the age nor the authority of the classics.

Other Han thinkers also rejected *hsien* practices. The philosopher Wang Ch'ung in his *Lun Heng*, especially book 7, "Taoist Untruths," mercilessly attacked such legendary stories. Wang Ch'ung lived from 27 C.E. to C.E. 97, but "it was only after the Later Han had entered its final stages that Wang Ch'ung's book became current, for during his own time and immediately thereafter the power of the very fashionable 'mystical doctrines' and superstitious practices was in no way curtailed."[355] If *hsien* practices were seen at the end of the Han as alien to their classical tradition by at least some cultured Chinese, then these practices could hardly serve as an effective cultural bridge for the *Li-huo lun's* importation of Buddhist doctrine and practice.

Similarly, in his championing of Confucian orthodoxy, Yang Hsiung strongly repudiated *hsien* notions and practices. "Hsiung refused to allow his associates to identify the sage with the so-called 'immortals' (*hsien*) of popular Taoism who were evidently a current source of much fascination."[356] The *Li-huo lun* follows this pattern, perhaps at least in part because such a stance was grounded in the roots of the classical tradition.

ARTICLE 30.
FASTING: BUDDHIST AND TAOIST

A critic asked: Among the Taoists, some abstain from eating grain, yet they drink their wine and eat their meat. They claim that this is the method of Lao-tzu. But the Buddha Tao considers wine and meat to be absolutely prohibited, while it does allow one to eat grain. Why such a stark difference?

Mou-tzu said: Such doctrines are trivial and trifling.[357] None of their ninety-six teachings surpasses the Buddha in tranquillity and nonaction. I have inspected the two sections of the Lao Tzu *and have heard of his prohibition against the five tastes,[358] but I have never found any place where he says that we should stop eating the five grains. The sage [i.e., Confucius] has arranged the text of the Seven Classics, but they contain no method of abstaining from grains. Lao wrote the Five Thousand Words, but there is no mention of avoiding grains. The sage says, "Those who eat grain are wise; those who eat grasses are fools. Those who eat meat are violent. Those who feed on the air are long-lived." Ordinary people do not understand these things, and when they see that the six birds hold their breath, neither inhaling nor exhaling, and do not eat in fall or winter, they want to emulate them. They do not realize that each being has its own specific nature. A magnet will attract iron, but it cannot move soft hairs!*

Source Codes

The passage Mou-tzu attributes to "the sage" apparently refers to Confucius, for he was thought to have arranged the text of the classics. Yet the quotation Mou-tzu presents does not occur in the present text of the *Analects*. A close parallel, and probably the *Li-huo lun's* source, does, however, occur in *The Family Discussions of Confucius* (*K'ung-tzu chia-yü*): "Those who eat water travel easily but suffer from the cold. Those who eat earth are without consciousness, but do not breathe. Those who eat trees are quite strong but unregulated. Those who eat grasses run easily, but are stupid. Those who eat mulberry [leaves], are gossamer but turn into moths. Those who eat meat are brave, but violent. Those who eat the air are spiritually bright and live long. Those who eat grains are wise and skillful. Those who do not eat are immortal and spirits."[359]

The *Chuang Tzu* has a passage about the proper nourishment of birds, which perhaps is alluded to by Mou-tzu's phrase about imitating the birds: "Haven't you heard this story? Once a sea bird alighted in the suburbs of the Lu capital. The marquis of Lu escorted it to the ancestral temple, where he entertained it, performing the Nine Shao music for it to listen to and presenting it with the meat of the T'ai-lao sacrifice to feast on. But the bird only looked dazed and forlorn, refusing to eat a single slice of meat or drink a cup of wine, and in three days it was dead. This is to try to nourish a bird with what would nourish you instead of what would nourish a bird. If you want to nourish a bird with what nourishes a bird, then you should let it roost in the deep forest, play among the banks and islands, float on the rivers and lakes, eat mudfish and minnows, follow the rest of the flock in flight and rest, and live any way it chooses."[360] Another relevant allusion from the *Chuang Tzu* might be: "To pant, to puff, to hail, to spit, to spit out the old breath and draw in the new, practicing bear-hangings and bird-stretchings, longevity his only concern—such is the life favored by the scholar who practices Induction, the man who nourishes his body, who hopes to live to be as old as P'eng-tsu."[361]

The Rectification of Unjustified Criticism, drawing on the *Chuang Tzu*, rejects such practices: "Furthermore, 'bear stretchings,' and 'bird-pantings,' 'drawing in deep breaths,' expelling [the old] and inhaling the revitalizing [breath], ceasing [to partake of] glutinous and panicled millet, and making use [instead] of flower pistils; consuming the wind and dew in order to replace ordinary rations; depending on [such as] these to prolong one's longevity, after all, still belongs to the class of having to rely on [things external to oneself]. [People who rely on] such methods as these [still] have a time when they will die, and they are unable to have an inexhaustible [span of life]."[362]

The last sentence of Mou-tzu perhaps refers to the *Huai-nan Tzu*, which states: "A magnet is capable of attracting iron, but if one touches it to copper, it does not work."[363]

Reader-Response Criticism

The critic's question here is quite polite, merely a request for information about the different dietary practices of the Taoists, some of whom abstain from grain, and the Buddhists, who neither eat meat nor drink wine. This question allows the implied author to address his implied reader without bothering about the story-level critic at all.

In his reply, Mou-tzu enters directly into a reading of the Chinese classics, showing from the text of the *Lao Tzu* that there is no prohibition about the five grains.[364] He is concerned not only with directly answering the critic's question—how the Buddhist teachings and the Chinese practices can be so much at variance—but also with showing that such Chinese practices are not condoned by the classical tradition itself. He becomes a champion of the Chinese classical tradition. The dialogue structure of the narrative has now all but disappeared, with the implied author speaking directly to his reader in an attempt to define the Chinese classical tradition as excluding the practices of *hsien* Taoism.

ARTICLE 31.
MOU-TZU AS A STRICT CLASSICIST

A critic asked: Can one indeed abstain from grains?

Mou-tzu said: Before I understood the Great Way, I too studied these things. The teachings about abstaining from grains include several hundreds of thousands of recipes. I practiced them without effect and engaged in them without result. Therefore, I abandoned them.

Look at the three masters from whom I received instruction! Although they claimed to be seven hundred, five hundred, and three hundred years old respectively, in less than three years after I had begun to study with them, they were all dead! This was because they abstained from grains, and gorged on fruit. They would enjoy their meat and take second helpings of it. They would drink their wine and empty their goblets. Their humors were irregular and their spirits dulled. Their intake of life-giving grain was insufficient. Their ears were muddled and their eyes were out of focus. Yet they did not desist from this excessive depravity. When I asked why, they responded that "Lao-tzu said that 'One does less and less until one does nothing at all.' His followers must diminish every day." But as I observed them, they increased every day and did not diminish at all! Thus, each of them died before the age of understanding the Decree [of Heaven, i.e., fifty years]. Neither Yao nor Shun, the Duke of Chou, nor Confucius was able to live a hundred years, and yet later generations stupidly and willingly place credence in the abstinence from grain in their search for inexhaustible longevity! What a pity!

Source Codes

Mou-tzu's quotation refers to the *Lao Tzu*: "In the pursuit of learning one knows more and more every day; in the pursuit of the way one does less and less every day. One does less and less until one does nothing at all, and when one does nothing at all there is nothing that is undone."[365]

His reference to "the age of understanding" alludes to the *Analects*: "The Master said, 'At fifteen I set my heart on learning; at thirty I took my stand; at forty I came to be free from doubts; at fifty I understood the Decree of Heaven; at sixty my ear was attuned; at seventy I followed my heart's desire without overstepping the line.'"[366] Thus, the age of understanding is fifty.

In *A Refutation of Hsi K'ang's Essay on Nourishing Life* (*Nan Yangsheng lun*), Hsiang Hsiu has a passage that parallels Mou-tzu's list of dead sages: "If the length of one's life is related to being skilled or clumsy, then the sages, who thoroughly understood the principles and exhausted their natures, ought to have enjoyed very long lives. But of Yao, Shun, Yü, T'ang, Wu, [the Duke of] Chou, and Confucius, the oldest lived to one hundred while the youngest died at seventy."[367]

Reader-Response Criticism

Again the critic merely provides the occasion for the implied author to speak through Mou-tzu to the implied reader. Again, the question directed to Mou-tzu is a request for information, this time about *hsien* practices concerning which Mou-tzu, a man of his times, has had some experience. Yet, despite this experience with *hsien* practices, Mou-tzu once more takes the role of the classical scholar, speaking for the normative value of the Chinese traditions of antiquity as against the ineffective, harmful practices of *hsien* adepts, even against the *Chuang Tzu*, which censures Chien Wu for belittling Chieh Yü, who "had said that there is a holy man (*hsien*) on faraway Ku-she Mountain, with skin like ice or snow, and gentle and shy like a young girl. He doesn't eat the five grains, but sucks the wind, drinks the dew, climbs upon the clouds and mists, rides a flying dragon, and wanders beyond the four seas. By concentrating his spirit, he can protect creatures from sickness and plague and make the harvest plentiful. I thought this was all insane and refused to believe it."[368] And that, of course, is the point: that Mou-tzu is a thoroughly orthodox scholar despite his Buddhist beliefs. On one level, the question merely launches his answer: you can abstain, but nothing of benefit will occur to you! By implication, however, our text might also be criticizing *hsien* practices among early Chinese Buddhists, thus disassociating itself from the popular Neo-Taoist practices that had undoubtedly coalesced to some degree with Buddhist practices. Indeed, Mou-tzu's confession of a *hsien* interlude witnesses to the popularity of such practices among his contemporaries, and his present rejection of such constitutes an invitation for others to go and do likewise.[369] *Hsien* Taoist practice may indeed have constituted a bridge for many from the Confucian classical tradition to Buddhism, but Mou-tzu offers another option.

ARTICLE 32.
SICKNESS AND HEALTH

A critic asked: Taoist practitioners say that one can drive away disease, be freed from illness, and heal oneself without recourse to acupuncture or medicine. Don't you believe this is true? Why then is it that Buddhists get sick and visit the acupuncturist and the alchemist?

Mou-tzu replied: Lao-tzu said, "When a being becomes strong [in asserting itself], it then grows old. We term this going against the Way. Now, that which goes against the Way will come to an early end."[370] *Only those who have attained the Way will not be reborn nor reach their "strength" [by going against the Way]. And, not reaching their strength, they will not grow old. Not growing old, they will not get sick. Not getting sick, they will not see corruption. This is why Lao-tzu considered his body to be such a lot of trouble.*[371] *When King Wu was ill, the Duke of Chou entreated the fates. When Chung-ni [i.e., Confu-*

cius] was sick, Tzu-lu asked to pray for him. I am aware that the sages were all afflicted with sickness, but not that they were ever free from disease. Shen Nung tested his herbs, yet those thereby brought close to death were several tens [of people]. The Yellow Emperor bowed his head and received acupuncture from Ch'i Po. Are these three sages not the equal of today's Taoist practitioners? If you study these words, they will be sufficient for you to reject those ideas!

Source Codes

The *Analects* report Confucius's illness: "The Master was seriously ill. Tzu-lu asked permission to offer a prayer. The Master said, 'Was such a thing ever done?' Tzu-lu said, 'Yes, it was. The prayer offered was as follows: pray thus to the gods above and below.' The Master said, 'In that case, I have long been offering my prayers.' "[372]

On the sickness experienced by the sages, the *Huai-nan Tzu* states: "Yen Hui, Chi Lou, Tzu Hsia, Jan Pei Niu were the expert disciples of Confucius. Nevertheless Yen had an untimely death. Chi Lou was mutilated in the war with Wei. Tzu Hsia lost the sight of his eyes through weeping for the loss of his son. Jan Pei Niu became leprous. All these men, great though they were, were buffeted by nature, and laboring under the restraints of life's handicaps, failed to reach the harmony of life."[373] *The Book of Documents (Shu Ching)* reports that when King Wu was ill, the Duke of Chou entreated their ancestors to be taken in his place.[374]

Shen Nung, the legendary Emperor "Spirit Farmer" is credited with the discovery of the medicinal properties of plants. The *Huai-nan Tzu* says: "People of old fed on grass, drank spring water, plucked the fruits of the trees for their food and fed on the flesh of wasps and mussels. They often were sick and poisoned. Then Shen Nung appeared and taught them, for the first time, the art of sowing and planting cereals, how to discern the relative values of lands and the seeds suitable to the soil; he taught them to differentiate between the dry and the humid, the rich and the poor, the high and low lands. By empirical methods of tasting the flavours of the various grasses, of testing the bitter and sweet waters in the springs, he enabled the people to avoid the noxious. It was then, under his regime, that, in one day, 70 kinds of poisonous plants were discriminated."[375] Pelliot surmises that this is the story Mou-tzu has in mind when he speaks about the tens of people who nearly died from employing his remedies.[376]

Ch'i Po, one of the assistants of the Yellow Emperor, was reputed to be the founder of the art of healing.[377] He is said to have been the interlocutor of the Yellow Emperor in the *Huang Ti su-wen*, perhaps the oldest work of Chinese medicine.[378]

Reader-Response Critcism

The critic's question is again one asking for information, not targeting Buddhist practices or doctrine. The issue is the place of Neo-Taoist methods of avoiding illness within Chinese classical tradition. The critic seems to assume that Buddhists do in fact practice the *hsien* arts and should not get sick or have need of remedies.

Again Mou-tzu dons the robes of the fully orthodox Chinese scholar, criticizing departures from the classical norms. He employs Lao-tzu to argue that those who attempt to assert themselves inevitably grow old and die, as have all the sages of old. The only ones who will not see corruption are those who have attained the Way, that is, the awakened ones, who, like the Buddha described in Article 1, escape the wheel of rebirth. All others, no matter what practices they adopt, will continue to be reborn and experience sickness and suffering. Mou-tzu's advice is then to find the awakened Tao, wherein one need not worry about the occurrence of old age or sickness. As for the rest, simply follow the accepted medicinal practices of acupuncture and pharmacology, and pay no attention to claims for any *hsien* immortality.

As in the previous article, one may detect here a critique on the part of the *Li-huo lun* of the popular Buddhist acceptance of *hsien* practices. That is what the critic's question implies, and such practices are firmly excluded by Mou-tzu's response.

ARTICLE 33.
NONACTION MEANS NO DIFFERENCES BETWEEN
TEACHINGS

A critic asked: In all of the teachings nonaction is identical. Why then do you differentiate and rank [nonaction], saying they are different? This engenders fox doubts in students. I think this is all a waste of time and profitless!

Mou-tzu said: If everything were called "grass," then we would be unable to designate with words the different kinds of grass. If everything were called "metal," then we would be un-

able to designate with words the different kinds of metals. Things may be of the same general category, but they are of different kinds. If this is the way it is with the ten thousand things, how can doctrines alone [be different]? Formerly Yang Chu and Mo Tzu blocked the Way of the Confucian group, their carts could not move ahead, and their people could not take a step forward. Only when Mencius opened that [Way] did they know where to follow.

When Shih K'uang played his ch'in, he hoped that people who could appreciate pitch would exist in the future. The sages have fixed the pattern in the hope that future [generations of] gentlemen would recognize them. But when jade and stone were placed in the same box, I Tun became upset about it. And when vermilion and purple clashed, Chung-ni [i.e., Confucius] sighed.

It is not that sun and moon are not bright, but that shadows hide their light. It is not that the Buddha Tao is incorrect, but that selfishness occludes its appeal. Therefore, I differentiate and rank these [teachings]. The wisdom of Tsang Wen and the uprightness of Wei-sheng were not approved by Confucius. These words [of Confucius] reform the world! How can they be a waste of time and unprofitable?

Source Codes

The critic says that Mou-tzu's teachings engender "fox doubts" (*hu-i*), which denote a deep state of indecision and perplexity. This refers to the story of a fox who, wanting to cross a frozen river but doubting the thickness of the ice, listens carefully for the sound of running water before proceeding.[379] The phrase is used in *The Book of Documents*: "In the autumn, when the grain was abundant and ripe, but before it was reaped, Heaven sent a great storm of thunder and lightning, along with wind, by which the grain was all beaten down, and great trees torn up. The people were greatly terrified" (*hu-i*).[380] It is not then simply intellectual doubt, but fearful and upsetting doubt, that the critic evinces.

Mou-tzu's reference to Yang Chu and Mo Tzu is found in the *Mencius*, which says: "... the words of Yang Chu and Mo Ti fill the Empire.... If the way of Yang and Mo does not subside and the way of Confucius is not proclaimed, the people will be deceived by heresies and the path of morality will be blocked."[381]

Mou-tzu's reference to Shih K'uang's music is apparently taken from Yang Hsiung's *Explaining Away Difficulties* (*Chieh Nan*), which was intended to refute the criticism that his *Classic of the Great Mystery* (*T'ai Hsüan Ching*) was unintelligible.[382] The passage reads: "When Master K'uang tempered his bells, he hoped that men who understand pitch would exist in the future [*szu chih yin che zai hou yeh* 竢知音者在後也, the exact phrase used in the *Li-huo lun*]; when Confucius wrote *The Spring and Autumn Annals*, he expected that gentlemen of the future would appreciate it."[383] The *Huai-nan Tzu* has a parallel passage: "Of old Duke Ping of Ts'in, Shansi, ordered his foundry-man to cast a bell. When this was done, he asked the minister of music, Shih K'uang, for his opinion on its tone. Shih K'uang replied that it was imperfect. Duke Ping, in turn, said that the opinions of the expert artificers were all favourable. How then did he consider it imperfect? Shih K'uang replied that it might do if posterity were without a person who understood music: but a true musician would at once discern its imperfection. Thus the wish of Shih K'uang was for a perfect-toned bell to satisfy the ear of a musician of all times."[384]

I Tun is a fifth century B.C.E. figure who was famed for amassing a fortune. The *Huai-nan Tzu* says: "The diamond-cutter may mistake a piece of jade, thinking it to be an imitation stone, the P'i. But I Tun, alone, would never miss the lustre."[385]

On Confucius's sigh, the *Analects* say: "The Master said, 'I detest purple for displaying vermilion.'"[386] Purple was considered to be a mixed color, while vermilion was a pure color.

Tsang Wen-chung, who did have a reputation for wisdom, was criticized in the *Analects* by Confucius: "The Master said, 'When housing his great tortoise, Tsang Wen-chung had the capitals of the pillars carved in the shape of hills and the rafter posts in a duckweed design. What is one to think of his intelligence?'"[387]

Wei-sheng Kao was also criticized by Confucius, "The Master said, 'Who said Wei-sheng Kao was straight! Once when someone begged him for vinegar, he went and begged it off a neighbor to give it to him.'"[388]

Reader-Response Criticism

The critic argues that one should not make any distinction at all between the doctrines of Buddhism or any of the Chinese traditions, classical or popular, for Buddhism is but another expression of the age-old doctrine of nonaction. Thus, why bother about differentiating the Buddha teachings from the Tao of nonaction? The context is important. As Tsukamoto explains, after the social chaos subsequent to the fall of the Han dynasty

There was a sharp increase in the number of those persons who, turning their backs on politics for their own sakes as well as their families', aspired instead to a "life of seclusion" [*yin yi*], which was a legitimately Confucian attitude toward life acknowledged, for example, in the *Canon of Changes*, where one reads (under the hexagram *ku*), "Serving

neither kings nor princes, he keeps his own affairs sublime
and lofty. . . ." They did, to be sure, study the Confucian classics, but they did not necessarily on that account seek
appointments. Not only that, but they were fond of "dark
learning" (*hsüan hsüeh*), i.e., of the quest for the "Way"
(*tao*) . . . Given this preference they sought the realm of no-
ado (*wu wei*), of that which is so of itself (*tzu jan*), as proclaimed by Lao-tzu and Chuang-tzu, for they held that only
he is a Sage (*sheng*) who embodies this Way.[389]

Yet the *wu-wei* sought by these early Buddhists was understood in
terms of the Buddhist doctrine of *nirvāṇa*, so they were both using
it as the cultural vehicle for that notion and understanding it in a
specifically Buddhist sense. In Article 1, Mou-tzu equates the Buddha's cessation with nonaction: "Thus, even after his entrance
into cessation and departure on the fifteenth day of the second
month, his scriptures and discipline still remain. Those able consistently to follow them also attain nonaction, for [his] blessing
flows over into later generations." Article 16 states that "the
Way of Buddha venerates nonaction and takes delight in giving."
Article 25 repeats the refrain: "But when I understood the words
of the Buddhist scriptures and examined the essentials of the *Lao
Tzu*, I was able to maintain a tranquil nature and gaze at the operations of nonaction." This equation between *nirvāṇa* and *wu-
wei* was not unique to Mou-tzu. Yüan Hung in his *Record of the
Later Han* (*Hou Han chi*) describes the Buddhist monk as "re-
verting to nonaction."[390] The critic apparently objects to this ap-
propriation of the traditional notion of *wu-wei* to signify what is
still to him a foreign notion.

Mou-tzu's response alludes to times in classical Chinese history when mistaken beliefs were blocking the Way and had to be
refuted. Mou-tzu's task is similar, as pointed out in the Preface,
where he is likened to Mencius, who refuted Yang Chu and Mo
Ti. Mou-tzu attempts to remove the occlusion from the Buddha
Tao to show how bright it is, and in so doing, it is implied, he
clears away as well the clouds that have obscured the classical
Chinese Way.

In distinguishing different kinds of nonaction (*wu-wei*), the
Li-huo lun shows an awareness that it is adopting a creative hermeneutical strategy and not simply understanding Buddhism in
terms of *hsien* practice. Mou-tzu is clearly aware of the difference

between *hsien* Taoist and Buddhist understandings of nonaction. Otherwise, he could simply have identified them, as the critic urges. The adoption of Taoist terms was not, then, an unconscious mistaking of Buddhist teachings for indigenous ideas, but a conscious rhetorical strategy for enculturating the Buddha Tao within the classical Chinese tradition.

Furthermore, Mou-tzu champions the words of Confucius. Those words were meant to reform the world and are thus not unprofitable at all. Teachings have to be adjudicated in terms of their intent, for they are not all simply identical. Thus, while committed to the Way of Buddha, Mou-tzu is still an orthodox Confucian scholar.

ARTICLE 34.
THE IMPLICATIONS OF BEING ORTHODOX

A critic asked: You revile the spirits and immortals, restrain the uncanny, and refuse to believe in a way to avoid death. Why then do you believe that only the Buddha Tao can save the world? Buddha lived in a strange country. Your feet have never trod on his native soil and your eyes have never seen his abode. You believe in his actions only because you have read his writings. Now, one who gazes at a flower cannot see its inner reality. One who looks at shadows cannot perceive true forms. Perhaps your [faith] is mistaken?

Mou-tzu replied: Confucius said, "Look at the means a man employs, observe the path he takes, and examine where he feels at home. In what way is a man's true character hidden from view?"[391] *Formerly when the Duke of Chou examined the governance of Lü Wang, he foresaw how his posterity would end up. Yen Yüan, on the day when they were exercising their teams of horses, saw the chariot-driving skill of Tung-yeh Pi and knew that his [team] would break down. Tzu-kung witnessed the meeting between Chu and Lu and explained how they would be destroyed. Chung-ni [i.e., Confucius] heard the lute music of Shih K'uang and recognized King Wen's arrangement. Chi-tzu perceived the customs of all the different countries by listening to*

*their music. Why would my feet have to tread [on his native soil],
or my eyes have to see [where he lived]?*

Source Codes

The critic's initial salvo depicts Mou-tzu in terms that recall Confucius's advice about spirits: "Fan Ch'ih asked about wisdom. The Master said, 'To work for the things the common people have a right to and to keep one's distance from the gods and spirits while showing them reverence can be called wisdom.'"392

Lü Wang, Duke T'ai, was the first ruler of the state of Ch'i.393 The famous Duke of Chou, who was in charge of enfeoffing the various military officers who had taken part in the establishment of the Chou dynasty,394 had placed his son over the state of Lu. That son did not report to his father for three years. When asked to render account, his son answered that he had first to reform the local customs. By contrast, Duke T'ai (i.e., Lü Wang) did render a full report to the Duke of Chou in three months, explaining that he had been able to act swiftly because he had simplified the local customs. The Duke of Chou then foresaw that the state of Lu would render homage to the state of Ch'i, because the people preferred the gentler attitude of the Ch'i ruler, Lü Wang, over the more exacting stance of the Lu ruler. In fact, that is what happened when Duke Huan of Ch'i became the overlord.395 The *Huai-nan Tzu* has a different version, in which both states come to an end: "Long ago [early in the Chou dynasty] T'ai-kung Wang and Tan, Duke of Chou, met on occasion of being enfeoffed, and T'ai-Kung Wang asked the Duke of Chou, 'How will you govern Lu?' The Duke of Chou said, 'I shall honor the honorable men and treat kin as kin.' T'ai-Kung said, 'It will follow from this that Lu shall weaken.' The Duke of Chou asked T'ai-Kung, 'How will you govern Ch'i?' T'ai-Kung said, 'I shall raise up the worthy and elevate the meritorious.' The Duke of Chou said, 'In later generations assuredly there will be lords who are despoiled and killed.' After that Ch'i grew day by day until it became a hegemonic [state]. Having passed twenty-four generations the T'ien family displaced [the ducal dynasty]. [The territory of] Lu was pared away day by day until it barely existed. Having passed thirty-two generations [the state] perished."396

A story about the driving skill of Tung-yeh Chi (Tung-yeh Pi in the *Li-huo lun* text) occurs in the *Chuang Tzu*, but there the predictor of failure is Yen Ho: "Tung-yeh Chi was displaying his carriage driving before Duke Chuang. He drove back and forth as straight as a measuring line and wheeled to left and right as neat as a compass-drawn curve. Duke Chuang concluded that even [the legendary] Tsao Fu could do no better, and ordered him to make a hundred circuits and then return to the palace. Yen Ho happened along at that moment and went in to see the Duke. 'Tung-yeh Chi's horses are going to break down,' he said. The Duke was silent and gave no answer. In a little while Tung-yeh Chi returned, his horses in fact having broken down. The Duke asked Yen Ho, 'How did you know that was going to happen?' Yen Ho said, 'The strength of the horses was all gone and still he was asking them to go on—that's why I said they would break down.'"[397] Mou-tzu's source for the story is probably chapter 16 of the *Hsün Tzu*, where Yen Yüan is the predictor and the driver is identified as Tung-yeh Pi.[398] The same story is also found in the *K'ung-tzu chia-yü*, chapter 30,[399] and the *I-hsia lun*.[400]

The account of Tzu-kung explaining how Chu and Lu would be destroyed is found in the *Tso Chuan*. For the fifteenth year of Duke Ting we read: "When Duke Yin of Chu appeared at the court of Lu, Tzu-kung witnessed [the ceremony between the two princes]. The Viscount bore his symbol of jade [too] high, with his countenance turned upwards; the Duke received it [too] low, with his countenance bent down. Tzu-kung said, 'Looking on [and judging] according to the rules of ceremony, the two rulers will [soon] die or go into exile. Those rulers are [as] a stem from which grow life and death, preservation or ruin. We draw our conclusion from the manner in which the parties move to the right or left, advance or recede, look down or up, and we observe this at court meetings and sacrifices, and occasions of death and war. It is now in the first month that these princes meet at court, and they both violate the proper rules—their minds are gone. On a festal occasion like this, unobservant of such an essential matter, how is it possible for them to continue long? The high symbol and upturned look are indicative of pride; the low symbol and bent down look are indicative of negligence. Pride is not far removed from disorder, and negligence is near to sickness. Our ruler is the host, and will probably be the first to die.'"[401]

The report on Shih K'uang's music is found in *The Records of the Grand Historian*, where he is correctly called Shih Hsiang, not the *Li-huo lun's* Shih K'uang. Confucius, in listening to the lute of Master Hsiang, perceived the influence of King Wen, whereupon, filled with admiration, Master Hsiang concurred that the piece he was playing indeed was composed by King Wen.[402]

Chi-tzu is the *tzu* of Chi Cha, an early sage who served as an envoy from the state of Wu to the state of Lu. A rather extended passage from the *Tso Chuan* reports that as he listened to the various odes from different areas, he commented on the social character and future prospects of those areas.[403]

Reader-Response Criticism

The critic accuses Mou-tzu of having an attitude toward the spirits and immortals even in excess of Confucius's advice, for that sage had recommended respecting the spirits and gods, even though one should keep them at a distance, while Mou-tzu is depicted as reviling the spirits and restraining the uncanny. Even in the opening sentence Mou-tzu is placed for the reader on the side of Confucius, who is reported in the *Analects* never to have spoken about anything uncanny.[404]

The critic's objection repeats his refrain that Buddhism is foreign to Chinese cultural sensitivities and tries to draw a normative line between the Chinese traditions—with which one is familiar and which one can validate within the assumptions of a Chinese interpretative community—and the Indian faith, which cannot be grounded within those assumptions. The *Li-huo lun* has just rejected the popular equation of Buddha with the *hsien*, so even that social grounding for Buddhism is disallowed.

The *Li-huo lun* is attempting to offer a more philosophical enculturation of the Buddha Tao within the Confucian milieu. Mou-tzu quotes from Confucius to point out that one can validly infer the truth of the Dharma from observing its manifestations. In all of the examples Mou-tzu cites from the classics, one arrives at the inner truth by observing external manifestations. Thus one can also arrive at the truth of the Buddha Tao by examining its scriptures without having visited India. Few of the readers of the *Li-huo lun* would have traveled to India, and so they too must rely on the manifestations of the Buddha Tao without any firsthand tourism to support their evaluation.

ARTICLE 35.
THE MONKS OF KHOTAN

A critic asked: Once when I was traveling through Khotan, several times I met with some monks, adherents of the Way. But my concerns were too difficult for them and, rather than confront my questions, none of them would engage me in dialogue. They all excused themselves. Many of them reformed their minds and changed their ideas. Why is that you alone are so difficult to reform?

Mou-tzu said: When light feathers on a high place encounter the wind, they blow away. When small pebbles in a valley meet a stream, they roll away. But Mount T'ai is not moved by a whirlwind and a great boulder is not budged by raging torrents. Plum trees lose their leaves at the first frost; only pines and cedars resist withering. The adherents of the Way whom you met were not immersed in learning nor had they depth of insight, so they sub-

mitted and withdrew. But you cannot exhaust me, dense as I am! How [helpless you would be] with one who truly understood the Way! You cannot reform yourself, and yet you would reform others! I have never heard that Chung-ni [i.e., Confucius] followed the Robber Chih or that T'ang and Wu modeled themselves on Chieh or Chou.

Source Codes

Our knowledge of Buddhism in Khotan is rather meager. The first direct literary description is given by Tao An (312–85), who tells us in his preface to the *Tao-hsing po-jo ching* (a partial translation of the *Pañcaviṃśatisāhasrikāprajñāpāramitāsūtra*) that the monk Chu Shih-hsing went as a pilgrim to Khotan to obtain a better copy of that scripture. When he arrived there and made known his desire, the Khotanese Hīnayāna monks appealed to the king to prevent the spread of such a Mahāyāna text as the *Prajñāpāramitāsūtra*. The king relented only when Chu Shih-hsing demonstrated the indestructibility of Mahāyāna doctrine by throwing his copy of that scripture into a fire and witnessing its incombustibility. The text was brought to Lo-yang, where in 291 "the original was taken into hand by the Khotanese śramaṇa Wu-ch'a-lo, while the upasāka Chu Shu-lan rendered it into Chinese script."[405] When Fa Hsien traveled there in 401, Khotan had become a Mahāyāna center, and he describes a splendid, citywide ceremony honoring the Buddha's birthday.[406]

Yet Chinese awareness of Khotan is apparent much earlier than this. In 220, the year of the accession of Emperor Wen to the Wei throne, an ambassador from Khotan came to the Chinese court, where he received a kindly welcome, and relationships with Central Asia once more opened after the chaos that marked the warfare during the last years of the Later Han. At this time, the Buddhism of Khotan was still of the Hīnayāna variety.

Mou-tzu's reference to pines and cedars alludes to the *Analects*: "The Master said, 'Only when the cold season comes is the point brought home that the pine and the cypress [i.e., perhaps cedar is better] are the last to lose their leaves.'"[407]

Chih is a famous bandit often mentioned in the *Chuang Tzu*, especially in chapter 29, which has a dialogue between Confucius and Robber Chih. Chieh and Chou were the tyrant rulers at the ends of the Hsia and the Yin dynasties, who respectively lost the mandate to the virtuous founders of the Yin and Chou dynasties, that is, to T'ang and Wu.

Reader-Response Criticism

This article has been central to the dating of the *Li-huo lun*, for it seems to presuppose Chu Shih-hsing's trip to Khotan and thus would date some years after knowledge of Khotan had become current—that is, sometime after 291 when the Prajñā-pāramitā text he brought back was translated. Yet "although Khotanese Buddhism was made famous by him, no doubt reports about Khotan were not unknown before Chu Shih-hsing."[408] From a Reader-Response perspective, however, another interpretation is perhaps preferable.

The critic's objection is a bit strange. He not only claims that the monks of Khotan were unable to face him in dialogue, but that many of them "reformed their minds and changed their ideas." That would apparently mean that these foreign practitioners of Buddhism were converted to the Chinese traditions Mou-tzu's critic represents, a most unlikely event for the author of the *Li-huo lun* to report. There is an account about the arrival of a Khotanese ambassador to the court of Emperor Wen in 220, after which that Emperor proclaimed: "The Western barbarian kings who have come, in admiration of Kingly Transformation, from the Ti and the Ch'iang praise the Odes and Documents of the Sages as things of beauty. Treat kindly the outer barbarians of the Western Regions who came a while ago to present themselves to the inner court!"[409] That is believable, for it relates to political sensitivities and expediencies. Yet it attests only that the Khotanese appreciated the Chinese classics, not that they were reformed by them. By contrast, in the rhetorical context of the *Li-huo lun*, the critic's report of a non-Chinese acceptance of Chinese cultural hegemony by fledgling Buddhist monks in Khotan lacks historical plausibility.

The underlying point of this dialogue seems to be the denigration of the monks of Khotan. Mou-tzu says only that his critic met with uninformed and inexperienced monks in Khotan, as if there were no intelligent monks to be found there. Such a caricature is understandable only if the Khotanese monks encountered by the critic are not historical persons, but literary characters who have a symbolic value for the intended audience. The *Li-huo lun* seems to evince a particularly low esteem for the "monks of Khotan."

It is significant that this article is sandwiched between articles that form a broader discussion of the *hsien* practices associated with Taoist adepts. The preceding Articles 28 through 34 treat the theme, and it is continued immediately hereafter in Articles 36 and 37. It is better, then, to see Article 35 as an organic part of this broader argumentation than to see it as an independent source for historical judgments on the actual state of Khotanese Buddhism. The "monks" in this article are better seen as ciphers for *hsien* Buddhists nearer home, practitioners of Taoist methods for obtaining numinous powers and long life. They are unlearned and lacking in insight. These Khotanese monks represent Buddhist practitioners in China—naturalized Chinese monks who practiced and preached a *hsien* version of the Buddha Tao.

There are many indications that early Chinese Buddhists, many of whom were themselves naturalized Chinese from the western regions, indeed understood Buddhism as a *hsien* practice. The critic's objections from Articles 28 through 37 presuppose that the intended readers of the *Li-huo lun* in fact conflated Buddhism with such practices. At precisely the same time as Buddhism was first being enculturated in China, Lao-tzu himself was regarded as a *hsien* and sacrifices were made to him at court in the year 166. There was in the minds of cultured Chinese a broad overlap between Buddhism and the cult of superhuman immortals. From the middle of the second century C.E., there was an upsurge in the use of magic spells for the healing of illness and elixirs for the achievement of immortality. Indeed, for many, Buddhism was received and enculturated precisely through such beliefs and practices.[410] The first Buddhist missionaries, foreign in origin and weak in Chinese culture, did resort to presenting the Buddha in terms such as these. Mou-tzu, however, rejects *hsien* practice altogether, aligning himself with such Han scholars as Yang Hsiung and Wang Ch'ung, and regarding all claims of *hsien* Buddhism as untrue bragging. So the criticism of the monks of Khotan in this article serves not to provide information about that distant land or its understanding of Buddhism, but to reject the foreign-born or recently naturalized monks in China, for it is they—by their equation of the Buddha with a *hsien*—who lack depth of insight and are unable to stand up to an orthodox critique.

ARTICLE 36.
TAOIST PRACTICES OF TRANQUILLITY

A critic asked: The method of the spirit immortals is to fast in autumn and winter, or to enter the chamber and stay many weeks without coming out.[411] *They call this "the perfection of tranquillity." I think it is to be respected and valued. Why doesn't the Buddha Tao conform to this?*

Mou-tzu said: You point south and say it is north, yet you are not confused? You take the west to be east, yet you are not myopic? Together with the owl you ridicule the phoenix! You clutch the cricket and the earthworm, but make fun[412] *of the tortoise and the dragon! The gentleman does not value the cicada's lack of fasting. The frog and the boa constrictor lurk in hidden places, but the sage doesn't consider that so important. Confucius said, "Among the species in heaven or on earth, I regard humans as precious."*[413] *I have never heard that he respected frogs or boa constrictors. Yet among men of this age there are certainly some who chew calamus and reject cinnamon and ginger, who refuse sweet tastes and sip vinegar juice.*[414] *A filament of hair, although small, can be seen if one looks closely. But the immensity of Mount T'ai cannot be seen if one looks in the opposite direction! The will may or may not be restrained; the mind may or may not be sharp. [The State of] Lu respected the Chi clan and disregarded Chung-ni [Confucius]. [The State of] Wu thought Chief Minister P'i to be illustrious and slighted [Wu] Tzu-hsü. Are not your doubts just what one would expect of you?*

Source Codes

The *hsien* practices that the critic mentions include "entering the chamber and staying many weeks without coming out." To enter into the chamber (*ju shih* 入室) might refer simply to retiring into an inner room to study the deep meaning of things; that is, it might be a spatial metaphor for an inner realm of meaning, as in the *Analects*, where Confucius says that "Yu may not have entered the inner room (*ju yü shih* 入於室), but he has ascended the hall."[415] That, however, hardly seems a *hsien* practice. Perhaps when the critic talks about entering the chamber for "many weeks," he is cryptically referring to sexual relationships between man and woman,[416] for that practice, too, continued for several weeks (i.e., several tens of days). The arts of the bedchamber (*fang shu* 房術) were prized by Taoist practitioners as a method of increasing the yang forces, and this was at times accompanied by fasting.[417]

Mou-tzu's reference to the owl and the phoenix alludes to the

Chuang Tzu: "When Hui Tzu was prime minister of Liang, Chuang Tzu set off to visit him. Someone said to Hui Tzu, 'Chuang Tzu is coming because he wants to replace you as prime minister!' With this Hui Tzu was filled with alarm and searched all over the state for three days and three nights, trying to find Chuang Tzu. Chuang Tzu then came to see him and said, 'In the south there is a bird called the Yüan-ch'u, I wonder if you've ever heard it? The Yüan-ch'u rises up from the South Sea and flies to the North Sea, and it will rest on nothing but the Wu-t'ung tree, eat nothing but the fruit of the Lien, and drink only from springs of sweet water. Once there was an owl who had gotten hold of a half-rotten old rat, and as the Yüan-ch'u passed by, it raised its head, looked at the Yüan-ch'u, and said, "Shoo!" Now that you have this Liang state of yours, are you trying to shoo me?' "[418]

The reference to worms and cicadas perhaps alludes to a passage from the *Huai-nan Tzu:* "The worm feeds from bristle and does not drink and in twenty-two days, it is transformed. The cicada drinks but does not eat and in thirty days, it sheds its skin. The ant neither eats nor drinks, and in three days it dies."[419]

The reference to those who chew calamus and sip vinegar broth perhaps alludes to Taoist *hsien* practitioners attempting to gain immortality through diet.

The state of Lu was Confucius's state, yet it did not recognize his worth. The *Analects* mention the Chi clan: "Confucius said of the Chi family, 'They use eight rows of eight dancers each [i.e., a prerogative of the Emperor] to perform in their courtyard. If this can be tolerated, what cannot be tolerated?'"[420] Confucius criticized the Chi, one of the noble houses of Lu, yet they received respect and honor from the state, while Confucius himself was ignored.

Wu Tzu-hsü was an aged servant of King Fu Ch'ai, who lost favor and was encouraged to commit suicide in 484 B.C.E. His body was cooked in a caldron, sewed into a sack, and thrown into the river. Stories grew that this restless spirit roiled the waves and drowned the inattentive, stories refuted by Wang Ch'ung in his *Lun Heng.* Wu Tzu-hsü was replaced by Po P'i in the esteem of the king, but, alas, Po P'i led the king to defeat and the land to ruin.[421]

The last phrase of Mou-tzu's reply about expected doubts is drawn from the *Analects*, where it ironically expresses dismay that anyone would regard Tzu-kung as superior to Confucius.[422]

Reader-Response Criticism

Here the critic attempts to harmonize the Buddhist Tao with *hsien* practices of fasting and seclusion in the chamber. Mou-tzu rejects them out of hand, citing example after example of just how the sages never devoted themselves to such dieting or withdrawal. His argument is simply a heaping of ridicule on such practices, which he never bothers to identify. That is understandable if indeed the reference is to sexual practices that are deemed to prolong life. That would contextualize his reference to the restraining of the will, and perhaps to the dark and musty haunts of frogs and boa constrictors. Yet the practices to which he refers are so deeply coded that it is difficult to ascertain just what is really being discussed.

ARTICLE 37.
MUST ONE DIE?

A critic asked: The Taoist practitioners say that Yao, Shun, the Duke of Chou, and Confucius, together with his seventy-two disciples, did not die, but became immortals. You Buddhists say that all must die, that nobody can escape. What about this?

———————

Mou-tzu said: These bewitching and wild words are not the speech of sages. Lao-tzu said, "Heaven and earth do not go on forever, much less can man."[423] *Confucius said, "The worthy leaves the world, but benevolence and filial piety remain." I have inspected the six arts and examined the commentaries and the records. Yao perished. Shun is buried at Mount Ts'ang-wu. Yü has his grave on Mount Kuei-chi. Po Yi and Shu Ch'i have their tombs on Mount Shou-yang. King Wen had not yet put an end to [the tyrant Chou] when he died. King Wu passed away before he was able to see Ch'eng reach adulthood. There are accounts that before they died, the Duke of Chou changed burial [customs] and Confucius had a dream about two pillars. Po Yü died before his father. Tzu-lu is said to have been chopped up and pickled. When Po Niu died it was said, "It must be Destiny! It must be Destiny!" There is the report that Tseng Ts'an uncovered his feet. A saying is recorded of Yen Yüan that, "Unfortunately, his allotted span was a short one," and a metaphor that "there are young plants that fail to produce blossoms." These things are all written in the classics and are the august words of the sages. I take these classics and commentaries as my evidence and rely on the experience of everyday people as my proof. Isn't it foolish to say that they did not die!*

Source Codes

The first part of Mou-tzu's citation from Confucius is found in the *Analects*, but with the sense of shunning the world, not dying: "The Master said, 'Men who shun the world come first; those who shun a particular place come next; those who shun a hostile look come next; those who shun hostile words come last.'"[424]

Mou-tzu refers to the six arts of a gentleman enumerated by Liu Hsin: rites, music, archery, chariot driving, writing, and mathematics, as well as to the classical texts that treat them.[425]

Mou-tzu presents a catena of classical passages reporting the deaths of sages and rulers. In stating that Yao died, Mou-tzu makes reference to a phrase from the *Documents*: "After twenty-eight years the Emperor [met his] demise [*tsu lo* 殂落], when the people mourned for him as for a parent for three years."[426] *The Record of Rites* and *The Records of the Grand Historian* both mention the tradition that Emperor Shun was buried in the solitude of Ts'ang-wu. *The Record of Rites* reports: "Shun was buried in the wilderness of Ts'ang-wu."[427] *The Records of the Grand Historian* report that Yü was buried on Mount Kuei-chi, as does the *Mo-tzu*: "Yü went east to instruct the nine tribes of Yi. He died on the way and was buried at Mt. Kuei Chi."[428] The *Huai-nan Tzu*, arguing that customs must fit circumstances, cites the case where "long ago when [the Emperor] Shun was buried in Ts'ang-wu, the marketers did not have to change [the location of] their displays. When [the Emperor] Yü was buried in the mountain of Kuei-chi, the farmers did not have to alter [the location of] their plots. They were enlightened in the distinction between the dead and the living, and they understood the suitable [times] for dissoluteness and frugality."[429] Po Yi and Shu Ch'i are the sages discussed in the source codes for Article 10. The *Records* also report that King Wen was imprisoned by Chou, the tyrant and last ruler of the Yin dynasty, and received the title of king only posthumously. King Wu was the son of King Wen and the father of King Ch'eng, but he died while Ch'eng was still young, and the new Chou dynasty prospered only through the services of the Duke of Chou. *The Record of Rites* reports that the burial customs changed after the Duke of Chou. Mou-tzu's report might, however, refer to the change in the actual burial location of the Duke of Chou, who wanted to be buried at Ch'eng-chou to be near to his nephew, King Ch'eng. Yet King Ch'eng had him buried at Pi together with King Wen.[430]

Confucius's dream is found in *The Record of Rites*, which reports that one day Confucius said to his disciple Tzu-kung, "'The people of

Yin performed the same [burial] ceremony between the two pillars, so that the steps for the host were on one side of the corpse, and those for the guest on the other. I am a man (descended from the house) of Yin, and last night I dreamt I was sitting with the offerings to the dead by my side between the two pillars. Intelligent kings do not arise; and what one under heaven is able to take me as his Master? I apprehend I am about to die.' With this he took to his bed, was ill for seven days, and died."[431]

The *Documents* reports that Po Yü, the son of Confucius, is reported by *The Records of the Grand Historian* to have died before his father.[432]

In the *Analects* Tzu-lu is characterized as a man of great resolve but poor judgment. He is both praised and criticized by Confucius, and seems to have been more of a close friend than merely a disciple. The *Analects* presents the relevant passage: "When in attendance on the Master, Min Tzu looked respectful and upright; Tzu-lu looked unbending; Jan Yu and Tzu-kung looked affable. The master was happy. A man like Yu will not die a natural death."[433] But the reference seems to be to Jan Yu, not to Tzu-lu. D. C. Lau thinks that the last sentence has been misplaced from some other context. In fact Tzu-lu died fighting for his lord in 480 B.C.E.[434] The account is reported in the *Tso Chuan*, describing how Tzu-lu refused to abandon his lord who had supported him, reentered the city, now occupied by rebels, and was struck down by their spears "cutting also the strings of his cap," a fact cited by Mou-tzu in Article 11.[435] He is reported in *The Record of Rites* to have been "chopped up and pickled."[436]

The account of Po Niu is given in the *Analects*: "Po-niu was ill. The Master visited him and, holding his hand through the window, said, 'We are going to lose him. It must be Destiny! Why else should a man be stricken with such a disease? Why else should a man be stricken with such a disease?'"[437]

On Tseng Ts'an (Tseng Tzu), the *Analects* say: "When he was seriously ill, Tseng Tzu summoned his disciples and said, 'Take a look at my hands. Take a look at my feet. The Odes say, "In fear and trembling, as if approaching a deep abyss, as if walking on thin ice." Only now am I spared, my young friends.'"[438]

On Yen Yüan, Mou-tzu cites two passages from the *Analects*: "When Duke Ai asked which of his disciples was eager to learn, Confucius answered, 'There was Yen Hui who was eager to learn. He did not vent his anger upon an innocent person, nor did he make the same mistake twice. Unfortunately his allotted span was a short one and he died. Now there is no one. No one eager to learn has come to my notice.'"[439] Again it reports Confucius saying, "'There are, are there not, young plants that fail to produce blossoms, and blossoms that fail to produce fruit?'"[440]

A similar listing of dead sages is given by Yang Hsiung in his *Model*

Sayings: "Alas, I have heard that Fu Hsi and Shen Nung died, that the Yellow Emperor, Yao and Shun dwell with their ancestors and are dead, King Wen came to an end, Confucius lies alone north of the walls of Lu. Did these masters want to die? [Immortality] is simply beyond the reach of humans. The immortals are also to no avail, they are the same as you."[441]

Reader-Response Criticism

Mou-tzu again dons the mantle of the orthodox Chinese scholar to negate the wild talk of the *hsien* practitioners. He doesn't even mention Buddhist scriptures or notions to argue that all must die. It is enough for him to ground himself in the classics and their commentaries, for the implied reader, if he has been following, has already recognized Mou-tzu not as a strange and alien person but as a scholar grounded in Chinese culture and its normative traditions, despite the fact that he now also belongs to the community of the Buddha Tao.

The argument, however, is rather disingenuous, for the Taoist practitioners of *hsien* methods did not deny apparent physical death. There are numerous accounts of Taoist adepts who appeared to have died but in fact transformed themselves into immortals. *The Records of the Grand Historian* reports that Li Shao-chün expounded to Emperor Ching (ca. 140 B.C.E.) dietary methods for achieving immortality, and that when Li himself died, "the emperor, however, believed that he was not really dead but had transformed himself into a spirit."[442] It also reports that the Yellow Emperor himself had become an immortal *hsien*.[443] When Ch'in Shih Huang Ti journeyed to Mount Chao to offer sacrifices at the tomb of Huang Ti, he asked how Huang Ti could be an immortal if indeed he had a tomb. He was then informed that he had risen to Heaven as an immortal *hsien*, leaving behind only his garments and cap to be interred.[444] Max Kaltenmark explains that "'Ascended to Heaven at the height of the day' was ... the stock formula to describe the final apotheosis of a Taoist who had succeeded in transubstantiating his physical being. True, some departed more discreetly; they seemed to die like ordinary mortals but their death was merely apparent, for if the coffin was opened after a lapse of time the body had disappeared and been replaced by the dead man's staff, sword, or sandals."[445] Such "resurrection" stories were not confined to Taoist adepts, for there are accounts of Buddhists who also managed somehow to avoid the finality of death. For example, *The Record of Mysterious Good Fortune* gives an account of Sun Tsun, an official under the Tsin, who had a beloved son, Chih, a true follower of the Buddha Tao. He died at age eighteen, and his parents were so distraught that they moved to Wu-ch'ang, where during a Buddhist *hsing hsiang* ceremony (carrying the image of the Buddha through the city on his birthday), they saw to their amazement their deceased son Chih in the entourage of a float led by the monk Yü Fa-k'ai.[446] There is another story told of Fo-t'u-ch'eng, the great Buddhist missionary and wonder-worker, that when Generalissimo Jan Min of the Later Chao opened Fo-t'u-ch'eng's tomb, he found nothing but an alms bowl and a staff but no corpse, and that someone saw Fo walking through the desert in the very month after he had died.[447]

The implied author cannot have been unaware of these beliefs, for he has his character Mou-tzu study for some three years under Taoist adepts. The critic, as usual unresponsive to Mou-tzu's arguments, offers no objection to the catena of classical sources on the death of the sages and worthies. But the implied reader soon catches the point that Mou-tzu rejects such preternatural happenings. He echoes Yang Hsiung, quoted in the source codes above, and Wang Ch'ung, who wrote: "The Grand Annalist in his eulogy on the Five Emperors also says that, having performed the hill-sacrifice, Huang Ti disappeared as a genius [i.e., an immortal *hsien*], and that his followers paid their respects to his garments and cap and afterwards buried them. I say that this is not true."[448] The implied reader is to accept the critical thought of such orthodox thinkers as Yang Hsiung and Wang Ch'ung that all people do in fact die, but then of course he may interpret it through the Buddhist notion of transmigration, as outlined in Article 12.

POSTSCRIPT.
THE THIRTY-SEVEN FACTORS

A critic asked: Your understanding is truly comprehensive, and assuredly we have never heard the like. But why do you limit yourself to these thirty-seven articles? Do you have a model?

Mou-tzu said: Tumbleweeds drifted about and cartwheels were invented. Hollow wood floated and boats and oars were made. A spider spun his web and fine nets were woven. Bird prints were seen and written words were devised. Thus it is easy to complete a task with a model but difficult to do so without one. I have examined how the essence of the Buddha's scriptures have thirty-seven factors of awakening and how Lao-tzu's classic on the Tao also has thirty-seven chapters. These are my models.

When the doubters heard this, they became nervously deferential, paled, clasped their hands together, and backed away from their mats. Shrinking back in humility and prostrating themselves, they said, "We are really backward and blind persons, born into a benighted backwater. We have presumed to utter foolish words and have not distinguished happiness from sorrow. But now, upon hearing your pronouncements, as suddenly as hot water melts the snow, we beg to change our feelings, cleanse our minds, and reform ourselves. May we please receive the five precepts and become lay followers?

Source Codes

The thirty-seven factors of enlightenment are a classic Mahāyāna teaching, found most prominently in the *Bodhisattvabhūmi*. They were stressed by the early Buddhist teaching of the Parthian An Shih-kao, who arrived in Lo-yang around 148, as essential for the overcoming of primal ignorance.[449] Mou-tzu aligns his articles not only with those factors but also with the thirty-seven chapters of book 1 of the *Lao Tzu*.

Mou-tzu's initial response seems to allude to the *Lun Heng*: "The observation of the foot-prints of birds gave rise to the invention of writing, and the aspect of creeping plants flying about led to the construction of carts."[450] The *Huai-nan Tzu* has a similar report: "[People] observed how wood floated and knew how to make boats. They saw tumbleweeds and knew how to make carts. They saw the prints of birds and knew how to write books."[451]

Reader-Response Criticism

In this Postscript Mou-tzu explains the rhetorical structure of his apologetic, almost as if to emphasize that one should not think that it represents any actual dialogue that ever took place. He reveals that it is crafted on literary models: the thirty-seven factors of Buddhist awakening, and the thirty-seven chapters of the first part of Lao-tzu's classic.

The final conversion scene of the critics is clearly a stage direction for how the implied author wishes his implied readers to respond. It appears to be modeled on the conclusion of many a Mahāyāna scripture, where the listeners all are converted on the spot, and not to represent an actual acceptance of the precepts. Indeed, can one imagine that the layman Mou-tzu, despite his ardent faith in Buddha, did in fact take over the role of a monk and administer the five precepts?[452] But if the readers of the *Li-huo lun* have been following, they can now conclude that Buddhism is not really so very alien. They themselves can seek to become lay followers, convinced by now that Buddhism presents a better option for practicing the Tao and *wu-wei*.

In this final paragraph, the narrator/character Mou-tzu falls silent, and the voice of the implied author of our text speaks through his suddenly overt narrator directly to his implied readers.

A Reader-Response interpretation of the *Mou-tzu Li-huo lun* urges upon the critical reader an awareness that the text is engaged in a hermeneutical argument over the interpretation of the classical Chinese literature. The author is not writing an apologetic for Buddhist doctrinal teachings.

It further clarifies the process whereby literate Chinese adapted Buddhist ideas to their cultural milieu. The initially alien Indian religion became enculturated in China through a consciously adopted rhetoric of assimilating the Dharma teachings, whenever possible, to the established patterns of classical learning. Therefore, early Chinese understandings of Buddhism are not simply Chinese misunderstandings of Indian ideas, but conscious cultural adaptations of Indian ideas.

The dialogue of the *Mou-tzu Li-huo lun* is always aimed at an implied reader versed in the Chinese classics, urging him to entertain and embrace a Buddhist reading of his own tradition.

Notes to Articles

1. See Dubs, "The Victory of Han Confucianism." But see Peerenboom, *Law and Morality*, 84–85, 176–78, on the differences between Lao-tzu and Huang-Lao thought, as presented in the Silk Manuscripts from Ma-wang-tui.

2. Tsukamoto, *Early Chinese Buddhism*, 33–35, describes the debilitating internal turmoil of the court, beset with emperors who acceded to the throne while still boys, ruled by the competing forces of the Empress Dowager, her relatives, and the eunuchs. Such a divided court was unable to address the major changes in Han society, the development of commercial capital, the transformation of the bureaucracy into a hereditary power elite, the deepening poverty of an increasingly landless and marginalized underclass scarcely distinguishable from agricultural slaves. "It was in this society that Chang Chüeh, preaching the religious faith contained in such writings as *The Book of Pure Acceptance of Grand Tranquillity*, gained the hearts of the uneducated peasantry and welded their dissatisfaction into a weapon to be wielded by warriors intent on overthrowing a government, pushing the Latter Han into the abyss of destruction not long after 220."

3. But see Michaud, "The Yellow Turbans," 81–97, who argues against describing the Yellow Turbans as Taoists. "It seems impossible," he says at p. 92, "to determine what the religion of the Yellow Turbans was."

4. According to Yang Hsien-feng, Tung Chung-shu was in fact a representative of the conservative landlord class, writing in reaction to the peasant uprisings of the previous Ch'in period. See Pokora, "Notes on

New Studies of Tung Chung-shu," 265–66. It is ironic then that Tung's philosophical ideas of cyclical movements of the world, both cosmic and human, were reduced to slogans by the Yellow Turbans.

5. Tsukamoto, *Early Chinese Buddhism*, 115–16.

6. Ibid., 116.

7. Ibid., 73.

8. Ibid., 74.

9. Maspero, "Le songe et l'ambassade de l'empereur Ming," 102–5.

10. See Michaud, "The Yellow Turbans," for a detailed account of the countervailing forces that led to the demise of the Han dynasty.

11. Link, "Cheng-wu lun," 160.

12. de Crespigny's description of the military campaigns at the end of the Han and into the subsequent state of Wu makes no mention of Chiao-chih, for all the activity was situated to the north. See "The Military Geography of the Yangtse and the Early History of the Three Kingdoms State of Wu." Michaud, "The Yellow Turbans," 57–58, observes that Chiao-chou witnessed only a few barbarian outbreaks during the Later Han.

13. Loewe, *Military Operations in the Han Period*, 3. Also see Loewe, *Records of Han Administration*, 1:49–50: "Between 112 and 108 B.C. Chinese forces were deployed in establishing colonial settlements and official outposts in the north-east, south-west and south-east, with the subsequent foundation of some fourteen commanderies which lay at a considerable distance from the centre of government." These included the commanderies of Chiao-chih and Ts'ang-wu, mentioned in the *Li-huo lun*.

14. *Hou Han shu*, 116:9a; 118:4b.

15. *Liang shu*, T'ung-wen ed., 54:17a.

16. Yü, *Trade and Expansion in Han China*, 175–78. See also Tsukamoto, *Early Chinese Buddhism*, 142, on the movement of Buddhism into China both from the north and from the south, from the Chiao-chou area.

17. Fukui, "Dōkyō no kisoteki kenkyū," 368–70.

18. Tsukamoto, *Early Chinese Buddhism*, 191, writes: "As is widely known, Chiao-chih at the time, though at the southernmost tip of territory that was politically Chinese, had become a haven of refuge for

scholars fleeing the Middle Plain toward the end of the Han, in addition
to flourishing as the center of the southern trade route. It was the point
of arrival for Buddhism too, i.e., for that Buddhism that came over the
sea without passing over the Central Asian Silk Route. *The Treatise on
the Removal of Doubt*, ascribed to Mou-tzu, if one may take it to be a
work produced in this area during the late Han or early Wu, leads one
to suppose that the said area was one in which Buddhism, still a foreign
religion, became so intermingled with the indigenous Confucianism,
Lao-Chuang study, and recipes for 'supernatural sylphhood' that it was
presumably impossible to know which was which." Yet the *Li-huo lun*
itself clearly rejects sylphic practices and has no trouble distinguishing
the classical Confucian texts from the deeper Buddhist scriptures, which
it conflates only with its version of the *Lao Tzu*.

19. Zürcher, *The Buddhist Conquest of China*, 13, quoting Yü
Chia-hsi.

20. Following the interpretation of *huo* given by Cua, *Ethical Argumentation*, 146: "Erroneous beliefs are the products of *pi* [蔽, obscura-
tions]. Men who are beset by *pi* may be said to be in the state of *huo*
[惑]. *Huo* refers to *cognitive delusion*, that is, to erroneous beliefs tena-
ciously held by persons without critical examination. A victim of *huo*
may also be said to be a self-deceiver. It is *huo* that is likely to generate
perplexities when a person is unaware that he is in that state. A person
who lives with his prejudices, for instance, may be puzzled when others
hold different beliefs."

21. Cited from Chan, *Two Visions of the Way*, 91.

22. Maspero translates the phrase *i-jen* 異人 as "strangers" in his
"Le songe et l'ambassade de l'empereur Ming," 99, while Pelliot, "Meou-
tseu," 287, renders it as "le gens remarquables," arguing that it means
exceptional people. This harmonizes with Hu Shih's examination of a
number of Chinese scholars reported in the *Wu Chih* to have fled the
chaos of the times to Chiao-chou, for which see Fukui, "Dōkyō no kisoteki kenkyū," 368. Makita, *Gumyōshū kenkyū*, 5, reads it as "Taoist
practitioners," that is, those otherworldly people intent upon *hsien* practices mentioned in the very next sentence.

23. One of the seven commanderies of Chiao-chou, the province of
Chiao. See Künstler, "Activité culturelle et politique," 13 n. 18, where he
notes that of the biographies cointained in the *Hou Han shu*, only 0.2
percent treat persons from Chiao-chou.

24. I follow Dubs and de Crespigny for the translation of official
titles. See de Crespigny, "An Outline of the Local Administration for
the Later Han Empire," 67–68.

25. The phrase *chuan-tui* (專對) alludes to the *Analects* 13.5: "The Master said, 'If a man who knows the three hundred *Odes* by heart fails when given administrative responsibilities and proves incapable of exercising his own initiative (*chuan-tui*) when sent to foreign states, then what use are the *Odes* to him, however many he may have learned?'" (Lau, *Analects* 119).

26. The *Han shu*, 3190, says: "If a horse be not cared for and tamed, then he cannot be taken for a gallop on the road. If a gentleman of the Way be not provided for, then he cannot be of value for the Empire." Note that when criticized for his extravagence, Mencius (3.B.3) replied that since a worthy scholar contributes to society, he deserves to be fed. His critic P'eng Keng "questions whether the *youshi*—and here he has in mind particularly those who do not take office—really do make any contribution to society in return for the goods they consume: 'it is not right for a *shi* to take no part in affairs and yet to be fed.'" (Vervoorn, "The Origins of Chinese Eremitism," 272).

27. Lau, *Lao Tzu: Tao Te Ching*, 75 (19).

28. Maspero, "Le songe et l'ambassade de l'empereur Ming," 102.4, notes that these exact phrases occur in the commentary to the *Tao Te Ching* of Ho-shang Kung, which is generally considered to be a T'ang dynasty work. Maspero thinks the reference shows that Ho-shang Kung's commentary is much earlier. Pelliot, "Meou-tseu," 334.22, thinks Mou-tzu had another source that lies behind both his text and Ho-shang Kung's commentary. Fukui, "Dōkyō no kisoteki kenkyū," 395, mentions a passage from the *Chuang Tzu*: "A gentleman will not befriend the man who possesses them (i.e., the eight faults), an enlightened ruler will not have him for a minister" (Watson, *Complete Works of Chuang Tzu*, 347). But, Fukui continues, the exact phrase is found in the *Wei chih*, chapter 11, the biography of Kuan Ning. He concludes that the sentence is a stock phrase for a high gentleman. Tsukamoto, *Early Chinese Buddhism*, 171, notes similar phrases from the *I Ching*, under the hexagram *ku*: "Serving neither kings nor princes, he keeps his own affairs sublime," and from *The Record of Rites*: "Among scholars are some who neither subordinate themselves to the Son of Heaven nor serve the feudatories below."

29. The Chinese does not specify the subject of the last sentence. It can as well be translated: "I entitle [it] The Sayings of Mou-tzu on Removing Doubt." The *I* in such a case would be the narrator of the Preface.

30. Lau, *Mencius*, 114.

31. One may note that here there is indeed a sharp division between philosophical Taoism and *hsien* Taoism, despite more recent attempts to blur the distinction.

32. de Crespigny, "The Recruitment System of the Imperial Bureau-cracy of Later Han," 69, writes: "Many *hsiao-lien* [Filially Pious and In-corrupt persons] had served as junior civil officers in local governments, and others were recommended on account of their scholarship, and some for their importance or remarkable conduct in their own communities." Again he remarks, p. 75: "From our earlier examination of the system of local government in the empire, we have seen that the staffing of the pre-fectural and commandery offices was largely in the hands of the members of the leading local families, and it is clear that the nominations for *hsiao-lien* were also dominated by these magnates."

33. For the respective administrative duties and roles of these officials, see de Crespigny, "An Outline," 57–66.

34. Pelliot, "Meou-tseu," 289–90, translates this as "Comme celle-ci faisait la sieste, elle rêva [de quelqu'un] monté sur un éléphant blanc dont le corps avait six défenses," explaining, 336.35, that to follow the grammar of our text and translate that she dreamed she was riding on the elephant runs counter to all the traditions. It seems to me that indeed the *Li-huo lun* has amalgamated the traditions to arrive at its unique reading.

35. The *T'ai-tzu jui-ying pen-ch'i ching* says that the prince with his right finger touches her stomach and tells her that in six years she will give birth to a son. See Pelliot, "Meou-tseu," 341.48.

36. Lau, *Lao Tzu: Tao Te Ching*, 78 (21).

37. Lau, *Confucius: The Analects*, 117 (12.22).

38. Maspero, "Le songe et l'ambassade de l'empereur Ming," 106. Fukui, "Dōkyō no kisoteki kenkyū," 361, concurs that the *Li-huo lun* must have been written after the *T'ai-tzu jui-ying pen-ch'i ching*.

39. Tsukamoto, *Early Chinese Buddhism*, 48.

40. Tsukamoto, *Early Chinese Buddhism*, 78. On the development of Huang-Lao thought, see Ishikawa, "Go-Han no bukkyō ni tsuite," *Shigaku* 18 (1939): 60–72, and the recent and authoritative study by Peeren-boom, *Law and Morality*.

41. Tsukamoto, *Early Chinese Buddhism*, 109. Wright, *Buddhism in Chinese History*, 24, writes that during the troubles at the waning years of the Latter Han dynasty, "many thinkers turned to the long ne-glected 'classics' of Taoism, the *Chuang-tzu* and the *Tao-Te Ching*, and it was this tradition of Chinese thought—used first to refine and reform Confucianism—that was to become dominant from about the year 250 onward."

42. K. Ch'en, "Neo-Taoism and the Prajñā School," 45, discusses Hsi Ch'ao's (336–77) treatment of *nirvāṇa* in his *Feng-fa yao*: "Here Ch'ao appeared to have read the Buddhist translations well. He described this state as one in which existence is forgotten, the operation of karma ceased, and rebirth discontinued. In nirvana one was troubled neither by being nor non-being, possessed intuitive understanding, and was not conditioned by anything. It was, as he put it, one immeasurable mysterious abandon, and he designated it by the Taoist term, *wu wei*."

43. Pelliot, "Meou-tseu," translates *t'i* 體 as "ses membres," which follows the classical distinction between *shen* 身 as body and *t'i* as limbs. Yet I think that here it makes little sense to speak of the Buddha separating his limbs. Rather, the point is that the Buddha's transformations enable him to appear in diverse realms in body and in person. The discussion seems to refer to the transformation body of Buddha (*nirmāṇakāya*), for which see Griffiths et al., *The Realm of Awakening*, 70–72, 240–43, 251–58.

44. Pokora, "Notes on New Studies on Tung Chung-shu," 261.

45. Watson, *Complete Works of Chuang Tzu*, 143 (5:12b–13a).

46. Zürcher, who dates the *Mou-tzu Li-huo lun* to the fourth or early fifth century, considers the *Cheng-wu lun* to be the earliest Chinese Buddhist treatise in existence. See *The Buddhist Conquest of China*, 14, 304.

47. Link, "Cheng-wu lun," 142.

48. *Hung-ming chi* (Ssu-pu pei-yao ed.), 3.10a.

49. Makita, *Gumyōshū kenkyū*, 13.3.

50. Watson, *Complete Works of Chuang Tzu*, 198.

51. Graham, *The Book of Lieh-tzu*, 34.

52. Kohn, *Early Chinese Mysticism*, 44. See also the classic work of Seidel, *La Divinisation de Lao Tseu dans le Taoisme des Han*.

53. Lau, *Confucius: The Analects*, 136–37 (15:35).

54. The phrase is from the *Chuang Tzu* (5.13b, Watson, *Complete Works of Chuang Tzu*, 143), where it says that the Perfect Teacher, Heaven, "carves and fashions the countless forms, but does not think himself skillful."

55. Keenan, "A Study of Chapter Four," 45–46.

56. *Hou Han chi* 10, in Tsukamoto, *Early Chinese Buddhism*, 41.

57. Morgan, *Tao: The Great Luminant*, 92. Pelliot, "Meou-tseu," 292, translates this "Il peut se diminuer ou se grandir, devenir round ou carré ...," which does not make much sense if predicated of Buddha.

58. *Huai-nan Tzu*, Ssu-pu pei-yao ed., 8:8a. Also see Allan, *The Shape of the Turtle*, 75.

59. My translation. Compare Watson, *Complete Works of Chuang Tzu*, 198, also note 143. This Teacher of mine (i.e., Heaven) is "he [who] carves and fashions the countless forms, but does not think himself skilled."

60. Lau, *Lao Tzu: Tao Te Ching*, 70 (14).

61. Keenan, "A Study of Chapter Four," 40–41.

62. Morgan, *Tao: The Great Luminant*, 4.

63. Kohn, *Early Chinese Mysticism*, 43.

64. *Hung-ming chi* (SPPY ed.), 3.9a.

65. *Fa-yen*, 4:6b; Keenan, "A Study of Chapter Four," 76.

66. Henricks, *Lao-tzu: Te-tao ching*, chap. 25, 236, explains the distinction between name (*ming* 名) and style (*tzu* 字) is that "made in ancient China between a man's name and his style. The 'name' is given at birth, is very formal and rarely used in public address; the 'style' is taken at 'capping' age, when a young man becomes an adult, and is commonly used in public address with friends who are on familiar terms."

67. Watson, *Complete Works of Chuang Tzu*, 262.

68. Hawkes, *Ch'u Tz'u: The Songs of the South*, 23.

69. Morohashi Tetsuji, *Dai Kanwa jiten* (Tokyo: Taishūkan, 1957–60), 1:257.550 and 257.872.

70. Lau, *Mencius*, 77 (2.A.2). Whalen Lai in private conversation and correspondence has said that he thinks that this citation of *Mencius* by the *Li-huo lun* may be particularly significant, in that it was overlooked by Han scholars only to become central in the Sung. If that is the case, then perhaps the *Li-huo lun* is to be credited with discovering it. Also see Riegel, "Reflections on an Unmoved Mind," 434–49.

71. See Chan, "Philosophical Hermeneutics," 425–33, who argues in a Gadamerian framework that the notion of tradition in the *Analects* is not a static set of norms valid for all occasions, but the "unifying ground of Confucius' ethico-spiritual vision" (430).

72. See Balazs, "Entre révolte nihiliste et évasion mystique."

73. The *Hou Han shu*, chapter 65, in the commentary to the biography of Chang Shun, identifies these as *The Classic of Poetry*, *The Classic of History*, *The Record of Rites*, *The Record of Music*, *The Classic of Changes*, *The Spring and Autumn Annals*, and the *Analects*. See Makita, *Gumyōshū kenkyū*, 17.1.

74. Reading *ch'i-chi* (騏驥), in accord with Makita's *Gumyōshū kenkyū* critical text, not *ch'i-lin*, as in the SPPY edition. *Ch'i-chi* is one of the legendary horses of Mu Wang and is reported to have been capable of a thousand li a day. The reading of *ch'i-lin* was perhaps influenced by the allusion to the *Mencius* that is cited in the source codes.

75. Wright, *Studies in Chinese Buddhism*, 8; *Buddhism in Chinese History*, 33–34.

76. Shih, *The Literary Mind*, 223.

77. Makita, *Gumyōshū kenkyū*, 17.2.

78. Legge, *Sacred Books of the East*, 28:464.

79. Legge, *The Chinese Classics*, 2:195–96. See Lau, *Mencius*, 80 (2.A.3).

80. Morohashi, 10:37481.33.

81. Graham, *The Book of Lieh-tzu*, 152.

82. *Huai-nan Tzu* (Ssu-pu pei-yao), 6:10a.8.

83. *Lieh Tzu*, Ssu-pu pei-yao ed., 1:3a–b. Forke, *Lun Heng*, 15. See also Graham, *The Book of Lieh-tzu*, 18–19.

84. Watson, *Complete Works of Chuang Tzu*, 32.

85. Knoblock, *Xunzi*, 222–23.

86. Lewis Lancaster, "The Earliest Mahāyāna Sūtra," and Whalen Lai, "Before the Prajñā Schools," have identified an early Chinese Mahāyāna text that dates before the rise of Neo-Taoism, that is, sometime around 222–29. Yet the *Li-huo lun* shows no familiarity with any Mahāyāna notions at all, and apparently its author was not familiar with such teachings.

87. Watson, *Complete Works of Chuang Tzu*, 149.

88. *Fa-yen*, Ssu-pu pei-yao ed., 4:1a. For a translation, see Keenan, "A Study of Chapter Four," 38.

89. Lau, *Confucius: The Analects*, 64 (2:7–8).

90. *Fa-yen*, Ssu-pu pei-yao ed., 4:1a. See Keenan, "A Study of Chapter Four," 36–37.

91. *Ch'un-ch'iu Fan-lu* 5,3:10a. Quoted in Pokora, "Notes on New Studies on Tung Chung-shu," 264.

92. For example, see Watson, *Records of the Grand Historian*, 1:115–16: "When Kao-tsu was fighting against Ch'ing Pu, he was wounded by a stray arrow and on the way back he fell ill. When his illness continued to grow worse, Empress Lü sent for a skilled doctor. The doctor examined Kao-tsu and, in answer to his question, replied, 'This illness can be cured.' With this, Kao-tsu began to berate and curse him, saying, 'I began as a commoner and with my three-foot sword conquered the world. Was this not the will of Heaven? My fate lies with Heaven. Even P'ien Ch'üeh, the most famous doctor of antiquity, could do nothing for me!' In the end he would not let the doctor treat his illness, but gave him fifty catties of gold and sent him away." Also see Graham, *The Book of Lieh Tzu*, 106–7.

93. Link, "Cheng-wu lun," 155.

94. *Hsün Tzu*, Ssu-pu pei-yao ed., 19:2b.

95. Chavannes, *Les Mémoires historiques de Se-ma Ts'ien*, 1:222 and 4:34–40.

96. Lau, *Confucius: the Analects*, 156.

97. Legge, *Sacred Books of the East*, 27:339.

98. *Hou Han shu*, comment to the biography of Chang Shun. See Morohashi, 1:6.86.

99. *Fa-yen*, 2.3a, 5.3a, 7.2a.

100. For a table of classics, from three to fourteen, see Morohashi, 2:2695.146.

101. Following Makita, *Gumyōshū kenkyū*, 20.

102. See Makita, *Gumyōshū kenkyū*, 20.2, for citations from the *Po-hu t'ung*, the *Shih chi*, the *Huai-nan Tzu*, and the *Shen-hsien chüan*.

103. Forke, *Lun Heng*, 1:304.

104. Knoblock, *Xunzi*, 1:204.

105. For a discussion of Chinese physiognomy, see Knoblock, *Xunzi*, 1:196–203.

106. Lau, *Confucius: the Analects*, 92 (8:3).

107. Morgan, *Tao: the Great Luminant*, 162. Book 11 is devoted to the assertion that the proprieties must be appropriate to circumstances. See Wallacker, *The Huai-nan Tzu, Book Eleven*, 15–22.

108. Lau, *Confucius: the Analects*, 100 (9:30).

109. Chavannes, *Les Mémoires historiques de Se-ma Ts'ien*, 1:215–16, 4:1–2. Pelliot, "Meou-tseu," 363.143.

110. Lau, *Confucius: the Analects*, 92 (8:1).

111. Forke, *Lun Heng*, 1:358. The story is also found in Crump, *Intrigues*, 285–87.

112. Giles, *Biographical Dictionary*, n. 1565.

113. Legge, *The Chinese Classics*, 5:556. Pelliot, "Meou-tseu," 364.149.

114. See Pelliot, "Meou-tseu," 365.150.

115. Lau, *Lao Tzu: Tao Te Ching*, 105 (44).

116. Lau, *Mencius*, 127 (4.A.26).

117. Lau, *Confucius: The Analects*, 125 (14.11).

118. Lau, *Lao Tzu: Tao Te Ching*, 102 (41).

119. Watson, *Complete Works of Chuang Tzu*, 167–68. See Pelliot, "Meou-tseu," 366.160, for the equation of *t'ien-t'an* 恬惔 with *t'ien-tan* 恬澹.

120. Watson, *Complete Works of Chuang Tzu*, 313.

121. *Huai-nan Tzu*, 6:5b.8 (Ssu-pu pei-yao). Translation by Charles LeBlanc, *Huai-nan Tzu: Philosophical Synthesis in Early Han Thought*, 131, n. 65. See Makita, *Gumyōshū kenkyū*, 24.4.

122. Watson, *Complete Works of Chuang Tzu*, 32.

123. Pelliot, "Meou-tseu," 367.163.

124. Watson, *Complete Works of Chuang Tzu*, 322.

125. There are various versions of the story of Po Yi and Shu Ch'i, for which see Vervoorn, "Boyi and Shuqi: Worthy Men of Old?" Vervoorn disentangles these versions to adjudicate their historical authenticity. For the author of the *Li-huo lun*, they serve as unquestioned models of filial conduct and commitment to principle.

126. Lau, *Confucius: The Analects*, 87–88 (7.15). Also see 80 (5.23), 141 (16.12), and 151 (18.8).

127. Wallacker, *Huai-nan Tzu, Book Eleven*, 47. Also see Ssu-ma Ch'ien's biography, translated by Burton Watson in Birch, *Anthology of Chinese Literature*, 103–5.

128. Makita, *Gumyōshū kenkyū*, 26.7, explains that the *Wei shu*, 24, Shih Lao-chih, reports that during the Han dynasty the monks all wore red robes, but later changed to a variegated color. Mou-tzu's description accurately describes the Han custom.

129. Lau, *Lao Tzu: Tao Te Ching*, 99 (38).

130. A similar account is given in the *Hou Han shu*. See Forke, *Lun Heng*, 2:85.

131. The phrase *shu-yu* (孰尤) perhaps alludes to a similar expression found in the *Tso Chuan*, *tun-mang* (敦厖), which Legge translates as "consenting." See Legge, *The Chinese Classics*, 5:391, 396a.

132. Legge, *The Chinese Classics*, 3:108.

133. Wilhelm, *The I Ching*, 332.

134. Legge, *The Chinese Classics*, 3:320.

135. Ibid., 3:326. Cf. Creel, *Origins of Statecraft in China*, 456–58, on the history of this text.

136. Lau, *Confucius: The Analects*, 159–60 (20.2).

137. Watson, *Complete Works of Chuang Tzu*, 315–16.

138. Legge, *The Chinese Classics*, 5:843.

139. Lau, *Confucius: The Analects*, 129 (14:32).

140. Legge, *The Chinese Classics*, 1:287 (14.34).

141. Watson, *Complete Works of Chuang Tzu*, 32–33. For the literature on the development of the story about Hsü Yu washing out his mouth, see Pelliot, "Meou-tseu," 370.183.

142. Watson, *Complete Works of Chuang Tzu*, 34.

143. *Hou Han shu*, 32, cited in Tsukamoto, *Early Chinese Buddhism*, 48.

144. See Yü, "'O Soul, Come Back!'" 379, where he explains that *kuei* "had already acquired the meaning of 'the soul of the dead' as early as the Shang period. The *p'o* or the *hun*, on the other hand, was distinguished from *kuei* by being a name for 'the soul of the living.'"

145. Lau, *Lao Tzu: Tao Te Ching*, 69 (13).

146. Ibid., 65 (9) has: "To retire when the task is accomplished is the way of heaven." Mou-tzu apparently takes the phrase much more literally.

147. Perhaps a parallel in *Hsün Tzu*. See Morohashi 8:27372.53

148. Makita, *Gumyōshū kenkyū*, 27.7, explains: "For the Taoists there were seventy-two fortunate lands in which the spirit immortals dwell. For the Confucians the fortunate abodes refer to the realms above the heavens. For the Chinese Buddhists the fortunate abodes are frequently a name for the Pure Land of Bliss." But perhaps the reference here is to the higher "destinies" (*gati*) of the wheel of transmigration, viz., humans, titans, and gods, while the abodes of misery are the hells, hungry ghosts, and animals.

149. The text actually reads: "Good is to happiness as white is to black." Which makes little sense.

150. Yü, "'O Soul, Come Back!'" 365–69. Also see Loewe, *Ways to Paradise*, 9–16, 33–34, 49–50, on the paintings from tomb number 1 at Ma-wang-tui. Also see Loewe, *Chinese Ideas of Life and Death*, 114–26. Cf. Allan, *The Shape of the Turtle*, 84–86, and Major, *Heaven and Earth in Early Han Thought*, 49–53.

151. Yü, "'O Soul, Come Back!'" 376. See Loewe, *Chinese Ideas of Life and Death*, 26.

152. From Forke, *Lun Heng*, 208–9.

153. From the *Li Chi*, Li-yün chapter. Legge, *Sacred Books of the East*, 27:368–69.

154. Morgan, *Tao: The Great Luminant*, 68. Also see Major, *Heaven and Earth in Early Han Thought*, 48–49, linking the issue of immortality with cosmogony.

155. See Morohashi, 12:45787.6. Legge, *Sacred Books of the East*, 27:444, translates: "The intelligent spirit returns to heaven; the body and the animal soul return to the earth; and hence arose the idea of seeking (for the deceased) in sacrifice in the unseen darkness and in the bright region above."

156. See Morohashi, 12:45787.5.

157. Maspero, "Le Taoisme," 17. Translated in Needham, *Science and Civilization in China*, 2:153–54.

158. *Hou Han chi*, 10, in Tsukamoto, *Early Chinese Buddhism*, 476.3.

159. Whalen Lai, "Early Chinese Buddhist Understanding of the Psyche," 93. See also T'ang Yung-t'ung, *Han Wei liang-Chin nan-pei ch'ao fo-chiao shih*, 275.

160. Translation in Bodde, "The Chinese View of Immortality: Its Expression by Chu Hsi and its Relationship to Buddhist Thought," *Essays on Chinese Civilization*, 323–24. The text, entitled "Yang Chu," constitutes the present chapter 7 of the *Lieh Tzu*, for which see Graham, *The Lieh Tzu*, 140–41.

161. Watson, *Complete Works of Chuang Tzu*, 175.

162. On the various notions of the soul and life after death in Han China, see Yü, "Life and Immortality in the Mind of Han China."

163. T'ang, *Han Wei liang-Chin nan-pei ch'ao fo-chiao shih*, 89, 91. Quoted in Bodde, "The Chinese View of Immortality," 325–26.

164. See Lai, "Early Chinese Buddhist Understanding of the Psyche," 85–103, where he argues convincingly that the Chinese notion of "the indestructibility of the soul" is not a misunderstanding of the Buddhist notion of transmigration, for the "soul" here stands not for the permanent *ātman*, but for the continuity of personal identity. Also compare Liu, "Fan Chen's Treatise on the Destructibility of the Spirit and Its Buddhist Critics," and Pachow, "The Controversy over the Immortality of the Soul in Chinese Buddhism."

165. Although it notes that all texts give *chi* 紀, Makita's *Gumyō-shū kenkyū*, 28, reads *chüeh* 絕, and translates: "This [issue about the spirits, about life and death] was ignored by the sage [Confucius]."

166. *Hsiao Ching*, Sang-ch'in chapter, which goes on to conclude: "The basic duties of the living are thus fulfilled. The righteousness of both the dead and the living is completed. This is how the service of a filial son is perfected." See Legge, *The Chinese Classics*, 488.

167. Lau, *Lao Tzu: Tao Te Ching*, 113 (52).

168. Ibid., 113 (52) has: "Use the light but give up the discernment. Bring not misfortune upon yourself."

169. Lau, *Confucius: The Analects*, 107 (11.12).

170. Ibid., 84 (6.22).

171. Tsukamoto, *Early Chinese Buddhism*, 476.3.

172. Morohashi, 7:18421.65.

173. Lau, *Confucius: The Analects*, 91 (7.35).

174. Legge, *The Chinese Classics*, 3:354.

175. Hummel, "Some Basic Moral Principles in Chinese Culture," 603. See Cua, "The Concept of Paradigmatic Individuals."

176. Lau, *Confucius: The Analects*, 67 (3.5).

177. Lau, *Mencius*, 103 (3.A.4).

178. Lau, *Confucius: The Analects*, 98 (9.14).

179. For the biography of K'ung-tzu and his many travels throughout the Warring States period, see Creel, *Confucius and the Chinese Way*, 25–56.

180. Some texts read "gold." I follow the reading of Makita's *Gumyōshū kenkyū* text, 1:14, 2:30.1.

181. Lau, *Mencius*, 100–101 (111.A.4). See Needham, *Science and Civilization in China*, 2:12–21.

182. *Fa-yen*, Ssu-pu pei-yao ed., 4:3a. Keenan, "A Study of Chapter Four," 50–53.

183. Watson, *Records of the Grand Historian of China*, 2:158.

184. Ibid., 2:158.4.

185. Legge, *The Chinese Classics*, 3:26.

186. Creel, *Origins of Statecraft in China*, 73–75.

187. Chavannes, *Les Mémoires historiques de Se-ma Ts'ien*, 1:207, 245. See Pelliot, "Meou-tseu," 374.223.

188. See Pelliot, "Meou-tseu," 374.226.

189. Lau, *Confucius: The Analects*, 63 (2.1).

190. Francis, *The Jātaka or Stories of the Buddha's Former Births*, 6:246–305, n. 547. Wray, *Ten Lives of the Buddha*, 93–103.

191. Mochizuki Shinkō, *Bukkyō daijiten* (Tokyo: Bukkyō Daijiten Hakkōsho, 1931–36), no. 2484.

192. Fukui, "Dōkyō no kisoteki kenkyū," 360, notes that this

Jātaka was translated by K'ang Seng-hui in *The Scripture of the Collection of the Six Perfections* (*Liu Tu-chi ching* 六度集經) in 251, which argues that the *Li-huo lun* is a later text.

193. Makita, *Gumyōshū kenkyū*, 32.2.

194. Creel, *Origins of Statecraft in China*, 122.80.

195. Chavannes, *Les Mémoires historiques de Se-ma Ts'ien*, 1:215.

196. Legge, *The Chinese Classics*, 5:156.

197. Morgan, *Tao, The Great Luminant*, 145.

198. Lau, *Mencius*, 139 (5.A.2).

199. Chavannes, *Les Mémoires historiques de Se-ma Ts'ien*, 1:178.

200. Watson, *Complete Works of Chuang Tzu*, 320.

201. Lau, *Mencius*, 146 (5.A.7).

202. Ibid.

203. Ibid., 175 (6.B.6).

204. Ibid., Appendix 4: "Ancient history As Understood by Mencius," 230–31.

205. Knoblock, *Xunzi*, 25–26, 273.36.

206. Morgan, *Tao: The Great Luminant*, 111–12.

207. Lau, *Mencius*, 124 (4.A.17).

208. Ibid., 139 (5.A.2).

209. Peerenboom, *Law and Morality*, 123. On the logical structure of Mencius's analogy, see Reding, "Analogical Reasoning in Early Chinese Philosophy," 42–43.

210. Legge, *The Chinese Classics*, 5:333. The phrase is repeated in *Analects*, 8:3.

211. Lau, *Mencius*, 58 (1.A.7).

212. Lau, *Lao Tzu: Tao Te Ching*, 74 (18).

213. Lau, *Mencius*, 117 (4.A.1). Chapter 50 of the *Mo Tzu* is devoted to an exchange between Kung Shu and Mo-tzu, in which Kung Shu is bested. See Mei, *Ethical and Political Works of Motse*, 257–59.

214. Giles, *Biographical Dictionary*, n. 965.

215. Legge, *The Chinese Classics*, 3:44–45.

216. Lau, *Confucius: The Analects*, Appendix 2: "The Disciples As They Appear in the Analects," 215.

217. Ibid., 203.

218. Legge, *The Chinese Classics*, 3:84.

219. See Lai, "Looking for Mr. Ho Po," 335–50. Also Karlgren, "Legends and Cults in Ancient China," 319–20.

220. In his *Hsi-ching fu* (Fu on the Western Capital), contained in the *Wen-hsüan*, 2:59–60. Quoted from Wright, *Buddhism in Chinese History*, 21. This poem was written around 130.

221. See Maspero, "Communautés et moines bouddhistes chinois."

222. Tsukamoto, *Early Chinese Buddhism*, 72–73.

223. Link, "Cheng-wu lun," 160.

224. Ibid., 151.

225. Lau, *Confucius: The Analects*, 91 (7.36).

226. Following Pelliot, "Meou-Tseu," 381.264, in reading *tzu* 訾, to estimate, in place of *tzu* 貲, riches. See R. H. Mathews, *Chinese-English Dictionary* (Cambridge: Harvard UP, 1943), 6956 and 6957.

227. Legge, *The Chinese Classics*, 5:106–7.

228. Lau, *Mencius*, 94 (2.B.13). Legge, *The Chinese Classics*, 2:232.

229. Pelliot, "Meou-tseu," 378.255.

230. Chavannes, *Les Mémoires historiques de Se-ma Ts'ien*, 1:72.

231. Legge, *The Chinese Classics*, 2:206; Lau, *Mencius*, 84 (2.A.8).

232. See Pelliot, "Meou-tseu," 379.257.

233. Makita, *Gumyōshū kenkyū*, 35.3.

234. Lau, *Confucius: The Analects*, 108 (11.19).

235. Legge, *The Chinese Classics*, 5:185–87, 203–8. See also Morgan, *Tao: The Great Luminant*, 117.

236. Legge, *The Chinese Classics*, 5:290.

237. Cited in Makita, *Gumyōshū kenkyū*, 35.10 from *Huai-nan Tzu*, chapter 18, Jen-chien.

238. Lau, *Confucius: The Analects*, 59 (1.1).

239. Lau, *Lao Tzu: Tao Te Ching*, 61 (5).

240. Ibid., 91 (32).

241. Lau, *Confucius: The Analects*, 63 (2.1)

242. Ibid., 154 (19.12).

243. Lau, "On Mencius' Use of Analogy in Argument"; *Mencius*, 262–63. Also see Graham, *Disputers of the Tao*, 81, on Hui Shih, and 120 on Mencius.

244. Tsukamoto, *Early Chinese Buddhism*, 477.4. Passage translated by Hurvitz.

245. Shih, *The Literary Mind*, 37.

246. Lau, "On Mencius' Use of the Method of Analogy in Argument," *Mencius*, 193.

247. See also Cua, *Ethical Argumentation*, 65–87.

248. Forke, *Lun Heng*, 2:370–71.

249. Pokora, "Notes on New Studies on Tung Chung-shu," 262.

250. Yet Chuang-tzu seems to have differed. In discussing the notion of *lei*, "kind" or "category," Reding, "Analogical Reasoning in Early Chinese Philosophy," 51–52, notes that "Zhuangzi, like most of the early Chinese philosophers, reflected deeply upon the notion of *lei* and its role in the art of debating. When he shows in chapter 2 that disputation is impossible, he starts precisely by undermining the concept of *lei*. For Zhuangzi, disputation had come to a dead end. He thought to have administered the coup de grace to dialectics by proving that no suitable criterion of fixing the kind could be found."

251. Ch'en, "Neo-Taoism and the Prajñā School," 43.

252. Liebenthal, "Shih Hui-yüan's Buddhism As Set Forth in His Writings," 245.

253. Lau, *Confucius: The Analects*, 103 (10.8).

254. Ibid., 72 (4.5). Hsi K'ang has a similarly constructed dialogue about wealth and rank, citing also the example of Liu-hsia Hui, who

"was three times dismissed and his expression did not become sad." See Henricks, *Philosophy and Argumentation*, 38–40.

255. Lau, *Lao Tzu: Tao Te Ching*, 68 (12).

256. Soyen Shaku, *Sermons of a Buddhist Abbot*, 6.

257. Lau, *Mencius*, 188 (7.A.28).

258. Ibid., 112 (3.B.7).

259. Giles, *Biographical Dictionary*, n. 200.

260. Lau, *Lao Tzu: Tao Te Ching*, 113 (52). Lau notes that these "openings" and "doors" refer to the senses and the intelligence. Wang P'i's commentary explains that "the openings are the causes whereby desire arises, while the doors are the causes whereby desire is followed" (Ssu-pu pei-yao ed., 10b–11a).

261. Ibid., 102 (41).

262. Legge, *The Chinese Classics*, 5:143, 145.

263. Cited in Morohashi, 3323.300.

264. Lau, *Confucius: The Analects*, 132 (15.1).

265. Bodde, *China's First Unifier*, 3–5. Also see 196–97.

266. Ibid., 242.

267. Maspero, "Le songe et l'ambassade de l'empereur Ming," 124, speculates that this might have been the famous White Horse Monastery. Yet the evidence seems insufficient for any conclusion about actual historical events.

268. Tsukamoto, *Early Chinese Buddhism*, 482.8. The reference for the text is T. 55.42c.

269. Ibid., 42. Liu Chün cites the *Mou-tzu Li-huo lun* account in his commentary to the *Shih-shuo Hsin-yü*, discussing discrepancies among the various versions of the story. See Mather, *Tales of the World*, 104–5.

270. *Kuang Hung-ming chi*, 9.9a–b. See Tsukamoto, *Early Chinese Buddhism*, 487.22, and Zürcher, *The Buddhist Conquest of China*, 320, for partial translations.

271. Pokora, "An Important Crossroad of the Chinese Thought," 67.

272. Maspero, "Le Songe et l'ambassade de l'empereur Ming," 128.

273. Ibid., 107.2.

274. Loewe, *Everyday Life in Early Imperial China*, 135.

275. Nanjio, *A Catalogue of the Chinese Tripiṭaka*, 381.4. Cf. Hrdličková, "The First Translations of Buddhist Sūtras," 118.7.

276. Lau, *Lao Tzu: Tao Te Ching*, 117 (56).

277. Ibid., 106 (45).

278. The sentence is quoted from the *Analects*. Legge, *The Chinese Classics*, 1:286 (14:29), translates it: "The master said, 'The superior man is modest in his speech, but exceeds in his actions.'" Lau, *Confucius: The Analects*, 128 (14:27), emends the text to then translate: "The Master said, 'The gentleman is ashamed of his word outstripping his deed.'"

279. Lau, *Lao Tzu: Tao Te Ching*, 65 (9).

280. Lau, *Confucius: The Analects*, 128 (14.27).

281. Ibid., 145 (17.13).

282. *Hsün Tzu*, Ssu-pu pei-yao ed., 19.7a.

283. Lau, *Confucius: The Analects*, 133 (15.8)

284. Ibid., 137 (15.41).

285. *Lao Tzu Tao Te Ching*, chapter 3: *wei wu-wei tse wu bu chih* (爲無爲則無不治). See Lau, *Lao Tzu: Tao Te Ching*, 59.

286. Lau, *Confucius: The Analects*, 133 (15.7).

287. Ibid., 79 (21).

288. Tsukamoto, *Early Chinese Buddhism*, 21.

289. Chan, *Two Visions of the Way*, 25.

290. Ch'en, "Neo-Taoism and the Prajñā School," 38.

291. It is interesting to compare Mou-tzu, who never cites as an example any Han dynasty person, with the late Han figure Hsün Yüeh, who in his *Extended Reflections* (*Shen Chien*), constantly adduces Han dynasty examples to elucidate his thought. See Ch'en, *Hsün Yüeh and the Mind of Late Han China*, 81, 84, passim.

292. Watson, *Complete Works of Chuang Tzu*, 34.

293. Lau, *Lao Tzu: Tao Te Ching*, 94 (35).

294. Tsukamoto, *Early Chinese Buddhism*, 475.3.

295. See Allan, *The Shape of the Turtle*, 28, which explains the ancient Mulberry Tree myth of the ten suns bathing in a pool of water of the same name.

296. See Pelliot, "Meou-tseu," 398.325–328. The *Li Chi* (Legge, *Sacred Books of the East*, 28:106) states: "The *Ta-chang* (Great Chapter) expressed the brilliance [of Yao's virtue], the *Hsien-ch'ih* (Pool of Heaven) the completeness [of the Yellow Emperor's virtue], the Hsiao [Chao] showed how Shun continued [the virtue of his predecessors]...."

297. Lau, *Confucius: The Analects*, 133–34 (11).

298. Doeringer, "Yang Hsiung," 88. See Dubs, *History of the Former Han Dynasty*, 3:19.

299. Doeringer, "Yang Hsiung," 296.

300. Cited from Fung, *A History of Chinese Philosophy*, 1:317.

301. Pelliot, "Meou-tseu," 399.333.

302. Lau, *Confucius: The Analects*, 147–48 (19.5).

303. See Watson, *Complete Works of Chuang Tzu*, 298–99. Another version appears in the commentary to the *Huai-nan Tzu*, for which see Le Blanc, *The Huai-nan Tzu: Philosophical Synthesis in Early Han Thought*, 132 n. 66.

304. *Huai-nan Tzu*, Ssu-pu pei-yao ed., 16.3a.

305. Lau, *Mencius*, 76 (2.A.2); Legge, *The Chinese Classics*, 2:185. Riegel, "Reflections on an Unmoved Mind," 436.

306. Makita, *Gumyōshū kenkyū*, 45.2. See Major, *Heaven and Earth in Early Han Thought*, 154.

307. Legge, *The Chinese Classics*, 2:195–96; Lau, *Mencius*, 80 (2.A.2).

308. Soyen Shaku, *Sermons of a Buddhist Abbot*, 12 (Article 17).

309. See McRae, *The Northern School and the Formation of Early Ch'an Buddhism*, 132–36, 146–47, 246–50.

310. Knechtges, "Yang Shyong, the *Fuh*, and Hann Rhetoric," 199.

311. Burke, *A Rhetoric of Motives*, 55.

312. Morgan, *Tao: The Great Luminant*, 72–73.

313. Lau, *Mencius*, 117 (4.A.l). The *Tso Chuan* reports a speech of Shih K'uang criticizing inept governance and extolling the ideal behavior of a ruler. See Legge, *The Chinese Classics*, 5:466–67.

314. Makita, *Gumyōshū kenkyū*, 46.5. See Legge, *Sacred Books of the East*, 27:140, 28:226. See Pelliot, "Meou-Tseu," 402.348, where he says that Mou-tzu's reference is borrowed from the *Chan-kuo Ts'e* and notes the modern Chinese proverb "To play the lute in front of a donkey."

315. Watson, *Complete Works of Chuang Tzu*, 346 (10:4a). Graham, *Chuang Tzu: The Inner Chapters*, 249, has a similar translation, which marks the germane sentence about like hearing like as a proverb:

> Confucius bowed twice, stood up straight. 'From my childhood I have cultivated learning, by now for sixty-nine years, and found none from whom to learn the ultimate doctrine. What can I do but keep the space open in my heart?'
>
> 'The same in kind go along with each other,
> The same in sound respond to each other.
>
> That indeed is the pattern which is in us from Heaven. I propose not to talk about what belongs to my own sort, but to put you right on what concerns yourself.'

316. Hrdličková, "The First Translations of Buddhist Sūtras," 115, in discussing the development from the first scriptural translations to the secularized *pien-wen*, notes: "Here we must point out that the translated sūtras could become a weapon of religious propaganda only if they were made understandable for the common people. This the translations succeeded in doing at least in part and so were able to fulfill their main purpose. Their ordinary religious content gradually became in the course of the sermons enriched with descriptions and illustrations from daily life, till the religious elements finally receded into the background to make way for the new realistic stories which have left their indelible stamp on the Chinese literary tradition." The task of the *Li-huo lun* was somewhat different, for it was aimed at the spread of Buddhism not among the common people, but among the cultured literati, the keepers of the traditions. Perhaps its reticence in citing Buddhist scriptures as evidence for its readers is due to the relatively wide dispersion of those more "popular" texts among the common people, with the result that they would not be readily acceptable as evidence by the cultured elite.

317. The framework of Mou-tzu's rhetoric draws upon the *Lao Tzu*, chapter 41, presented in the source codes for Article 10. Here clearly

Mou-tzu not only paraphrases, but completely alters the words of the *Lao Tzu*, lending more weight to the possibility that he has done so in the preceding two sentences also.

318. Makita, *Gumyōshū kenkyū*, 48.2.

319. Reischauer and Fairbank, *East Asia: The Great Tradition*, 106.

320. Henricks, *Lao-tzu: Te-tao ching*, xv.

321. Lau, *Lao Tzu: Tao Te Ching*, 105.

322. Henricks, *Lao-tzu: Te-tao ching*, 200 and 224.

323. Ibid., 126, 158. But see Lai, "The Public Good That Does the Public Good," in which he argues that Mencius turned the Mohist term *li* (利) into a pejorative "private gain," which then colored subsequent interpretations.

324. Henricks, *Lao-tzu: Te-tao ching*, 194, 196, 146.

325. Lau, *Lao Tzu: Tao Te Ching*, 74, and Henricks, *Lao-tzu: Te-tao ching*, 138.

326. Blofeld, *I Ching (The Book of Changes)*, 108. Wilhelm, *The I Ching*, 437, translates this more literally as: "'The perseverance of a dark man brings good fortune.' He is central and does not get confused."

327. Lau, *Lao Tzu: Tao Te Ching*, 119 (58).

328. See Doeringer, "Yang Hsiung," 4.

329. But Whalen Lai, in private conversation and correspondence, sees it as an indication that the *Li-huo lun* was written before the demise of that academy.

330. Tsukamoto, *Early Chinese Buddhism*, 116.

331. Balazs, "Entre révolte nihiliste et évasion mystique," 33.

332. Fukui, "Dōkyō no kisoteki kenkyū," 370.

333. Balazs, "Entre révolte nihiliste et évasion mystique," 54–55.

334. Holzman, "Les Sept Sages," 319–25.

335. Pokora, "Notes of New Studies on Tung Chung-shu," 264.

336. Tsukamoto, *Early Chinese Buddhism*, 26. For such practices in the Han dynasty, see Shima Kunioto, *Gogyō shisō to Reiki Getsuryō*

no kenkyū (An Investigation into the Five Element Theory and the Yüeh Ming Li Chi [Chapter of the *Lü-shih Ch'un ch'iu*]), 234–99, on the Han, and 314–39 on Yang Hsiung, which treats his *T'ai Hsüan Ching*, a book on cosmic harmonies and prognostications modeled on *The Classic of Changes*. Yang was influential in the formulation of Han classical orthodoxy, as argued by Franklin Doeringer, "Yang Hsiung," 2–7, and his *T'ai Hsüan Ching* is exemplary of the attempts to read future events in terms of classical patterns of cosmic harmony. For a translation of the latter, see Walters, *The T'ai Hsüan Ching, The Hidden Classic: A Lost Companion of the I Ching*, although it was in fact never very lost.

337. For stories and legends about these eight immortals, see Ho and O'Brien, *The Eight Immortals of Taoism*. Wang Ch'iao and Ch'ih Sung do not figure in the traditional list, which dates from the tenth century. See Pelliot, "Meou-tseu," 404–6.363.

338. Giles, *Biographical Dictionary*, nn. 2149 and 2140.

339. Ibid., n. 377.

340. Ibid., n. 88.

341. On the history of this text, Pelliot, "Meou-tseu," 407.366, has an extended note.

342. Pokora, "On the Origin of the Notions T'ai-p'ing and Ta-t'ung in Chinese Philosophy," 448: "We even do not know the author of the original version of the *T'ai-p'ing ching* which was first mentioned in 166 A.D. in a memorial by Hsiang K'ai to Emperor Huan. Hsiang K'ai spoke only of a 'Divine Book' (*Shen shu*) which was received by Kung Ch'ung from his master Yü Chi. Fan Yeh, the author of the *Hou Han shu*, remarked that Kung Ch'ung presented the book to Emperor Shun (126–144) and that its name has been *T'ai-p'ing ch'ing ling shu*. Li Hsien's (654–684) commentary identifies again the latter text with the *T'ai-p'ing ching*. Some decades after Hsiang K'ai's mention of Yü Chi's (?) *T'ai-p'ing ching*, the same statement was repeated almost verbatim by Mou-tzu, who said that the book consisted of 170 fascicles." It seems that the available evidence does not allow any firm conclusion about the provenance or identity of the *T'ai-p'ing ching*, for which see Michaud's discussion, "The Yellow Turbans," 81–86.

343. Tsukamoto, *Early Chinese Buddhism*, 32. See 472.16 for a translation of the *Han shu's* biography of Hsiang K'ai. On Yü Chi, see 69–71.

344. Lau, *Confucius: The Analects*, 143 (17.1).

345. Lau, *Mencius*, 112 (3.B.7)

346. Lau, *Confucius: The Analects*, 113 (12.8).

347. Ibid., 94 (8.15).

348. *Aṅguttaranikāya*, 12. See Morohashi, 1:167.330; Nakamura, 255.

349. See Yü, "Life and Immortality," 93ff.

350. Tsukamoto, *Early Chinese Buddhism*, 28. See the exchanges on practices of extending one's life span between Hsi K'ang (223–62) and Hsiang Hsiu (d. 312) in Henricks, *Philosophy and Argumentation in Third-Century China*, 21–70.

351. Henricks, *Philosophy and Argumentation in Third-Century China*, 22–23.

352. Tsukamoto, *Early Chinese Buddhism*, 36. See also the passage on p. 78, quoted in the source codes for Article 1.

353. Tsukamoto, *Early Chinese Buddhism*, 475.a.

354. See Henricks, *Lao-tzu: Te-tao ching*, 252, on the absence of the character *wang* 亡, to perish, in the Ma-wang-tui texts, which he then translates "To die but not to be forgotten (忘)—that's [true] long life." In this reading the Lao-tzu is not evincing a belief in any kind of physical immortality.

355. Tsukamoto, *Early Chinese Buddhism*, 27.

356. Doeringer, "Yang Hsiung," 157.

357. I take Mou-tzu's phrase *ts'ung-ch'ien* 叢殘 to allude the phrase *ts'ung-ts'o* 叢脞 in *The Book of Documents*, 2.4.11 (Legge, *The Chinese Classics*, 3:90), where Kao Yao addressed the Emperor, saying, "When the head (i.e., the Emperor) is vexatious (*ts'ung-ts'o* 叢脞), the members are idle and all affairs will go to ruin." In the commentary Ch'ing observes that *ts'ung-ts'o* means "a general collection of small affairs."

358. Lau, *Lao Tzu: Tao Te Ching*, 68 (12): "The five colours make man's eyes blind; the five notes make his ears deaf; the five tastes injure his palate...."

359. See Pelliot, "Meou-tseu," 413.381, where he gives the text from the *K'ung-tzu chia-yü* (6:25) and mentions a parallel in the *Huai-nan Tzu*, Ssu-pu pei-yao ed., 4:6b–7a. The passage is repeated in the *Po-wu chih*, Ssu-pu pei-yao ed., 7.1b, which inserts the phrase: "Those who eat stones are fat, but do not live long."

360. Watson, *Complete Works of Chuang Tzu*, 194–95.

361. Ibid., 167.

362. Link, "Cheng-wu lun," 158.

363. *Huai-nan Tzu*, Ssu-pu pei-yao ed., 16.5a.

364. Hsiang Hsiu similarly rejects any refusal to consume the five grains. Henricks, *Philosophy and Argumentation in Third-Century China*, 31: "Such things as restraining grief and joy, calming delight and anger, moderating food and drink, and tempering hot and cold—these were also practiced by the ancients. But to turn to elimination of the five grains, rejection of rich flavors, lessening of emotions and desires, and repression of wealth and rank—these they never presumed to allow."

365. Lau, *Lao Tzu: Tao Te Ching*, 109 (48).

366. Lau, *Confucius: The Analects*, 63 (2.4).

367. Henricks, *Philosophy and Argumentation in Third-Century China*, 35.

368. Watson, *Complete Works of Chuang Tzu*, 33. It is perhaps significant that the *Li-huo lun* never quotes the *Chuang Tzu*, perhaps because of its sympathy toward *hsien* practice.

369. Thanks to Whalen Lai for pointing out to me the significance of this confession by Mou-tzu.

370. Lau, *Lao Tzu: Tao Te Ching*, 88 (30) and 116 (55). Lau emends *tse* 則 (rule, standard; thus, then) to *ts'e* 賊 (harm, injure), and thus translates: "A creature in its prime doing harm to the old is known as going against the way. That which goes against the way will come to an early end." Chan, *The Way of Lao Tzu*, 152 (30), keeps the reading *tse* and translates: "(For) after things reach their prime, they begin to grow old, which means being contrary to Tao. Whatever is contrary to Tao will soon perish." Pelliot, "Meou-tseu," 320, is, I think, closer to the *Li-huo lun's* understanding: "Lao-tseu dit: Quant quelque être est devenue fort, il vieillit; c'est qu'on peut dire que [l'être fort] est contraire au *tao*; tout ce qui est contraire au *tao* finit prématurément." He reads the passage in light of Lao-tzu's preceding maxims against the use of military force.

371. Lau, *Lao Tzu: Tao Te Ching*, 69 (13): "The reason I have great trouble is that I have a body. When I no longer have a body, what trouble have I?"

372. Lau, *Confucius: The Analects*, 91 (7.35).

373. Morgan, Tao, the Great Luminant, 76.

374. Legge, The Chinese Classics, 3:354. See the citation under Article 13.

375. Morgan, Tao: The Great Luminant, 220–21.

376. Pelliot, "Meou-tseu," 416.396.

377. Giles, Biographical Dictionary, n. 311.

378. Forke, Lun Heng, 2:446.

379. Morohashi, 7:20333.7.

380. Legge, The Chinese Classics, 3:359.

381. Lau, Mencius, 114 (III.B.9).

382. Knechtges, "Yang Shyong, the Fuh, and Hann Rhetoric," 82. On the T'ai Hsüan Ching, see the translation by Walters. The passage from Chieh Nan is included in Yang Hsiung's biography in the Han shu, 3578.

383. Morohashi, 8:23935.8. Doeringer, "Yang Hsiung," 296–97.

384. Morgan, Tao: The Great Luminant, 241.

385. Ibid., 170.

386. Lau, Confucius: The Analects, 146 (17.18).

387. Ibid., 78 (5.18).

388. Ibid., 80 (5.24).

389. Tsukamoto, Early Chinese Buddhism, 171.

390. Ibid., 41.

391. Lau, Confucius: The Analects, 64 (2.10).

392. Ibid., 84 (6.22).

393. For references, see Creel, Origins of Statecraft in China, 343–45.

394. Ibid., 71–80.

395. Chavannes, Les Mémoires historiques de Se-ma Ts'ien, 4:100–112; Pelliot, "Meou-tseu," 417.408.

396. Wallacker, Huai-nan Tzu, Book Eleven, 30. Wallacker, 16, in-

terprets the account: "T'ai-kung Wang (i.e., Lü Shang) and the Duke of Chou were each able to predict the downfall of the other's domain from the stated policies of elevating certain members of the population to positions of honor."

397. Watson, *Complete Works of Chuang Tzu*, 206.

398. *Hsün-tzu*, Ssu-pu pei-yao ed., 20:14a–b.

399. Kiyota, *Kōshi kago*, 137–40.

400. *Hung-ming chi*, 7:7b–8a.

401. Legge, *The Chinese Classics*, 5:791.

402. Chavannes, *Les Mémoires historiques de Se-ma Ts'ien*, 5:349–51.

403. Legge, *The Chinese Classics*, 5:549–50. Giles, *Biographical Dictionary*, n. 287.

404. Lau, *Confucius: The Analects*, 88 (7.21): "The topics the Master did not speak of were prodigies, force, disorder, and gods." Prodigies (怪), also used in the critic's accusation (怪), I render as "uncanny."

405. Tsukamoto, *Early Chinese Buddhism*, 1:234, 555.4. See Demiéville, "La Pénétration du bouddhisme dans la tradition philosophique chinoise," 23.

406. Tsukamoto, *Early Chinese Buddhism*, 109–12, 274–75.

407. Lau, *Confucius: The Analects*, 100 (9:28).

408. Fukui, "Dōkyō no kisoteki kenkyū," 361–62.

409. From *The Records of the Three Kingdoms*, quoted in Tsukamoto, *Early Chinese Buddhism*, 124.

410. Tsukamoto, *Early Chinese Buddhism*, 26, 31, 78–79, 121–22.

411. Needham, *Science and Civilization in China*, 2:148, remarks that the phrase *ching shih* (精室) in the ancient Taoist works on sexual practice refers to the seminal vesicles, i.e., the seminal chambers. If that is its sense in the critic's comment about "entering the chamber" (入室), then perhaps one could translate: "Some draw up their vesicles and accumulate [their seminal energy] for days on end without emissions." If such a reading is possible, then the reference is to the practice of *coitus reservatus*, the purpose of which was to increase one's amount of life-giving seminal essence (*yang*) by sexual stimulation. Note also that the *Yangsheng yao-chi* (Compendium of Essentials for Nourishing Life), which

contained materials from the Former Han, devoted a chapter to the "art of the inner chamber." See Despeux, "Gymnastics: The Ancient Tradition," 228–29. I surmise that this art was also a sexual method for nourishing long life.

412. Following Makita, *Gumyōshū kenkyū*, 58.2, translation of *t'iao* 調 as "to tease," "to make fun of," "to ridicule." Reference is made to the *Shih-shuo Hsin-yü*, P'ai-t'iao chapter (Ssu-pu pei-yao ed., hsia chih hsia, 5a.), which is translated by Mather, *Tales of the World*, 410: "K'ang Seng-yüan's eyes were deep set and his nose high. Chancellor Wang Tao often teased (p'iao) him about it. Seng-yüan replied, 'The nose is the face's mountain, and the eyes are its pools. If the mountain's not high, it has no power, or the pools not deep, they are not clear.'" Also compare *The Record of Extensive Things* (*Po-wu chih*), Ssu-pu pei-yao, 7.2, where the compound "to make fun of and ridicule" *p'iao hsiao* (調笑) is used.

413. Pelliot, "Meou-tseu," 420.423bis, notes that the phrase is not found in the *Analects*, but that an identical sentence is found in the *T'ien jen san ts'e* of Tung Chung-shu, and there also attributed to K'ung-tzu. A similar passage occurs in the *Li Chi*: "among all creatures that have blood and breath, there is none which has intelligence equal to man; and hence the feeling of man on the death of his kindred remains unexhausted even till death" (Legge, *Sacred Books of the East*, 28:392). However, *The Classic of Filial Piety*, Sheng-chih chapter, has a direct parallel: "The Master said, 'Among the beings in heaven and earth, I regard humans as precious. Among the actions of humans, none is greater than filial piety.'"

414. Compare Hsi K'ang, Henricks, *Philosophy and Argumentation in Third-Century China*, 26: "Rich flavors fry the entrails [of the uninformed people of the world]; unstrained wine boils their bowels; fragrant sweet smells rot their marrow."

415. Lau, *Confucius: The Analects*, 108 (11.15).

416. Morohashi, 1:1415.100.

417. Needham, *Science and Civilization in China*, 2:146–52.

418. Watson, *Complete Works of Chuang Tzu*, 188.

419. Quoted by Pelliot, "Meou-tseu," 420.422.

420. Lau, *Confucius: The Analects*, 67 (2.1). See also his criticism of the Chi family in 2.3.

421. Chavannes, *Les Mémoires historiques de Se-ma Ts'ien*, 4:211–33.

422. Lau, *Confucius: The Analects*, 156 (19.23). Also see Pelliot, "Meou-tseu," 420.428, and Forke, *Lun Heng*, 2:247–51.

423. Lau, *Lao Tzu: Tao Te Ching*, 80 (23).

424. Lau, *Confucius: The Analects*, 130 (14.37).

425. Pelliot, "Meou-tseu," 378.249.

426. Legge, *The Chinese Classics*, 3:40.

427. Legge, *Sacred Books of the East*, 27:132.

428. Mei, *Ethical and Political Works of Motse*, 130.

429. Wallacker, *The Huai-nan Tzu, Book Eleven*, 37.

430. See Pelliot, "Meou-tseu," 422.435–40.

431. Legge, *Sacred Books of the East*, 27:138–39.

432. Chavannes, *Les Mémoires historiques de Se-ma Ts'ien*, 5:424–25.

433. Lau, *Confucius: The Analects*, 107–8 (11:13).

434. Ibid., "The Disciples As They Appear in the Analects," 209–13.

435. Legge, *The Chinese Classics*, 5:843.

436. Legge, *Sacred Books of the East*, 27:123–24: "Confucius was wailing for Tzu-lu in his courtyard. When any came to condole with him, he bowed to them. When the wailing was over, he made the messenger come in, and asked him all about (Tzu-lu's death). 'They have made him into pickle,' said the messenger; and forthwith Confucius ordered the pickle (in the house) to be thrown away."

437. Lau, *Confucius: The Analects*, 82 (6.10).

438. Ibid., 92 (8.3).

439. Ibid., 81 (6.3).

440. Ibid., 99 (9.22).

441. *Fa Yen*, 12:4b.

442. Watson, *Records of the Grand Historian of China*, 2:39.

443. Ibid., 2:52.

444. Forke, *Lun Heng*, 1:332.

445. Kaltenmark, *Lao Tzu and Taoism*, 117.

446. Tsukamoto, *Early Chinese Buddhism*, 276.

447. Ibid., 284.

448. Forke, *Lun Heng*, 1:332.

449. Ch'en, "Neo-Taoism and the Prajñā School," 33.

450. Forke, *Lun Heng*, 2:27.

451. *Huai-nan Tzu*, Book 16 Shuo Shan, cited in Makita, *Gumyōshū kenkyū*, 61.1.

452. Compare the confessional *uposatha* ceremony for *upāsaka* described in the Wei dynasty *T'i-wei Po-li Ching*, in Lai, "Folk Religious Practice in China," 20–26.

Bibliography

Abrams, M. H.
1979   "How to Do Things with Texts." *Poetics Today* 46:566–88.

Allan, Sarah
1991   *The Shape of the Turtle: Myth, Art, and Cosmos in Early China.* Albany: State University of New York Press.

Aurousseau, L.
1922   Review of "Meou–tseu ou les doutes levés," by Paul Pelliot. *Bulletin de l'École francais d'Extrême-Orient* 22: 276–98.

Austin, J. L.
1975   *How to Do Things with Words.* Edited by J. O. Urmson and Maria Sbisà. Cambridge: Harvard University Press.

Balazs, Étienne
1948   "Entre révolte nihiliste et évasion mystique: Les courants intellectuels en Chine au IIIe siècle de notre èra." *Asiatische Studien: Zeitschrift der Schweizerischen Gesellschaft für Asienkunde* 2:27–55.
1964   *Chinese Civilization and Bureaucracy.* Translated by H. M. Wright. New Haven and London: Yale University Press.

Beal, Samuel
1871   *A Catena of Buddhist Scriptures from the Chinese.* Reprint, Delhi: Sri Satguru, 1989.

1882   *Buddhist Literature in China*. Reprint, Delhi: Sri Satguru, 1988.

Birch, Cyril
    1965   *Anthology of Chinese Literature: From Early Times to the Fourteenth Century*. New York: Grove Press.

Blofeld, John, trans.
    1965   *I Ching* (The Book of Changes). New York: Dutton.

Bloom, Harold
    1973   *The Anxiety of Influence: A Theory of Poetry*. London: Oxford University Press.

Bodde, Derk
    1953   "Harmony and Conflict in Chinese Philosophy." In *Studies in Chinese Thought*, edited by Arthur F. Wright. Chicago: University of Chicago Press.
    1967   *China's First Unifier: A Study of the Ch'in Dynasty As Seen in the Life of Li Ssu*. Hong Kong: Hong Kong University Press.
    1981   *Essays on Chinese Civilization*. Edited by Charles Le Blanc and Dorothy Borei. Princeton: Princeton University Press.
    1991   *Chinese Thought, Society, and Science: The Intellectual and Social Background of Science and Technology in Premodern China*. Honolulu: University of Hawaii Press.

Booth, Wayne
    1983   *The Rhetoric of Fiction*. 2nd ed. Chicago: University of Chicago Press.

Burke, Kenneth
    1950   *A Rhetoric of Motives*. New York: Prentice Hall.

Cammann, Schuyler van R.
    1956   "Archaeological Evidence for Chinese Contacts with India during the Han Dynasty." *Sinologica* 5 (1): 1–19.

Chan, Alan K. L.
    1984   "Philosophical Hermeneutics and the *Analects*: The Paradigm of 'Tradition.'" *Philosophy East and West* 34:421–36.
    1991   *Two Visions of the Way: A Study of the Wang Pi and the Ho-shang Kung Commentaries on the Lao-Tzu*. Albany: State University of New York Press.

Chan, Wing-tsit
    1963   *A Source Book in Chinese Philosophy*. Princeton: Princeton University Press.

Chang, Cung-yung
1974   "Tao: A New Way of Thinking." *Journal of Chinese Philosophy* 1 (2): 137–52.

Chatman, Seymour
1978   *Story and Discourse: Narrative Structure in Fiction and Film.* Ithaca: Cornell University Press.

Chavannes, Edouard
1895–1905   *Les Mémoires historiques de Se-ma Ts'ien.* Paris: E. Leroux.

Ch'en Ch'i-yün
1980   *Hsün Yüeh and the Mind of Late Han China: A Translation of the Shen-Chien with Introduction and Annotations.* Princeton: Princeton University Press.

Chen, Ellen Marie
1973   "Is There a Doctrine of Physical Immortality in the Tao Te Ching?" *History of Religions* 12 (3): 231–49.

Ch'en, Kenneth
1957   "Neo-Taoism and the Prajñā School during the Wei and Chin Dynasties." *Chinese Culture* 1 (2): 33–46.
1964   *Buddhism in China: A Historical Survey.* Princeton: Princeton University Press.
1973   *The Chinese Transformation of Buddhism.* Princeton: Princeton University Press.

Ch'ü, T'ung–tsu
1957   "Chinese Class Structure and Its Ideology." In *Chinese Thought and Institutions,* edited by John K. Fairbank, 235–50. Chicago and London: University of Chicago Press.

Creel, Herrlee G.
1960   *Confucius and the Chinese Way.* New York: Harper & Row; Torchbook edition, 1969.
1970   *The Origins of Statecraft in China.* Chicago and London: University of Chicago Press.

Crump, J. I., Jr.
1964   *Intrigues: Studies of the Chan-kuo ts'e.* Ann Arbor: University of Michigan Press.

Cua, A. S.
1971   "The Concept of Paradigmatic Individuals in the Ethics of Confucius." *Inquiry* 14:41–55.
1975   "Uses of Dialogue and Moral Understanding." *Journal of Chinese Philosophy* 2:131–48.

1985   *Ethical Argumentation: A Study in Hsün Tzu's Moral Epis-temology.* Honolulu: University of Hawaii Press.

Culler, Jonathan
1975   *Structuralist Poetics: Structuralism, Linguistics, and the Study of Literature.* Ithaca: Cornell University Press.

de Bary, Theodore, ed.
1960   *Sources of Chinese Tradition.* 2 vols. New York: Columbia University Press.
1969   *The Buddhist Tradition in India, China, and Japan.* New York: Random House; New York: Vintage Books, 1972.

de Crespigny, Rafe
1966   "The Military Geography of the Yangtse and the Early History of the Three Kingdoms State of Wu." *Journal of the Oriental Society of Australia* 4 (1): 61–76.
1966   "The Recruitment System of the Imperial Bureaucracy of Later Han." *Chung Chi Journal* 6:67–78.
1967   "An Outline of the Local Administration of the Later Han Empire." *Ching Chi Journal* 7:57–71.

de Jong, J. W.
1979   "Buddha's Word in China." In *Buddhist Studies*, edited by Gregory Schopen. Berkeley: Asian Humanities Press.

Demiéville, Paul
1956   "La Pénétration du bouddhisme dans la tradition philoso-phique chinoise." *Cahiers d'histoire mondiale* 3 (1): 19–38.

Despeux, Catherine
1989   "Gymnastics: The Ancient Tradition." In *Taoist Meditation and Longevity Techniques*, edited by Livia Kohn. Ann Arbor: University of Michigan, Center for Chinese Studies.

Doeringer, Franklin Melvin
1971   "Yang Hsiung and His Formulation of a Classicism." Ph.D. diss., Columbia University.

Dubs, Homer H.
1937   "The 'Golden Man' of Former Han Times." *T'oung Pao* 33: 1–14.
1938   "The Discussion of the Classics in the Shih-ch'ü Pavilion." In *History of the Former Han Dynasty*, vol. 2, 271–74.
1938   "The Victory of Han Confucianism." *Journal of Asian Studies* 58:435–49. Also published in *History of the Former Han Dynasty*, vol. 2, 341–53.

1938-55   *History of the Former Han Dynasty by Pan Ku.* 3 vols.
          Baltimore: Waverly Press.

Duyvendak, J. J. L.
1928   *The Book of Lord Shang.* London: Probsthain.

Eberhard, Wolfram
1957   "The Political Function of Astronomy and Astronomers in
          Han China." In *Chinese Thought and Institutions,* edited
          by John K. Fairbank, 33–70. Chicago and London: Univer-
          sity of Chicago Press.

Fish, Stanley
1980   Is There a Text in This Class? The Authority of Interpre-
          tive Communities. Cambridge: Harvard University Press.
1989   *Doing What Comes Naturally: Change, Rhetoric, and the
          Practice of Theory in Literary and Legal Studies.* Durham,
          N.C., and London: Duke University Press.

Forke, A., trans.
1962   *Lun Heng: Wang Ch'ung's Essays.* 2 vols. Princeton: Prince-
          ton University Press.

Fowler, Robert M.
1991   *Let the Reader Understand: Reader-Response Criticism
          and the Gospel of Mark.* Minneapolis: Fortress Press.

Francis, H. T., trans.
1957   *The Jātaka or Stories of the Buddha's Former Births.* Lon-
          don: Pali Text Society.

Freer, Léon
1868   *Le Sūtra en quarante-deux articles. Textes chinois, tibétain
          et mongol.* Paris: Maisonneuve et Cie, Libraires.

Freund, Elizabeth
1987   *The Return of the Reader: Reader-Response Criticism.* Lon-
          don and New York: Methuen.

Fukui Kōjun
1952   "Dōkyō no kisoteki kenkyū" (Basic Research on Taoism).
          In *Fukui Kōjun chosaku shū* (A Collection of the Works of
          Fukui Kōjun). Tokyo: Hōzōkan.

Fung, Yu-lan
1947   *The Spirit of Chinese Philosophy.* Translated by E. R.
          Hughes. Boston: Beacon Press.

1953   *A History of Chinese Philosophy.* Translated by Derk
        Bodde, 2 vols. Princeton: Princeton University Press.

Genette, Gérard
1966   "Frontières du récit." *Communications* 8:152–63.
1968   "Vraisemblance et motivation." *Communications* 11:5–21.
1970   "Time and Narrative in *A la recherche du temps perdu.*"
        Translated by Paul de Man. In *Aspects of Narrative,* edited
        by J. Hillis Miller, 93–118. New York: Columbia University
        Press.

Gernet, Jacques
1956   *Les Aspects économiques du bouddhisme dans la société
        chinoise du V au X siècle.* Paris: École francais d'Extrême-
        Orient.

Graham, A. C.
1960   *The Book of Lieh–tzu.* London: John Murray. Reprinted
        1973.
1981   *Chuang Tzu: The Inner Chapters.* London: Allen & Unwin.
1989   *Disputers of the Tao: Philosophical Argument in Ancient
        China.* LaSalle, Open Court.

Granet, Marcel
1934   *La pensée chinoise.* Reprint, Paris: Éditions Albin Michel,
        1968.

Griffiths, Paul J., Noriaki Hakamaya, John P. Keenan, and Paul L. Swanson
1989   *The Realm of Awakening: Chapter Ten of Asaṅga's Mahā-
        yānasaṅgraha.* New York and Oxford: Oxford University
        Press.

Hakamaya Noriaki
1989   *Hongaku shisō hihan* (Critique of the Notion of Original
        Enlightenment). Tokyo: Daizō Shuppan.
1990   *Hihan bukkyō* (Critical Buddhism). Tokyo: Daizō Shuppan.
1992   *Dōgen to bukkyō* (Dōgen and Buddhism). Tokyo: Daizō
        Shuppan.

Hall, David L., and Roger T. Ames
1987   *Thinking Through Confucius.* Albany: State University of
        New York Press.

Hawkes, David
1959   *Ch'u Tz'u: Songs of the South.* London: Oxford University
        Press; Boston: Beacon Press, 1962.

Henricks, Robert G.
1983   *Philosophy and Argumentation in Third Century China:*

The Essays of Hsi K'ang. Princeton: Princeton University Press.

1989   *Lao-tzu: Te-tao ching: A New Translation Based on the Recently Discovered Ma-wang-tui Texts.* New York: Ballantine.

Ho, Hwok Man, and Joanne O'Brien

1990   *The Eight Immortals of Taoism: Legends and Fables of Popular Taoism.* New York: Meridian.

Holub, Robert

1984   *Reception Theory: A Critical Introduction.* London and New York: Methuen.

Holzman, Donald

1956   "Les Sept Sages de la forêt des bambous et la société de leur temps." *T'oung Pao* 44:317–46.

Hrdličková, Praha

1958   "The First Translations of Buddhist Sūtras in Chinese Literature and Their Place in the Development of Storytelling." *Archiv Orientalni* 26:114–44.

Hummel, Arthur

1952   "Some Basic Moral Principles in Chinese Culture." In *Moral Principles of Action,* edited by Ruth Nanda Ashen. New York and London: Harper.

Hurvitz, Leon

1957   "'Render Unto Caesar' in Early Chinese Buddhism: Huiyüan's Treatise on the Exemption of the Buddhist Clergy from the Requirements of Civil Etiquette." *Sino-Indian Studies* 5:80–114.

1961   "Wei Shou, Treatise on Buddhism and Taoism." *Yun-Kang, the Buddhist Cave-Temples of the Fifth Century A.D. in North China: Detailed Report of the Archaeological Survey Carried Out by the Mission of the Tōhōbunka Kenkyūsho 1938–45.* Appendix 2. Kyoto: Kyoto University, Jimbunkagaku Kenkyūsho.

1975   "The First Systematizations of Buddhist Thought in China." *Journal of Chinese Philosophy* 2 (4): 361–88.

Iser, Wolfgang

1972   "The Reading Process: A Phenomenological Approach." *New Literary History* 3:279–99.

1978   *The Act of Reading: A Theory of Aesthetic Response.* Baltimore and London: John Hopkins University Press.

Ishikawa Hiromichi
    1939   "Go-Han bukkyō ni tsuite." *Shigaku* 18:43–75, 599–642.

Jan, Yun-hua
    1978   "Silk Manuscripts on Taoism." *T'oung Pao* 63:65–84.
    1980   "Tao, Principle, and Law: The Three Key Concepts of the Yellow Emperor Taoism." *Journal of Chinese Philosophy* 7:205–28.
    1980   "Tao Yüan on Tao: The Origin." *Journal of Chinese Philosophy* 7:195–204.
    1990   "Human Nature and Its Cosmic Roots in the Huang-Lao Taoism." *Journal of Chinese Philosophy* 17 (2): 215–34.

Kaltenmark, Max
    1969   *Lao Tzu and Taoism*. Translated from the French by Roger Greaves. Stanford: Stanford University Press.

Karlgren, Bernhard
    1946   "Legends and Cults in Ancient China." *Bulletin of the Museum of Far Eastern Antiquities* 18:199–366.

Keenan, John P.
    1976   "A Study of Chapter Four of the Fa-Yen by Yang Hsiung." Master's thesis, University of Pennsylvania.
    1990   "The Doctrine of Buddha Nature in Chinese Buddhism: Hui K'ai on Paramārtha." In *Buddha Nature: A Festschrift in Honor of Minoru Kiyota*, edited by Paul J. Griffiths and John P. Keenan. Reno: Buddhist Books International.

Kermode, Frank
    1975   "The Reader's Share." *Times Literary Supplement*, 11 July, 751–52.

Kiyota Kiyoshi
    1957   *Koshi kago*. Tokyo: Meitoku.

Knechtges, David R.
    1968   "Yang Shyong, the *Fuh*, and Hann Rhetoric." Ph.D. diss., University of Washington.

Knoblock, John
    1988–90   *Xunzi: A Translation and Study of the Complete Works*. 2 vols. to date. Stanford: Stanford University Press.

Kohn, Livia
    1992   *Early Chinese Mysticism: Philosophy and Soteriology in the Taoist Tradition*. Princeton: Princeton University Press.

Künstler, Mieczyslaw Jerzy
  1966   "Activité culturelle et politique des différentes régions de la
          Chine sous les Han orientaux." *Rocznik Orientalistyczny*
          30:7–29.

Lai, Whalen
  1981   "Beyond the Debate on 'The Immortality of the Soul': Re-
          covering an Essay by Shih Yüeh." *Journal of the American
          Oriental Society* 19 (2): 139–45.
  1983   "Before the Prajñā Schools: The Earliest Chinese Commen-
          tary on the Aṣṭasāhasrikā." *Journal of the International
          Society of Buddhist Studies* 6 (1): 91–108.
  1986   "The Early Chinese Buddhist Understanding of the Psyche:
          Chen Hui's Commentary on the Yin Ch'ih Ju Ching." *Jour-
          nal of the International Association of Buddhist Studies* 9
          (1): 85–103.
  1987   "The Earliest Folk Buddhist Religion in China: *T'i-wei Po-li
          Ching* and Its Historical Significance." In *Buddhist and
          Taoist Practice in Medieval Chinese Society: Buddhist
          and Taoist Studies II*, edited by David W. Chappell. Hono-
          lulu: University of Hawaii Press.
  1990   "Looking for Mr. Ho Po." *History of Religions* 29, no. 4
          (May): 335–50.
  forthcoming "The Public Good That Does the Public Good."
          Asian Philosophy.

Lancaster, Lewis
  1975   "The Earliest Mahāyāna Sūtra: Its Significance to the Study
          of Buddhist Development." *Eastern Buddhist* 8 (1): 30–41.

Lau, D. C.
  1963   "On Mencius' Use of the Method of Analogy in Argu-
          ment." *Asia Major*, n.s., 10:173–94.

Lau, D. C. trans.
  1963   *Lao Tzu: Tao Te Ching.* London and New York: Penguin.
  1970   *Mencius.* London and New York: Penguin.
  1979   *Confucius: The Analects.* London and New York: Penguin.

Le Blanc, Charles
  1985   *Huai-nan Tzu: Philosophical Synthesis in Early Han
          Thought.* Hong Kong: Hong Kong University Press.

Legge, James, trans.
  1885   *The Li Ki, Sacred Books of the East.* Edited by Max Müller,
          vols. 27 and 28. Oxford: Clarendon Press.
  1893   *The Chinese Classics.* 5 vols. Oxford: Clarendon Press.

Leslie, Donald
    1956   "Contribution to a New Translation of the Lun Heng."
             T'oung Pao 44:100–149.

Liebenthal, Walter
    1950   "Shih Hui-yüan's Buddhism As Set Forth in His Writings."
             Journal of the American Oriental Society 70:243–59.
    1968   *Chao Lun: The Treatise of Seng-chao.* Hong Kong: Hong
             Kong University Press.

Link, Arthur E.
    1957   "Shyh Daw-an's Preface to Saṅgharakṣa's Yogācārabhūmi-
             sūtra and the Problem of Buddho-Taoist Terminology in
             Early Chinese Buddhism." *Journal of the American Orien-
             tal Society* 77:1–14.
    1958   "Biography of Shih Tao-an." *T'oung Pao* 46:1–48.
    1961   "The Cheng-wu lun: The Rectification of Unjustified Criti-
             cism." *Oriens Extremus* 8:136–65.
    1969–70   "The Taoist Antecedents of Tao-an's Prajñā Ontology."
             History of Religions 9 (2–3): 181–215.

Liu, Jiahe
    1992   "Early Buddhism and Taoism in China (A.D. 65–420)."
             Translated by Dongfang Shao. *Buddhist-Christian Studies*
             12:35–42.

Liu, Ming-Wood
    1987   "Fan Chen's Treatise on the Destructibility of the Spirit
             and Its Buddhist Critics." *Philosophy East and West* 37 (4):
             402–28.

Loewe, Michael
    1959   "Some Notes on Han-time Documents from Chüyen."
              T'oung Pao 47 (3–5): 294–322.
    1961   *Military Operations in the Han Period.* London: China
             Society.
    1967   *Records of Han Administration.* Vol. 1, *Historical Assess-
             ment.* Cambridge: Cambridge University Press.
    1968   *Everyday Life in Early Imperial China during the Han Pe-
             riod 202 B.C.–A.D. 220.* New York and Evanston: Harper &
             Row.
    1979   *Ways to Paradise: The Chinese Quest for Immortality.*
             London: George Allen & Unwin.
    1982   *Chinese Ideas of Life after Death: Faith, Myth and Reason
             in the Han Period (202 B.C.–A.D. 220).* London: George
             Allen & Unwin.

Mailloux, Steven
1977   "Reader-Response Criticism?" *Genre* 10:413–31.
1979   "Learning to Read: Interpretation and Reader-Response Criticism." *Studies in the Literary Imagination* 12:93–108.
1982   *Interpretive Conventions: The Reader in the Study of American Fiction.* Ithaca and London: Cornell University Press.

Major, John S.
1993   *Heaven and Earth in Early Han Thought: Chapters Three, Four, and Five of the Huainanzi.* Albany: State University of New York Press.

Makita Tairyō
1974   *Gumyōshū kenkyū* (A Study of the *Hung-ming chi*). 2 vols. Kyoto: Kyōto Daigaku Jinbunkagaku Kenkyūsho.

Malbon, Elizabeth Struthers
1983   "Structuralism, Hermeneutics, and Contextual Meaning." *Journal of the American Academy of Religion* 51:207–30.

Maspero, M. H.
1901   "Le songe et l'ambassade de l'empereur Ming: Étude critique des sources." *Bulletin de l'École francaise d'Extrême-Orient* 10:95–130.
1910   "Communautés et moines bouddhistes chinois au IIe et IIIe siècles." *Bulletin de l'École francaise d'Extrême-Orient* 10: 222–32.
1950   "Le Taoisme." In *Mélanges posthumes sur les religions et l'histoire de la Chine*, edited by P. Demiéville, no. 58. Paris: Civilisations du Sud.

Mather, Richard B.
1969–70   "The Controversy over Conformity and Naturalness during the Six Dynasties." *History of Religions* 9 (2–3): 160–80.
1976   *Shih-shuo Hsin-yü: A New Account of Tales of the World, by Liu I-Ch'ing with Commentary by Liu Chün.* Minneapolis: University of Minnesota Press.

McRae, John R.
1986   *The Northern School and the Formation of Early Ch'an Buddhism.* Honolulu: University of Hawaii Press.

Mei, Yi-Pao
1929   *The Ethical and Political Works of Motse.* London: Arthur Probsthain; Westport, Conn.: Hyperion Press, 1973.

Michaud, Paul
    1958   "The Yellow Turbans." *Monumenta Serica* 17:47–127.

Miyakawa, Hisayuki
    1960   "The Confucianization of South China." In *The Confucian Persuasion*, edited by Arthur F. Wright, 21–46. Stanford: Stanford University Press.

Moore, Stephen D.
    1986   "Negative Hermeneutics, Insubstantial Texts: Stanley Fish and the Biblical Interpreter." *Journal of the American Academy of Religion* 54 (4): 707–19.

Morgan, Evan
    1934   *Tao: The Great Luminant: Essays from Huai Nan Tzu*. Shanghai: Kelley & Walsh. Reprint, New York: Paragon Books, 1969.

Needham, Joseph
    1956   *Science and Civilization in China*. Vol. 2. Cambridge: Cambridge University Press.

Overmyer, Daniel L.
    1987   "Chinese Religion: An Overview." In *The Encyclopedia of Religion*. Editor in Chief, Mircea Eliade. New York: Macmillan.

Pachow, W.
    1978   "The Controversy over the Immortality of the Soul in Chinese Buddhism." *Journal of Oriental Studies* 16 (1–2): 21–38.
    1980   *Chinese Buddhism: Aspects of Interaction and Reinterpretation*. Boston: University Press of America.

Peerenboom, R. P.
    1993   *Law and Morality in Ancient China: The Silk Manuscripts of Huang-Lao*. Albany: State University of New York Press.

Pelliot, Paul
    1903   "Le Fou-nan." *Bulletin de l'École francais d'Extrême-Orient* 3:248–303.
    1920   "Meou-tseu ou les doutes levés: Traduit et annoté." *T'oung pao* 19:255–433.

Pokora, Timotheus
    1961   "An Important Crossroad of the Chinese Thought." *Archiv Orientalni* 29:65–79.

1961   "On the Origin of the Notions T'ai-P'ing and Ta-T'ung in Chinese Philosophy." *Archiv Orientalni* 29:448–54.
1965   "Notes on New Studies on Tung Chung-shu." *Archiv Orientalni* 33:256–71.

Prince, Gerald
1971   "Notes Toward a Categorization of Fictional 'Narratives.'" *Genre* 4:100–105.
1982   *Narratology: The Form and Function of Narrative*. Berlin, New York, and Amsterdam: Mouton.

Reding, Jean-Paul
1986   "Analogical Reasoning in Early Chinese Philosophy." *Asiatische Studien: Zeitschrift der Schweizerischen Gesellschaft für Asienkunde* 40:40–56.

Reischauer, Edwin O. and John K. Fairbank
1958   *East Asia: The Great Tradition*. Boston: Houghton Mifflin.

Richards, I. A.
1932   *Mencius on the Mind: Experiments in Multiple Definitions*. London: Kegan Paul; New York: Harcourt Brace.

Riegel, Jeffrey
1979   "Reflections on an Unmoved Mind: An Analysis of *Mencius* 2A2." *Journal of the American Academy of Religion* 47 (3S): 433–58.

Ro, Young-Chan
1988   "The Significance of the Confucian Texts as 'Scripture' in the Confucian Tradition." *Journal of Chinese Philosophy* 15:269–87.

Schmidt-Glintzer, Helwig
1976   *Das Hung-ming Chi und die Aufnahme des Buddhismus in China* (The Hung-ming Chi and the Beginnings of Buddhism in China). Wiesbaden: Franz Steiner Verlag GMBH.

Searle, John
1969   *Speech Acts: An Essay in the Philosophy of Language*. Cambridge: Cambridge University Press.

Seidel, Anna
1969   *La Divinisation de Lao Tseu dans le Taoisme des Han*. Vol. 71. Paris: Publications d'École francaise d'Extrême-Orient.

Shih, Vincent Yu-chung
1959   *The Literary Mind and the Carving of Dragons. Translated and Annotated*. New York: Columbia University Press.

Shima Kunioto
1971   Gogyō shisō to Reiki Getsuryō no kenkyū (An Investigation into the Five Element Theory and the Yüeh Ming Li Chi [a chapter of the Lü-shih Ch'un ch'iu]). Tokyo: Kyūko Shoin.

Soyen Shaku
1901   Sermons of a Buddhist Abbot. New York: Samuel Weiser, 1971.

Steiner, George
1979   "'Critic'/'Reader'." New Literary History 10:423–52.

Suleiman, Susan R., and Inge Crosman, eds.
1980   The Reader in the Text: Essays on Audience and Interpretation. Princeton: Princeton University Press.

T'ang, Yung-t'ung
1938   Han Wei liang-Chin nan-pei ch'ao fo-chiao shih. Peking: Chunghua Shuchu.

Tjan, Tjoe Som
1949   Po Hu T'ung, the Comprehensive Discussions in the White Tiger Hall: A Contribution to the History of Classical Studies in the Han Period. Leiden: Brill.

Tokiwa Daijō
1911   "Kan-min guhosetsu no kenkyū." Tōyō Kyōkai Chōsabu 10:1–49.
1929   Shina ni okeru bukkyō to jukyō dōkyō. Tokyo: Tōyō bunko ronsō.

Tsukamoto Zenryū
1985   A History of Early Chinese Buddhism: From Its Introduction to the Death of Hui-yüan. Translated by Leon Hurvitz. Tokyo: Kodansha.

Vervoorn, Aat
1983   "Boyi and Shuqi: Worthy Men of Old?" Papers on Far Eastern History 29:1–22.
1984   "The Origins of Chinese Eremitism." Journal of the Institute of Chinese Studies of the Chinese University of Hong Kong, 15:249–95.

Waley, Arthur
1951   "The Fall of Lo-yang." History Today 1:7–10.
1953   "Life under the Han Dynasty: Notes on Chinese Civilization in the First and Second Centuries A.D." History Today 3:89–98.

Wallacker, Benjamin E.
1962   *The Huai-nan-tzu, Book Eleven: Behavior, Culture and the Cosmos.* New Haven: American Oriental Society.

Walters, Derek
1983   *The T'ai Hsüan Ching: The Hidden Classic.* Wellingborough, Northamptonshire: Aquarian Press.

Watson, Burton, trans.
1961   *The Records of the Grand Historian of China.* 2 vols. New York: Columbia University Press.
1968   *The Complete Works of Chuang Tzu.* New York: Columbia University Press.

Wilhelm, Richard, trans.
1950   *The I Ching.* Translated from the German by Cary F. Baynes. Princeton: Princeton University Press, 1967.

Wray, Elizabeth, Claire Rosenfield, and Dorothy Bailey
1972   *Ten Lives of the Buddha: Siamese Temple Paintings and Jataka Tales.* New York and Tokyo: Weatherhill.

Wright, Arthur F.
1951   "Fu I and the Rejection of Buddhism." *Journal of the History of Ideas* 12:33–47.
1959   *Buddhism in Chinese History.* Stanford: Stanford University Press; London: Oxford.
1990   *Studies in Chinese Buddhism.* New Haven and London: Yale University Press.

Yü, Ying-shih
1965   "Life and Immortality in the Mind of Han China. 206 B.C.– A.D. 220." *Harvard Journal of Asiatic Studies* 25:80–122.
1967   *Trade and Expansion in Han China.* Berkeley: University of California Press.
1987   " 'O Soul, Come Back!' A Study in the Changing Conceptions of the Soul and Afterlife in Pre-Buddhist China." *Harvard Journal of Asiatic Studies* 47:363–95.

Zach, Erwin von
1939   "Yang Hsiungs Fa Yen: Wörter Strenger Ermahung." *Sinologische Beiträge* 4:1–74.

Zürcher. E.
1959   *The Buddhist Conquest of China.* Leiden: Brill.
1987   "Buddhism: Buddhism in China." In *The Encyclopedia of Religion.* Editor in Chief, Mircea Eliade. New York: Macmillan.

Index